Hiking Trails

of the Cohutta & Big Frog Wildernesses

Tim Homan

Hiking Trails

of the Cohutta & Big Frog Wildernesses

PEACHTREE
ATLANTA

Ⓟ
Published by
PEACHTREE PUBLISHERS, LTD.
494 Armour Circle NE
Atlanta, Georgia 30324

Text © 2000 by Tim Homan
Photographs © 2000 by William Houghton, Page Luttrell
Cover photograph © 2000 by Page Luttrell

Interior illustrations © 1999 by Vicky Holifield
Maps © 2000 by XNR Productions, Middleton, Wisconsin
Book design by Loraine M. Balcsik
Book composition by Robin Sherman

Manufactured in the United States of America

10 9 8 7 6 5 4 3 2 1
First Edition

Library of Congress Cataloging-in-Publication Data

Homan, Tim.
  Hiking Trails of Cohutta and Big Frog Wildernesses / Tim Homan. — 1st ed.
    p. cm.
  ISBN 1-56145-209-2
  1. Hiking—Tennessee—Citico Creek Wilderness—Guidebooks. 2. Hiking—Joyce Kilmer–Slickrock Wilderness (N.C. and Tenn.)—Guidebooks. 3. Citico Creek Wilderness—Guidebooks.
  4. Joyce Kilmer–Slickrock Wilderness (N.C. and Tenn.)—Guidebooks.
  I. Homan, Tim. Hiking Trails of Joyce Kilmer–Slickrock and Citico Creek Wilderness areas.
  II. Title.

  GV199.42.T22C585 1998
  917.56'97—DC21   98-9326
                                                        CIP

Cover photo: Cohutta Wilderness stream
Photo credits: page 5, Museum of North Idaho; pages 39, 81, 91, and 237 by Page Luttrell; pages 155 and 173 by William Houghton

Acknowledgments

I WISH TO EXTEND SPECIAL THANKS to the following people for their help:

■ David Acton Brown, Steve Craven, Elizabeth Little, Charles Ratliff, and Page Luttrell for hiking with me;

■ Larry Thomas with the Chattahoochee National Forest and Quentin Bass with the Cherokee National Forest for their time and wilderness history information;

■ Margaret Quinlin of Peachtree Publishers for giving me the opportunity;

■ Vicky Holifield for her editing and artwork;

■ David Acton Brown, Page Luttrell, and William Houghton for their photographs;

■ Loraine Balcsik for her map and design work;

■ Page Luttrell, my wife, for her typing, editing, and computer lessons.

—*Tim Homan*

Contents

Part I—Cohutta Wilderness

Part II—Big Frog Wilderness

Preface

I WALKED DOWN TO JACKS RIVER for the first time in 1975, the year the Cohutta received wilderness designation. Back then, Beech Bottom had two small houses and a large hunting cabin with a screened-in porch. On the Jacks River Trail that day, railroad spikes were much easier to find than other hikers.

My Cohutta hiking first turned systematic in 1979, when I walked all of the wilderness trails for inclusion within my guide, *The Hiking Trails of North Georgia*. I saw my first wild hog—a large, prominently tusked male—early on a May morning along Rough Ridge.

I employed a pedometer to measure mileage for the first edition. When it came time for a major revision of the little book in 1986, I rolled an incessantly clicking, orange measuring wheel borrowed from the Forest Service. By using this pain-in-the-ass apparatus I was able to record distances in feet, such as 87,013 feet for the Jacks River Trail, then easily convert the large numbers to the nearest tenth of a mile. If a measurement fell exactly between tenths, 2.75 miles for example, the figure was rounded upward to the nearest tenth. (On my second go-around in the Cohutta Wilderness, I saw a bobcat from Rice Camp Trail, my first and thus far only sighting of that predator from a Southern Appalachian Trail.)

I wheeled the trails in neighboring Big Frog and those in the Cohutta yet again in 1990 in order to write a hiking guide for the combined wilderness. Even though the hiking was completed, I failed to finish the book for reasons that seemed compelling at the time.

Life is short, but it is sometimes long enough for second chances. In 1998, from April through November, on weekends, vacation days, and three-day holidays, I hiked and wheeled the trails in the combined wilderness again—and enjoyed every river-wading and ridge-walking day of it, even the backpacking trip when tent, canteens,

Therm-a-rests, and some other seemingly necessary items didn't make that all-important trip from living room to car. But the weather was dry, the ground soft enough, and best of all, the packs were very light.

I didn't see any new critters this time around, but I did encounter Dillard—a habitual, hard-core solo hiker in the Big Frog—on two different occasions. Both times he was the only person I saw all day. He often carries a bow saw so that he can cut a few deadfalls as he moves up the trail. You'll know it's Dillard when you see him.

Happy Trails.

Tim Homan

Climb the mountains and get their good tidings. Nature's peace will flow into you as sunshine flows into trees. The winds will blow their own freshness into you, and the storms their energy, while cares drop off like autumn leaves.

—John Muir

The Combined Wilderness

THE COHUTTA MOUNTAINS ARE the westernmost mass of the high Southern Appalachians. Geographers have designated the Cohuttas as a distinct physiographic subunit—the Cohutta Mountains District—within the Western Blue Ridge. In Georgia, the Cohutta Mountains District is disjunct from the rest of the Blue Ridge to the southeast, south, and west. To the southeast a thin sliver of Piedmont separates the Western Blue Ridge from the eastern. To the south the district descends to the foothills of the upper Piedmont. The escarpment peaks along the western flank of the Cohuttas fall away to the Paleozoic sedimentary rocks of the Ridge and Valley Province.

The Cohutta Mountains District contains the westernmost land over 4,000 feet in elevation in the eastern United States. No matter how far north within the U.S., the terrain west of the Cohuttas does not rise to the 4,000-foot level again until it reaches the Great Plains, far across the Mississippi.

Cohutta hikers tread on ancient metamorphic rock. Swirlholes cutting into the streambeds of the Jacks and Conasauga Rivers drill into rock originally deposited as sediment layers in the late Pre-Cambrian Era—approximately 570 to 700 million years ago. During the early Paleozoic Era (430–570 million years ago), tectonic forces deformed these sedimentary layers—faulted and folded them, shoved, overthrust, and buried them deep below the Earth's surface. Down there in subterranean hell the heat and pressure cooked the sedimentary rocks, metamorphosing them into what they are today—hard metamorphic rocks resistant to erosion and weathering.

Another round of tectonic sumo wrestling wrenched the cooked rocks back up to the surface and beyond, even higher than when the cycle started as sediment. And although today's surface rocks were way above the surrounding plains, they were buried deep in the bellies of sky-scraping mountains that made the upstart Rockies look like foothills. Weather and vast time eroded vertical miles from the once great mountains. Hundreds of millions of years have brought the rock outcrops atop Wolf Ridge to the light of day and slow dissolution. Geologists have named the layers of rock extending southward into the Cohutta Mountains the Ocoee Series. Major rock types in this series include quartzite, phyllite, metagraywacke (metamorphosed graywacke), gneiss, and shist.

The Cohutta Mountains District is the southernmost link in the much longer mountain chain known as the Unaka. The Cohuttas are roughly outlined by a rectangle of very recent Holocene highways—US 76 to the south, US 411 to the west, US 64 to the north, plus TN 68, GA 5, and US 76 to the east.

Preserving the heart of the Cohutta Mountains in north-central Georgia and southeastern Tennessee, the Cohutta–Big Frog Wilderness straddles two states, two national forests, four counties, and two natural features: the Blue Ridge and the Tennessee Valley Divide. Tennessee's Cherokee National Forest manages all of the protected tract north of the state line. Georgia's Chattahoochee National Forest administers all of the wilderness below the border.

The 71-square-mile combined wilderness stretches into portions of Gilmer, Murray, and Fannin Counties in Georgia, and Polk County in Tennessee. The southern tip of the Cohutta Wilderness dips into northernmost Gilmer County. The westernmost mountains in the Cohutta Wilderness, a north-south strip generally from 1¼ to 2 miles wide, range into easternmost Murray County. Most of the Cohutta Wilderness and the southernmost 89 acres of the Big Frog Wilderness add to the beauty of western Fannin County. The northernmost 1,795 acres of the Cohutta and all of the Big Frog Wilderness (except those 89 acres) lie within Tennessee's Polk County.

The long, prominently labeled ridge nearly synonymous with Southern Appalachia winds through the wilderness. From the state line at Double Spring Gap, the Blue Ridge serves as the dividing crest between the two wildernesses northwestward across Big Frog Mountain to the Wolf Ridge–Chestnut Mountain junction.

Separating watersheds, the Tennessee Valley Divide follows the keel of the Blue Ridge throughout the combined wilderness. Water flowing south and west of the divide enters the Gulf of Mexico at

Alabama's Mobile Bay. Water dropping down the other side of the Blue Ridge, from north and east of the divide, takes a vastly different journey in our country's largest drainage. Conveyed in turn by the Tennessee, Ohio, then Mississippi Rivers, the cold Cohutta Mountain water, along with contributions from Montana and Pennsylvania, turns salty in the Gulf of Mexico near New Orleans.

Encompassing 45,059 acres, the Cohutta–Big Frog is either the largest or second largest national forest wilderness, single or combined, in the eastern United States. (New Hampshire's Pemigewasset Wilderness is listed as 45,000 acres—a rounded-off, unsurveyed figure.) The irregularly shaped contiguous wilderness is roughly twice as long north to south as it is wide east to west. The area's greatest width is approximately 8½ miles; its maximum length, from north-northeast to south-southwest, is approximately 15½ miles.

The highest peaks in the Cohutta Mountains, all within the combined wilderness, rise to over 4,000 feet. Elevations within the preserved tract range from 4,224 feet atop Big Frog Mountain down to approximately 970 feet where the Jacks River enters Alaculsy Valley. Unlike the Southern Highlands to the north and east, many of the unnamed knobs and mountains in the Cohuttas are round topped and flat crowned. And many of the prominent ridges have wide-crested sections that are nearly level side to side. The Cherokee were certainly well aware of these characteristics when they established their ball field atop Little Bald Mountain, now the Group Camping Area across the road from Tearbritches Trailhead. Several of the wide ridgelines have deep, dark, fertile soil that supports a much richer flora than is normally found on ridgetop habitats.

Though the South's largest national forest wilderness may seem hopelessly puny by out-West standards, it nevertheless offers the flexibility of numerous routes and room enough to roam. This guide details a network of 26 trails totaling 127 miles. You can dayhike a short trail in and right back out. Or you can backpack a long, circuitous route—with loops off of loops—and walk for most of a week with scarcely a backtrack.

Not only is there room to roam, but there is also plenty to look at while you are walking. Southern Appalachia, where northern cold dips deep into southern warmth, is an ecological crossroads—a zone of rapid transition and great biological diversity. The Southern Appalachians provide sanctuary for the world's second richest temperate zone flora; only eastern China is more diverse.

Numerous factors help explain the incredible array of trees, shrubs, vines, herbaceous wildflowers, ferns, and fungi found in our Southern Highlands. A partial list of reasons for this diversity include heavy rainfall, relative warmth, orientation of the mountains, and the wide range of exposures and elevations that match climatic conditions all the way to Canada. The three most important components, however, were favorable location, nearly unimaginable time, and long-term stability. Their location allowed the Southern Appalachians the time and stability to remain a refugia in which the evolutionary development of plants could proceed without major interruption. The height and location of our southern mountains protected them from the twin threats of glaciation from the north and submersion from the south. All of the slow oscillations of Pleistocene ice stopped well short of the Smokies, and the Southern Appalachians stood high enough to avoid seawater submersion for over 200 million years.

Time, stability, and steady speciation created today's bewildering botanical diversity. The Great Smoky Mountains National Park alone harbors over 1,500 kinds of flowering plants, more than in any other North American park. More than 100 species of native trees grow in the Great Smoky Mountains National Park, more than in any other North American park and more than in all of northern Europe. The entire Southern Appalachian region boasts approximately 140 types of native trees, more than are found in all of Europe. Within the combined wilderness, hikers can easily differentiate twenty-five to thirty-five tree species along a 1-mile stretch of the lower Jacks River Trail.

Cohutta History

Until recently a wolf-howl and panther-scream wilderness—one with fiercer predators, thicker trees, and now and forever extinct birds—overspread the Cohutta Mountains. Not very long ago, these mountains were also home to bison and elk. Stands of magnificent chestnut trees, some so large as to seem mythological by today's

Southern Appalachian chestnut grove prior to the blight.

diminished standard, rained mast down upon the wild harvest fall after fall without fail. Astonishing congregations of passenger pigeons swirled down from the sky to glean the forest, then after a short respite stormed away to quench another hunger. Flocks of chattering Carolina parakeets flashed yellow, green, and orange-red as they flew across the lowermost Jacks River. Much has been lost, yet much remains.

The Cohuttas were once in Cherokee country, high hunting land that stretched down the mountains from today's southernmost West Virginia into northeastern Alabama. Cohutta is the anglicized pronunciation of *Gahuti*, the Cherokee word for "a shed roof supported on poles." The mountains were thought to be the poles that supported the roof—the sky.

There were no towns within the present-day wilderness, but the Cherokee hunted extensively on the lower elevations of the Cohuttas. They hunted, and they held athletic contests on the very edge of what is now designated wilderness. The grassy opening atop Little Bald (Ball) Mountain—today's Group Camping Area where children throw baseballs and Frisbees—was yesterday's Cherokee playground. Young men from towns east and west of the Cohuttas met in the middle and competed in a sort of Cherokee field hockey league.

These old mountains also contributed to the spiritual well-being of the Cherokee. One of the myths in their cosmology, the legend of the great serpent, *Ustu'tli* (foot snake), originated in the Cohuttas. The *Ustu'tli* had suckerlike feet at either end of its huge, serpentine body. Instead of slithering side to side like other snakes, it humped up and reared forward, moving with great speed like an immense inchworm. This monstrous creature bleated like a fawn to lure deer and Cherokee hunter alike. If deer or Cherokee ran up- or downhill, the *Ustu'tli* could catch and eat the fastest among them. But if the pursued ran along the contour of the slope, the serpent quickly fell behind because it slipped slightly downward with each spanning stride.

One day a brave Cherokee hunter from the north set out to kill the *Ustu'tli*. He heard the bleat and crept closer to see the great reptile, whose scaly head was reared up high among the pines. The monster quickly spotted the man and immediately lunged forward to grasp and devour him. The warrior was so frightened that he completely lost his wits and ran as fast as he could—straight uphill. At the last possible moment, just as the foot snake had closed the gap to striking distance, the Cherokee hunter, remembering the serpent's weakness, veered out across the slope.

He quickly outpaced the slipping snake and was soon well out of sight. Determined to kill the *Ustu'tli*, the warrior opened his fire pouch and soon ringed the serpent's mountain with a fast burning blaze. The reptile retreated to the top of the mountain. The fire's circumference grew smaller and smaller as the flames climbed the mountain; the *Ustu'tli* worked its way to the topknot of the rocky summit. Fanned by strong updrafts of heated air, the fire rapidly reached the giant serpent's final refuge, caught a grove of dead pines ablaze, and burned the ferocious creature to death.

The Cherokee came to know their own ring of fire—the reality of encroachment on all fronts—which was much more deadly than the literal flames of myth. Despite the fact that the Cherokee had acculturated to pioneer ways—many of them had become independent farmers, merchants, and craftsmen—they were not allowed to remain in their homeland. In fact, shortly after gold was discovered near Dahlonega, Georgia, the Cherokee nation was ethnically cleansed. As is well documented, the United States government rounded up the Cherokee from their Appalachian homes in 1838 and forced them to endure the Trail of Tears westward across the Mississippi to the Oklahoma Territory.

After The Removal, pioneers quickly settled in the bottomland valleys surrounding the Cohutta Mountains. By the late 1800s, the surrounding settlements had penetrated further into the mountains, into halfway level areas such as Bray Field and Beech Bottom. Small-operation loggers, using oxen and horses to skid boles to the saw, began to harvest the trees in the mountains. From the cleared bottomlands, they gnawed away at the edges of the forest onto a few lower slopes. But their inroads were slight. Until early in the twentieth century, the ruggedness of the Cohutta Mountains provided de facto protection for the last major tract of largely virgin forest for miles around in Murray and Fannin Counties.

But in 1912 another removal began. That year Conasauga River Lumber Company, located in Conasauga, Tennessee, began full-tilt industrial logging in the Cohutta Mountains. The company owned the land, hired the men, built the railroad system, and brought in the huge skid horses and locomotives. They constructed numerous trestles over the Conasauga and Jacks Rivers. Today's trails, short-cutting across the same river bends and pinched in by the same topography, often ford the rivers where trestles once spanned high overhead.

The cutting began in the Conasauga River watershed well to the northwest of today's wilderness. The men felled the trees, cut them to length, skidded the logs one way or another, then loaded the timber onto railcars bound for the mill in Conasauga. The sawyers slashed deeper and deeper into the Cohuttas, cutting east then southeast up the Conasauga. By 1929, the lumber company had sawed and skidded all the merchantable trees it wanted out of the Conasauga River drainage up to headwater slopes.

Before the last load came out of the Conasauga, cutting began up the Jacks—the next large watershed to the east. Not long after the Jacks River lumbering started, the Great Depression brought the felling to a three-year halt. Many of the loggers worked for the CCC during the lull. Lake Conasauga and most of the major roads in the Cohuttas were built with CCC labor in the early 1930s. The lumberjacking resumed but ended for good in the Jacks River Basin in 1935.

Much of our Cohutta Wilderness, cut off and often burned over, was purchased by the Forest Service in 1934 and 1935 for as little as two or three dollars per acre. The railroad was dismantled and the rails removed in 1937. Trestles fell to disrepair and flood.

Most written accounts of Cohutta Wilderness history state that only 70 percent of the wilderness was logged. If that were true, there should be roughly 11,000 acres of near-virgin forest out there somewhere. While there are occasional old-growth hemlocks down along streams, and occasional logger's cull blackgums and oaks on ridges, there are no large tracts of virgin timber tucked away in the high coves. My research and observations indicate that virtually all of the Cohutta was logged.

Under government stewardship, the forest regenerated; it made an especially impressive comeback where fertile soil remained intact. The trees able to stump sprout brushed out quickly. Trees that had been too thin or crooked to cut had a head start in the open canopy and seeded the forest floor below. The light gaps quickly filled with briers and large-leafed saplings.

Time passed, the Southern Appalachian rain fell, and the forest healed itself. Forty years after the logging ended, on January 3, 1975, Public Law 93-622 designated approximately 34,100 acres as the Cohutta Wilderness. Eleven years later, on October 27, 1986, Congress passed Public Law 99-555, which added approximately 2,900 acres to the Cohutta Wilderness. The most recent Forest Service survey set the Cohutta's acreage at 36,977.

The 58-square-mile Cohutta Wilderness is longer trending southwest to northeast than it is wide west to east. Its greatest southwest-northeast length, from Potatopatch Mountain to the Blue Ridge west of Big Frog Mountain, is roughly 12 miles. The Cohutta's maximum east-west extent, straddling the Georgia-Tennessee border, is approximately 8½ miles. The highest and lowest elevations, the same as those for the combined wilderness, range from 4,224 feet atop Big Frog Mountain to approximately 970 feet where the Jacks River enters Alaculsy Valley.

Two trout streams, the Conasauga and Jacks Rivers, flow in deep furrows across the wilderness from southeast to northwest. With the exception of the 1986 wilderness addition—the roughly 2,900 acres to the east of Hemp Top Trail and the Tennessee Valley Divide—all of the land and water flows toward these two rivers. Most of the long ridges—Rough, Hickory, Fork, and Blue—and most of the named mountains—Buckeye, Ken, Cohutta, Chestnut, Bald, Cowpen, and Big Frog—stretch across the land in varying degrees of north-south alignment.

Following the wilderness from southwest across the rivers to the northeast, the land falls away then humps up in well-defined folds from ridge to river and back to ridge. The terrain first descends along small stream valleys and parallel spurs to the Conasauga River. Across the clear Conasauga, the wilderness rises up and over Panther Bluff to Cohutta Mountain, the long ridge that divides drainages. Dropping to the bottom of the second fold, the topography—long ridges to either side of deeply entrenched streams—pitches down to the Jacks River. Much of this section is exceedingly steep. The most precipitous slope on the east side of the upper Rough Creek valley loses 1,050 feet of elevation in one third of a mile (1,760 feet).

Beyond the Jacks, the land heaves up again, up Murray and Beech Creeks, to the crest of the next fold—Big Frog Mountain and the Tennessee Valley Divide.

The Cohutta Wilderness trail system—following these rivers, ridges, and smaller stream valleys—interlaces seventeen paths totaling approximately 93 miles.

Big Frog History

The history of the Big Frog is essentially the same as that of the Cohutta, its neighboring wilderness to the south. And like Cohutta, the appellation Big Frog comes to us from its former inhabitants. The Cherokee named the highest mountain around after their nearby town—Two Big Spring Frogs Fighting Town—once located near today's Fightingtown Creek, east of the combined wilderness in Georgia's Fannin County. The Cherokee revered the spring frog for its ability to climb and its instinct to emerge early from hibernation to breed. The spring frog was not only a harbinger of spring, but also a symbol of fertility and rebirth. The Cherokee frequently honored natural features with the spring frog name. Maps from the early nineteenth century labeled the highest peak in today's wilderness as Big Spring Frog Mountain. Most of the spring frog place names have been shortened to just spring or frog.

After the Cherokee were driven out in 1838, settlers quickly moved onto the best bottomlands along the outer edges of the Cohutta Mountains. The first settlement near present-day Big Frog occurred along Dutch and Sylco Creeks, just to the west of the wilderness. There, in the 1840s, German and French settlers attempted to establish a vineyard beside the creeks at the Dutch Settlement. The wine making was never commercially successful, and the last family left the community in the late 1920s. Just to the west of Pace Gap, Dutch Fields remains a place name on the Caney Creek Quadrangle. The gap itself—the current site of the Wolf Ridge Trailhead—was named for the Pace Family who farmed the thin sliver of level land where Pace Branch meets Big Creek, near the Big Creek Trailhead. The last of the Paces left sometime around World War I.

From around 1875 to 1905, small numbers of land-poor settlers moved into the coves within the current wilderness. These farmers burned the forest each year, ran free-range hogs and sheep up on Big Frog Mountain, and scraped by on slash-and-burn subsistence agriculture, primarily cultivating small, short-rotation plots of corn. Their hardscrabble farming was rough on the land. Starting in the 1890s, small-time loggers began high-grading the forest—skidding out the best trees of the most valuable species. Full-scale, industrial logging began in 1904, when the Conasauga River Lumber Company and the Tennessee Timber Company began cutting the land south of the Ocoee River. Rather than using railroads to remove the timber as they did in the Jacks and Conasauga watersheds to the south, the Big Frog loggers processed the timber on site, using portable sawmills. The boards were then hauled to the nearest rail spur, where the wood was transported to the permanent mills for further processing.

The first round of cut-to-the-quick logging came to an end around 1918. From 1912 to 1918, the Forest Service bought the land that would become wilderness, often for a pittance per acre. In 1938, the Conasauga River Lumber Company built a road up Big Creek and quickly completed cutting the Big Creek watershed, the terrain that had been too steep for earlier efforts.

Three trails—Wolf Ridge, Licklog Ridge, and Big Frog—predate the Depression-era CCC construction efforts. These three trails probably began in the late 1800s as narrow, ridge-running herder paths to the highcountry grazing atop Big Frog Mountain. In the early 1930s, CCC crews constructed most of the main Forest Service roads in the area, improved the three existing paths, and built almost all of Big Frog's current trail system. Their masterpiece was Grassy Gap Trail, well surveyed and laboriously dug in on the midslope sidehill from Grassy Gap on Wolf Ridge to Low Gap on Peavine Ridge. The Big Frog Wilderness trail network now has nine paths totaling approximately 34 miles. All six trails heading on FS 221 have their beginning mileage outside of the wilderness.

On January 3, 1975, less than forty years after the Big Creek watershed was logged, Public Law 93-622—the law that created the Cohutta Wilderness—designated Big Frog as a wilderness study area. Public Law 98-578 designated approximately 5,055 acres as the Big Frog Wilderness on October 30, 1984. That same law, known as the

Tennessee Wilderness Act, also established another Big Frog Wilderness study area. The Big Frog's legal resumé grew again on October 16, 1986, when Public Law 99-490 added slightly over 3,000 acres to the wilderness. The most recent Forest Service survey lists the Big Frog's size as 8,082 acres.

Big Frog's maximum dimensions are approximately 4⅓ miles north to south and just over 4 miles east to west. This relatively small, 13-square-mile tract is surprisingly steep, especially from ridgetop down to narrow valley bottom. Slopes that lose 1,000 feet of elevation within half a mile—40-degree grades that turn maps brown with bunched contour lines—are common in the southern half of the wilderness. Big Frog's highest point, 4,224 feet atop its namesake mountain, is only 2⅗ line-of-sight miles from its lowest point, approximately 1,460 feet where Big Creek flows north out of the wilderness.

The grain of this land runs predominantly north and south. Big Frog Mountain, its peak along the southern boundary of the wilderness, is the focal point of the grain, the point of divergence. All of the wilderness slopes away from the mountain. The major ridges—Licklog, Peavine, Bark Legging, and Wolf—splay outward and down to the north away from the summit. Narrow watersheds of the longest streams—Peter Camp Branch, Big Creek, and the East and West Forks of Rough Creek—flow generally northward away from the mountain deep down between the fingers of the ridges. An east-west cross section through the middle of the wilderness would be regularly and sharply folded from ridgecrest down to stream, then back up to the next ridge and back down to the next stream.

Benton MacKaye Trail History

Benton MacKaye—forester, philosopher, visionary planner—was the first to envision and propose a continuous footpath along the crest of the entire Appalachian range. His completed dream, the Appalachian Trail (finished in 1937), is now nearly 65 years old. The father of the AT also foresaw the need to construct major loops that would join the master trail. His vision has become a tradition of hard-working volunteerism. In 1979 a trail association was established to make the concept of a long, AT-linking loop in the South—appropriately named the Benton MacKaye Trail—a reality.

The BMT was planned as an all-Appalachian, 250-mile footpath to be walked in conjunction with, or instead of, the heavily used Appalachian Trail. When completed, the BMT will cross or join the AT at three widely separated locations, forming a giant figure-eight trail system in the mountains of Georgia, Tennessee, and North Carolina. The Benton MacKaye shares the AT's famous southern terminus atop Springer Mountain in Georgia. From Springer the completed portion of the BMT heads northwest to the Cohutta–Big Frog Wilderness, then leads generally north to its crossing of US 64 in Tennessee. From there, the as-yet-unfinished route will wind to the northeast to its meeting and crossing of the AT in the southwestern corner of the Great Smoky Mountains National Park. The final leg, which remains within the park and roughly parallels the AT, traverses the remote southern, North Carolina section of the GSMNP. The end of the northeastern loop and Benton MacKaye's northern terminus is Davenport Gap, where the AT exits the eastern edge of the park.

Completed in the fall of 1989, Georgia's segment of the BMT stretches approximately 78.6 miles, from Springer Mountain to Double Spring Gap at the Tennessee border within the combined Cohutta–Big Frog Wilderness. At present, BMT trailbuilders have cleared a treadway northward to US 64 in Tennessee's Cherokee National Forest. Once the extensive and exhaustive approval process is completed, construction will continue toward the Smokies.

The Benton MacKaye Trail Association, a volunteer organization, is constructing and maintaining the trail. The association is always looking for more hard-working people to help them complete their project. Work trips are scheduled for the second Saturday of every month. If you are interested write:

Benton MacKaye Trail Association
P.O. Box 53271
Atlanta, GA 30355-1271

Things to Know Before You Go

WILDERNESS HIKING BRINGS MANY REWARDS—magnificent views into wild and undisturbed lands; peaks covered with spring wildflowers; and clear, cold, cascading mountain rivers—but this kind of hiking also presents challenges. Trails within this combined wilderness are unblazed, are maintained less rigorously than nonwilderness trails, and offer hikers eighty walk-in-the-water fords. The following information will help dayhikers and backpackers plan for trips into the wilderness and will help them become aware of what to expect on Cohutta–Big Frog trails.

Camping Areas

There are plenty of national forest campsites to either side of the combined wilderness. On the Tennessee side, the Cherokee National Forest has three campgrounds—Tumbling Creek, Thunder Rock, and Sylco—near the Big Frog Wilderness. Tumbling Creek and Sylco are no fee-pay, open all year, and have only tables and toilets. Situated beside the Ocoee River, Thunder Rock is fee-pay, open all year, and has tent pads, toilets, and water.

On the Georgia side, the Chattahoochee National Forest offers six camping areas—Lake Conasauga, Overflow, Group Camping, Jacks River Fields, Murray Lake, and Cottonwood Patch—very near the Cohutta Wilderness. All of these camping areas except Murray Lake are fee-pay. And all of these campgrounds except Lake Conasauga, which usually opens by the second weekend in April and closes after the last weekend in October (dates subject to change), remain open all year. The gate to the Group Campground is closed during winter, but camping is still permitted.

Lake Conasauga is by far the largest and most developed (tent pads, picnic tables, indoor toilets and sinks) of the six. The Overflow Camping Area was designed to accommodate additional campers when Lake Conasauga reaches capacity. It has chemical toilets and picnic tables, but no water. You can obtain water at Lake Conasauga when it is open. Located in the large field opposite the Tearbritches Trailhead, the Group Camping Area has chemical toilets but no water. Again, you can obtain water at Lake Conasauga when it is open. Murray Lake has no facilities whatsoever; however, you can camp beside the 4-acre lake if you want. Cottonwood Patch, designed as a horse riders' camp, has water and chemical toilets. A small, developed campground, Jacks River Fields has picnic tables, tent pads, chemical toilets, but no water as yet.

Fee-Pay Stations

The Cohutta Ranger District has recently instituted a fee-pay policy for several of its Cohutta Wilderness trailheads. At present the fee is $2.00 per night per vehicle. The stations accept checks as well as cash. The accumulated money funds information education (no-trace camping), a wilderness ranger position, trail maintenance, trailhead improvement, and bear-proof trash bins.

The fee-pay stations are currently located at the Beech Bottom Trailhead, Chestnut Lead Trailhead, East Cowpen's southern trailhead at Three Forks Mountain, and Hickory Creek's southwestern trailhead off FS 630. Jacks River Trail's northwestern terminus in Alaculsy Valley is slated for a fee-pay station during the hiking season of 2000.

There are no fee-pay stations at any of the Big Frog Wilderness Trailheads, nor are any planned for the near future.

Rivers

Many people, especially those from the West, think southern wilderness is chopped liver—low elevations, no large mammals, and scarcely any real danger. It's true: no grizzlies roam these ridges, the mountains are old and stoop-shouldered, and there has long since been no room for cougars or wolves. But this southern wilderness has its days. The Jacks and Conasauga Rivers remain as wild and indifferently dangerous as ever. After the right amount of rain (which varies from week to week), they rise quickly and run fast.

They test your resolve and nerve, knock you off your feet, and send you packing short of your goal—or worse if you read them wrong.

This is not hype or over-romancing what's left of the Southern Appalachian wilderness. When these two whitewater rivers roll fast and full, they will strand you between flooded fords. And then it's just you and the river and those old, steep-sided mountains jungled with rhododendron and mountain laurel—nothing at all like a walk in the park.

I write from personal experience. Late one November, on a day after steady rain, the Jacks kept rising as I attempted to work my way downstream from Beech Bottom. After the high water knocked me off my feet several times, lost nerve became found sense. The river ran me off the route and sent me bushwhacking for Horseshoe Bend Trail and the long, cold walk out to the shuttle car in Alaculsy Valley.

The water level in these two rivers is normally highest in late fall, winter, and early spring before leaf-out. Throughout this period of the year, many of the lower, downstream fords remain midthigh to waist deep (at their deepest) for weeks at a time. Of course when it really pours during the bare broadleaf season, these rivers flood and flood fast. The steep valleys of mountain rivers cause them to flood much faster than Piedmont rivers. If the soil is already saturated before it showers for an hour or two, the Jacks and Conasauga Rivers will rise significantly before the rain stops.

With normal spring precipitation, the Cohutta Wilderness rivers flow fairly full until bud break reaches the highest ridges in mid-May. The safest time to aquahike the two river trails, considering both depth and water temperature, is from late May through late October. During these months, except after substantial rainfall, the fords usually present no serious danger for adults, other than slipping and getting wetter than you wanted.

Fording Tips

■ A hiking stick is essential for balance on deep, swift fords.

■ Walk on the very bottom of the riverbed, on eddy sand and the smallest rocks possible. If you attempt to step from one large, slick, underwater rock to the next, you will probably fall and become much wetter than if you had waded on the bottom. A fall with the extra weight of a backpack greatly increases your chances of injury.

▪ Use good judgment. If one of the rivers becomes dangerous, do whatever you have to do—wait until it goes down, bushwhack alongside the river, abandon the route and work your way to a side trail—rather than risk a flooded ford.

▪ Don't pressure inexperienced, apprehensive hikers to attempt fords higher than their confidence levels. Hiking is supposed to be enjoyable, not threatening.

▪ If the current looks strong enough to knock you off your feet, unfasten the waist buckle of your backpack so you can quickly wriggle out of your pack.

▪ If you are concerned about heavy rain or already rising water, camp close to the nearest lead-in trail, so that you have a no-ford bailout route.

▪ Remember that downriver fords, the ones below major tributaries, are usually wider, deeper, and more powerful than those nearest the upper-elevation trailheads. The most challenging fords on the Jacks River Trail are downstream from Jacks River Falls, where three creeks—Rough, Murray, and Beech—add their collective volumes to the Jacks in a 1.5-mile stretch. The Conasauga's fords become considerably more difficult north of Bray Field after Tearbritches and Little Rough Creeks add their contributions. If the upstream fords are already demanding, or if it is raining hard as you head downriver, you may want to change your plans.

▪ A good backpack cover will enable your pack to float like a boat. If you need to make one ford to escape a high or soon-to-flood river, work your way to the longest pool you can find, take off your pack, and swim it across the pool. Or swim a rope across, then surf your pack over. This is a semi-emergency measure, to be employed only if you have decided you must get across the river. Once again, use good judgment. If the river is really flooded, don't attempt to ford by any method, including rope. Walk away, even if it means spending an extra night in the wet woods.

■ You may want to wear old running shoes or toe-protecting river sandals when you hike either the Jacks or the Conasauga River Trail. Boots quickly become heavy and waterlogged, and it is impractical and tough on the feet to take them off for each of the forty-two fords on the Jacks River.

Stream Crossings

The terrain detailed in this guide is wilderness, and with only one exception—the guywire spanning the thirty-third ford on the Conasauga River—there are no guywires or bridges to help hikers cross streams. That is how it should be. Stream crossings are simply part of wilderness travel, a necessary and potentially challenging part in this wilderness.

This guide employs two terms—cross and ford—to describe all of the wider stream crossings within the wilderness. When describing a trail that crosses a branch or creek, the term means that at more or less normal levels the water is below calf deep. When these streams are up and flowing fast, you are going to get your feet and footwear wet, but unless they are in flood, there is no danger of being knocked off your feet. Except right after rain, most crossings can be made dry-shod, or nearly so, by late June of the average hot, dry summer.

When describing a trail that fords a stream, the term means the water is or often can be calf deep or higher. Fording usually means wading and balancing on the slick stream bottom or submerged rocks. And perhaps slipping and becoming much wetter than you wanted.

Dividing the crossings into slightly wet (cross) and wading (ford) should give you a general idea of what to expect and what to plan for. However, water levels fluctuate widely with the seasons and, of course, the amount of recent rainfall. There are no guarantees. Once the two rivers become summer shallowed, however, they usually present few problems, and many of the upstream fords are below calf deep and very easy. Many winter and early spring fords become summer and fall crossings. During late August in the severe drought of 1986, two long-legged men in our backpacking group rock-hopped across all of

Conasauga River's thirty-eight fords and stayed completely dry. Conversely, in most years after heavy rains, especially in winter and spring before bud break reaches the high ridges, the longer side streams such as Rice Camp Branch, Beech Creek, and Rough Creek (Jacks River tributary) in the Cohutta Wilderness and both forks of Rough Creek in the Big Frog will rise well above their step-across rocks. After hard, heavy rains, all three of the Rough Creeks just mentioned can quickly rise to potentially dangerous depths.

All of the Conasauga and Jacks River crossings are rated as fords, even though the word "cross" is used occasionally for variety. All of the other stream crossings in the combined wilderness are rated as just that—crossings.

Deadfalls and Trail Maintenance

Wilderness trails are by regulation maintained to a more primitive standard than nonwilderness trails. This standard includes an acceptable number of deadfalls per mile. Under normal circumstances, the trails can easily be kept passable. After blizzards, hurricanes, and tornadoes, however, when the number of deadfalls becomes problematic, when trails most need maintenance, the prohibition against chain saws in wilderness makes clearing the way slow and strenuous.

Despite the exclusion of chain saws, the Cohutta Ranger District of the Chattahoochee National Forest does a very good job of maintaining the Cohutta Wilderness trails south of the Tennessee state line. In the spring of 1998, for example, a tornado ripped through the Jacks River Gorge, leaving jackstrawed trees piled along its path. The Cohutta Ranger District and its network of volunteers quickly got on the stick and cleared the Jacks River Trail. For all those who planned and worked, sweated and ached, thanks for a job well done. Although you may encounter path-blocking blowdowns after a major storm, the Cohutta Ranger District will clean up the windthrows within months, not years.

On the north side of Big Frog Mountain, however, the trails are not as well maintained. Judged against the Cohutta Ranger District standard, the Ocoee Ranger District of the Cherokee National Forest has fallen short; trail maintenance has been poor in the Big Frog Wilderness. Granted, they had numerous blowdowns after the blizzard in 1994 and Hurricane Opal in 1995. But despite the large pool of potential volunteers in nearby Chattanooga and Knoxville, the Ocoee Ranger District apparently made little effort to brush out or cut through wilderness trails until late 1998 and again late in 1999. The trail in the worst condition, Grassy Gap, may not be cleared out until the year 2000 or 2001.

I hope the Ocoee Ranger District will do a better job in the future. In the meantime, feel free to hold their feet to the fire—politely. And if you comment or complain, be sure to back it up with an offer to help—to volunteer your time and muscle, not just your mouth.

Signs and Blazes

Both wildernesses are currently employing the same scheme for sign and blaze usage within their boundaries. Trailheads and interior junctions are signed; trails are no longer being blazed by the Forest Service.

Vandalism of signs, including bear damage, is a recurring problem. If the sign is missing, use the post as your sign. If the post is gone, use the hole or the pile of rocks that once held it up as your sign. But most of all use your head—and your map and compass. Don't expect right-angle, red-line intersections like the ones on road maps, and don't expect all of the signs to be up all of the time, especially in Tennessee.

Horse Usage

Horses and their riders are allowed on eleven of the seventeen trails within the Cohutta Wilderness. At present, the entire length of eight trails—Hickory Creek, East Cowpen, Penitentiary Branch, Hemp Top, Hickory Ridge, Beech Bottom, Chestnut Mountain, and Rice Camp—are open to horse travel. Six trails—Tearbritches, Conasauga River, Chestnut Lead, Sugar Cove, Panther Creek, and

Benton MacKaye (from Watson Gap to its junction with Hemp Top)—are completely closed to horse usage.

The remaining three trails—Rough Ridge, Horseshoe Bend, and Jacks River—have split designations. Horses are allowed to Horseshoe Bend's view, but are prohibited beyond. On Rough Ridge horses are allowed northward only to mile 4.4, just beyond the pair of spring-run rivulets. Horses are prohibited on the Jacks River Trail except along two disjunct segments: the 1.4-mile stretch between the Beech Bottom and Penitentiary Branch junctions, and the first couple of miles on the old Bear Creek Road starting from Dally Gap. Horses are supposed to turn around before the first ford.

Horses are permitted in the Big Frog only on those sections of trails that follow the ridgeline boundary between the two wildernesses. The northernmost 0.8 mile of Hemp Top Trail, from Double Spring Gap to its end at Licklog Ridge Trail, is open to horse riders. Continuing to the west, the final 0.5 mile of Licklog Ridge Trail, from its Hemp Top junction to its end atop Big Frog Mountain, is legal for four-legged hikers. The next link to the west, Wolf Ridge Trail, is open to horseback riders along the 1.8-mile stretch from Big Frog Mountain's high point to its junction with Chestnut Mountain Trail.

Hunting Seasons

Hunting is a legal and somewhat popular pastime in the Cohutta–Big Frog Wilderness. Various overlapping seasons occur throughout much of autumn and early winter. There is also a spring season for turkey. (Not all barred owl hoots come from birds during this time of year.) To further complicate matters for hikers and hunters, the two states—Georgia and Tennessee—have different hunting seasons and laws.

All of the Cohutta Wilderness within Georgia lies at the core of the 95,000-acre Cohutta WMA. All of the combined wilderness north of the Tennessee border belongs to the 625,000-acre Cherokee WMA, which encompasses the same area as the Cherokee National Forest. This national forest, and therefore the WMA, is split into southern and northern sections by the Great Smoky Mountains National Park. The Big Frog Wilderness is located within the South Cherokee Portion, Ocoee Unit.

Big-game hunts within WMAs often last for a shorter period of time than those on non-WMA land. As a hiker, you should be particularly aware of the firearm season for deer. During a recent year the firearm season for deer in the Cohutta WMA was November 20–27. During that same year, the firearm season for deer in the Ocoee Unit of the South Cherokee Portion was split: November 5–7, November 12–14, November 20–28, and December 17–21.

Because nearby WMA land is much more accessible to motorized vehicles, most nonmounted big-game hunters don't venture very far inside the wilderness boundary. Hunters on horseback, however, can and do make hunt camps deep within the Cohutta Wilderness. Because horses are prohibited on most Big Frog Trails, there are even fewer hunters in the interior of the Big Frog Wilderness. Wearing orange would definitely be a good idea if you intend to hike during hunting season.

All of the Big Frog Wilderness in Tennessee's Cherokee National Forest is part of the roughly 52,800-acre Ocoee Bear Reserve. Bear cannot legally be hunted at any time of the year within the reserve.

For more information:

Cohutta WMA:

Wildlife Resources
2592 Floyd Springs Rd.
Armuchee, GA 30105
(706) 295-6041
www.dnr.state.ga.us/
    dnr/wild

Cherokee WMA:

Tennessee Wildlife Resources Agency
464 Industrial Blvd.
Crossville, TN 38555
(931) 484-9571
www. state.tn.us/twra/
    huntmain.html

Cohutta Wilderness Fishing Regulations

Every trailhead along the edge of Georgia's portion of the Cohutta Wilderness has a fishing regulation sign prominently posted. The two major watersheds within the wilderness—the Jacks and the Conasauga Rivers plus their tributaries—have different restrictions:

■ The Jacks River watershed is closed to all fishing from November 1 until the last Saturday in March.

■ Fishing within the Conasauga River watershed is restricted to artificial lures only from November 1 until the last Saturday in March.

Problem Bears

During the very late 1990s, a problem bear or two occasionally patrolled the Beech Bottom section of the Jacks River Trail. Bears become problems when they lose much of their fear of humans and grow habituated to backpacker food. Problem bears increasingly associate people with food rewards, and think that gorp is both tastier and easier to obtain than old-fashioned bear food, such as yellow jacket larvae. And just like bullies, bears that succeed in securing food with little resistance become bolder and more demanding. An emboldened bear will enter your camp, bluff you away, then drag off your pack and power bars. Or even rip into your tent looking for food.

Most often problem bears are created by problem campers. Campers cause problems when they throw substantial amounts of leftovers in the bushes, purposely leave food for animals, and worst of all, feed bears. When enough of these sloppy campers congregate in a small area, it doesn't take long for a bruin to learn that backpacks were put on earth to become bear buffets. People who feed bears create trouble for both the bears and other campers. Especially in areas where they are hunted, as in the Cohutta Wilderness, fed bears often quickly become dead bears.

Beyond being a good camper, there are three measures you can take to avert bear problems. The first, quite obviously, is to avoid camping in congested areas. The second is to hang your food—every bit of it—from a high tree limb right after supper. The third is to actively discourage bears from associating you with food. If a bear comes sniffing up to your camp, holler, bang pots and pans, throw rocks—do what you have to do short of seriously harming the bear to make it feel unwelcome.

Road Closures

At present, the Cohutta Ranger District (Cohutta Wilderness) does not gate roads during severe winter weather. This policy is due in large part to frequent destruction of gates in the past. The Ocoee Ranger District (Big Frog Wilderness), however, still gates roads—primarily the Big Frog Loop Road, FS 62—during periods of ice or snow.

Weather

Keep the following facts in mind when hiking Cohutta–Big Frog trails:

▪ **Elevation.** To a measurable extent, the higher the mountains, the more they create their own weather. As you climb a mountain, average wind speed and annual precipitation increase as temperature decreases—2 to 3 degrees for every 1,000-foot rise in elevation.

▪ **Shade.** High mountains help create their own cloud cover and shade their own lower slopes. When winter camping, it is important to remember that sunlight doesn't shine on some of the lowermost, north-facing slopes until after 10:00 A.M. If you have a choice, camp on the sunny south slope in winter.

▪ **Precipitation.** Depending upon elevation and location, annual rainfall averages 55 to 75 inches across the combined wilderness. The lowest amounts occur at the lowest elevations in the northwestern quadrant. The highest totals occur at the highest elevations in the southeastern quadrant. The driest period of the year is October to early November. A second, shorter dry period occurs in April.

▪ **Frost.** The last killing frost of spring is usually in mid-April. At the highest elevations, however, it often occurs from mid- to late April. The first killing frost of fall normally occurs during the middle of October. Above 3,800 feet, the first killing frost can occur as early as late September.

▪ **Wind.** Winter winds, sweeping across exposed ridges and funneling through gaps, are fierce. Steady winds of 10 to 20 miles per hour are common. Branch-cracking gusts of 30 to 40 miles per hour are not unusual on the higher ridges and gaps.

▪ **Unpredictability.** October, November, March, and April are the transition months. During these months the weather may be mild and sunny for two or three days, then it may suddenly turn cold and even snow in the highcountry.

■ **Low Temperatures.** Prepare for overnight lows in the 50s during June, July, and August. During May and September, prepare for overnight lows in the 40s, and even the 30s in early May and late September at the higher elevations. During the rest of the year prepare for overnight lows down to freezing and well below. During the average winter, ordinarily in January and February, but occasionally in late December or early March, the temperature drops to between 5 above to 5 below zero several times at the highest elevations of the combined wilderness. A real cold snap, a northern express that blows through every three to five years, can send the mercury down to 5 to 15 degrees below zero on top of Big Frog Mountain. And that does not include windchill.

How To Use This Guide

THIS GUIDEBOOK COVERS ALL OF THE TWENTY-SIX TRAILS within the Cohutta–Big Frog Wilderness. The trails are grouped geographically; a list of trails and a basic map are provided at the beginning of each section.

Trail Descriptions

A concise, at-a-glance summary of essential trail information appears at the beginning of each trail description. You can quickly refer to the foot trail number (as it is listed on the map), the trail's length, and its difficulty rating, often both for dayhiking and for backpacking. Also provided here are the starting and ending points of the trail, a list of junctions with other trails, topographic quadrangles, and a brief listing of some of the trail's outstanding features.

Following this information listing you will find a complete description of the trail, usually in the direction most frequently hiked, with special attention given to the type of terrain, stream crossings, trail junctions, and interior mileages to prominent physical features. At the conclusion of the trail description there is a section featuring some of the flora and fauna you may encounter while hiking.

Finally, the directions or references are given that will lead you to the exact trailhead or—if there is more than one path at a trailhead—to the specific trail.

When using this guidebook, keep in mind that conditions on wilderness trails are constantly changing and trails are occasionally rerouted. To be sure of current conditions, contact the appropriate Forest Service office before planning a hike.

Trail Ratings

Difficulty ratings are inherently subjective. Useful systems, however, are those that achieve consistency by limiting this subjectivity to a single source. To this end, I have walked and rated all of the trails described in this guide. Even if you do not agree with my ratings, I hope that you will find them consistent and, after a trip or two, useful. The trail ratings utilized in this book were based on the usual criteria: how much elevation changes, how that elevation change is accomplished, how difficult a trail is compared to others within the wilderness, how long the trail is, and how my legs and lungs felt during the hike. In general, to reflect the cumulative effect of the grade, the longer trails were rated as slightly more difficult than shorter trails with roughly the same number of feet gained per mile. Uneven footing, stream crossings, and fords were not taken into consideration; they are simply part of wilderness travel.

This rating system is also based on two assumptions. The first is that this scheme, or any other for that matter, does not apply to either end of the overall fitness spectrum—those in excellent condition and those in poor condition. Hikers who are able to run long distances with little effort already know that ratings are meaningless for them. Conversely, people who become winded after a flight or two of stairs would find difficulty classifications equally inaccurate, although much harder to ignore.

The other assumption is that a very high percentage of the people who walk or want to walk in this wilderness exercise, at least occasionally. After all, if you rarely exercise, it may not be wise to attempt to hike a mountain wilderness trail ranked more difficult than easy to moderate. Thus, this approach is designed to accommodate those people who exercise, at least sporadically, and who fall somewhere in that broad, general category between slightly below fair condition and slightly better than good condition.

Three categories of difficulty are utilized in this guide: Easy, Moderate, and Strenuous. As you will notice, many trails have been assigned two designations. These split designations are used to help span fitness levels when trail difficulty falls between obvious gradations. For instance, a trail may be rated "Dayhiking In: Moderate to Strenuous." A person in good cardiovascular condition would find this trail to be about moderate. A hiker in fair shape would probably rate the trail moderate to strenuous, and a person with a poor level of fitness would probably consider it strenuous.

The decision to walk a certain trail is a commonsense personal judgment. When planning a trip, you should be aware of the trail's difficulty, not intimidated by it; you should think of it as advice, not a warning. If you keep the intended mileage low, walk at a leisurely pace, and take frequent rest stops, you will often be surprised at what you can accomplish. If you want to walk a tougher trail, and think you can, give it a try.

Regional Directions and Maps

THE COHUTTA–BIG FROG WILDERNESS extends from north-central Georgia into southeastern Tennessee. Sixty-seven miles of road—almost all of it Forest Service and almost all of it dirt-gravel of varying width and roughness—wind around the two-state wilderness. To the south, the encircling road frequently doubles as the Cohutta Wilderness boundary. The northern arc of the road system generally remains from ⅔ to 1⅓ miles out from the border of the Big Frog Wilderness.

At irregular intervals dirt-gravel roads spoke away from the 67-mile loop, much longer north-south than east-west. These roads, which become paved at various distances away from the wilderness, link up with a 107-mile, roughly rectangular network of intersecting state and federal highways. Longer north to south than wide east-west, this rectangle of highways is defined by four small towns. The southern edge of the rectangle, GA 52, stretches from the southeastern corner, Ellijay, to the southwestern corner, Chatsworth. The quadrangle's northern highway, Tennessee's US 64, connects the northeastern corner, Ducktown, to the northwestern angle of the circuit, the community of Ocoee.

This guide utilizes a two-tiered system of directions. This arrangement is designed to avoid repetition, yet enable hikers to approach the inner loop from any point along the 107-mile rectangle of peripheral highways. The directions that follow are those to the access points: the intersections where the roads leading inward from the highways tie into the dirt-gravel loop. Detailed directions to all eight access points are given here at the beginning of the guide. These directions lead hikers, where necessary, from the two closest major intersections—one from the south and the other from the north, for example—to the roads that lead to the access points. The final segment of the access point directions guides you from the beginning of the connector road to the access-point intersection on the 67-mile dirt-gravel loop.

The second tier of directions, those that follow the trail descriptions, start at one or more of the closest access points. Final directions steer you from each of the appropriate access points to the trailhead via the dirt-gravel road.

Access Points

Access Point 1 (From the east): This access point is the three-way FS 68–FS 64 intersection near Potatopatch Mountain at the southernmost tip of the Cohutta Wilderness. The route to this intersection turns north from GA 52 onto Gates Chapel Road a short distance from Ellijay, Georgia.

Approach from the east: From the Ellijay Square, travel GA 52 West toward Chatsworth, Georgia, for a little over 5 miles before turning right onto Gates Chapel Road, marked with a street sign on the right and a brown Lake Conasauga/Bear Creek sign on the left.

Approach from the west: Hikers wishing to travel to the Potatopatch Mountain intersection from the west, from Chatsworth, will want to follow the directions to Access Point 1 from the west.

From Gates Chapel Road: Proceed on the main road slightly more than 7 miles (Gates Chapel Road becomes FS 90 where the pavement ends after slightly less than 5.5 miles) to the three-way FS 90–FS 68 intersection. Turn to the right and uphill onto FS 68, following signs for Lake Conasauga and the Cohutta Wilderness. Once on FS 68, continue straight ahead for approximately 3.5 miles to the three-way FS 68–FS 64 intersection.

The road forks where Gates Chapel Road becomes FS 90. Take the right fork, usually marked with a small FS 90 sign. From this point it is a dirt-gravel road.

Access Point 1 (From the west): This access point is the three-way FS 68–FS 64 intersection near Potatopatch Mountain at the southernmost tip of the Cohutta Wilderness. The route to this intersection turns east from US 411 onto CCC Camp Road in Eton, Georgia.

Approach from the south: From the US 411–GA 52 intersection in Chatsworth, Georgia, travel US 411 North for approximately 4.2 miles before turning right onto CCC Camp Road, designated with a green street sign, at the stoplight in Eton.

Approach from the north: From the US 411–US 64 intersection near Ocoee, Tennessee, travel US 411 South slightly less than 22 miles to the left turn onto CCC Camp Road at the stoplight in Eton. *From CCC Camp Road:* Proceed on the main road for a little more than 10 miles to the three-way FS 18–FS 68 intersection. After approximately 6 miles, the pavement ends and the road becomes FS 18. Following the sign for Lake Conasauga, turn left and uphill onto FS 68. Once on FS 68, continue straight ahead for approximately 6 miles to the three-way FS 68–FS 64 intersection at Potatopatch Mountain.

Access Point 2: This access point is the four-way FS 630–FS 17 intersection near Paint Bank Gap on the western side of the Cohutta Wilderness. The route to this intersection turns east from US 411 onto Grassy Street in Crandall, Georgia.

Approach from the south: From the US 411–GA 52 intersection in Chatsworth, Georgia, travel US 411 North for approximately 7.3 miles before turning right onto Grassy Street (green street sign).

Approach from the north: From the US 411–US 64 intersection near Ocoee, Tennessee, travel US 411 South for approximately 18.5 miles to the left turn onto Grassy Street.

From Grassy Street: Follow Grassy Street for 0.4 mile (cross over the railroad tracks), turn right onto Crandall-Ellijay Road, then after 0.1 mile or less turn left onto FS 630 (Mill Creek Road). Once on FS 630, proceed straight ahead (pavement ends after 0.6 mile) for approximately 9 miles to the four-way FS 630–FS 17 intersection.

Access Point 3: This access point is the three-way FS 16–FS 17 intersection approximately 2.5 miles west of where the Conasauga River leaves the Cohutta Wilderness. The route to this intersection turns east onto Old GA Hwy 2 from US 411 between Chatsworth, Georgia, to the south and the US 411–US 64 intersection in Tennessee to the north.

Approach from the south: From the US 411–GA 52 intersection in Chatsworth, Georgia, travel US 411 North for approximately 13 miles before turning right onto Old GA Hwy 2 (marked with a green street sign) immediately before the stone-sided Cisco Baptist Church.

Approach from the north: From the US 411–US 64 intersection near Ocoee, Tennessee, travel US 411 South for approximately 12.5 miles to the left turn onto Old GA Hwy 2 (marked with a green street sign) immediately after the Cisco Baptist Church.

From Old GA Hwy 2: Continue on the main road for slightly more than 3 miles (the pavement ends after approximately 2 miles) to the well-signed Old GA Hwy 2 (FS 16)–FS 17 intersection next to a WMA check station cabin.

Access Point 4: This access point is the three-way FS 221–FS 16 intersection next to the iron bridge over the Jacks River in Alaculsy Valley. Located on the Tennessee-Georgia border, this intersection is located at the end of the thin, northwestern tip of the Cohutta Wilderness. The route to this intersection turns east onto Ball Play Road from US 411 between the nearby communities of Oldfort and Conasauga, Tennessee.

Approach from the south: From the US 411–GA 52 intersection in Chatsworth, Georgia, travel US 411 North for approximately 19 miles before turning right onto Ball Play Road. Ball Play does not have a road sign, but it is well marked with signs for Ball Play Baptist Church and Mountain Springs Baptist Church. Highway 313 West heading toward Cleveland, Tennessee, is opposite the turn onto Ball Play Road.

Approach from the north: From the US 411–US 64 intersection near Ocoee, Tennessee, travel US 411 South for approximately 6.6 miles to the left turn onto Ball Play Road, marked by signs for Ball Play and Mountain Springs Baptist Churches.

From Ball Play Road: Continue on the main road for approximately 9 miles to the FS 221–FS 16 intersection next to the iron bridge over the Jacks River. The pavement ends after approximately 4 miles and the dirt-gravel road becomes FS 221.

Access Point 5: This access point is the three-way FS 55–FS 221 intersection at Blue Ridge Gap, several miles west of the Big Frog Wilderness. The route to this intersection turns south onto Cookson Creek Road from the segment of US 64 between US 411 and TN 68.

Approach from the west: From the US 64–US 411 intersection near Ocoee, Tennessee, travel US 64 East for approximately 2.5 miles before turning right onto Cookson Creek Road. Although Cookson Creek Road does not have a street sign, the turn—immediately after a gas station—is prominently marked with signs for Cookson Creek Baptist Church and Sylco Campground.

Approach from the east: From the US 64–TN 68 intersection near Ducktown, Tennessee, travel US 64 West for approximately 23.5 miles to the left turn onto Cookson Creek Road. The turn, just before a gas station, is marked with signs for Cookson Creek Baptist Church and Sylco Campground.

From Cookson Creek Road: Continue on the main road for approximately 11.5 miles to the FS 55–FS 221 intersection beyond Sylco Campground. Along the way, the pavement ends after approximately 4.0 miles, and the road becomes FS 55. A half-mile after FS 55 becomes dirt-gravel, it bears to the right, toward Sylco Campground, at a well-marked junction.

Access Point 6: This access point is the three-way FS 45–FS 221 intersection on Chestnut Ridge just north of the Big Frog Wilderness. The route to this intersection turns south from US 64 onto FS 45 at the Ocoee No. 3 Powerhouse.

Approach from the east: From the US 64–TN 68 intersection near Ducktown, Tennessee, travel US 64 West for approximately 7.5 miles before turning left onto FS 45 at TVA's Ocoee No. 3 Powerhouse. The turn is additionally marked with a sign for nearby Thunder Rock Campground.

Approach from the west: From the US 411–US 64 intersection near Ocoee, Tennessee, travel US 64 East for approximately 18.5 miles to the right turn onto FS 45 at TVA's Ocoee No. 3 Powerhouse.

From FS 45: Forest Service 45 crosses over the Ocoee River, passes close beside the powerhouse, then continues straight ahead, uphill, at the signed junction for Thunder Rock Campground, which is nearby to the right. Proceed on this steep, winding Forest Service road (the pavement ends just beyond the powerhouse) for slightly less than 3 miles to its three-way intersection with FS 221.

Access Point 7: This access point is the three-way FS 221–FS 65–County Road 251 intersection beside Tumbling Creek near the northeastern boundary of the combined wilderness. This intersection is approximately 1 mile north of the Georgia-Tennessee border. The route to this intersection turns west onto County Road 251 from TN 68 between McCaysville to the south and Ducktown to the north.

Approach from the south: From the three-way TN 68–GA 60–GA 5 intersection in McCaysville on the Georgia-Tennessee border, travel TN 68 North approximately 1.6 miles before turning left onto County Road 251 (unmarked) at the Tumbling Creek Campground sign.

Approach from the north: From the four-way TN 68–US 64 intersection near Ducktown, Tennessee, travel TN 68 South for approximately 2 miles, then turn right onto County Road 251 (unmarked) at the Tumbling Creek Campground sign.

From County Road 251: Continue straight ahead on the main paved road for approximately 5.5 miles to the paved, three-way intersection (another sign for Tumbling Creek Campground) just beyond the bridge over Tumbling Creek. Forest Service 221 and the campground are to the right; FS 65 continues straight ahead.

Access Point 8: This access point is the four-way intersection (FS 22, FS 64, Old Highway 2, and County Road 187) at Watson Gap near the eastern side of the Cohutta Wilderness. The route to this intersection turns west onto Old State Route 2 from GA 5 between Blue Ridge, Georgia, to the south and McCaysville on the Georgia-Tennessee border to the north.

Approach from the south: From the US 76–GA 5 intersection on the northern edge of Blue Ridge next to the McDonald's, travel GA 5 North approximately 3.7 miles before turning left onto Old SR 2. Three signs mark the turn: one for Watson Gap, another for Old SR 2, and a green Hwy 2 street sign.

Approach from the north: From the three-way TN 68–GA 60–GA 5 intersection in McCaysville, travel GA 5 South for approximately 6.5 miles to the right turn onto Old SR 2, marked with signs for Old SR 2 and a green Hwy 2 street sign.

From Old State Route 2: Continue on the main road for approximately 10.3 miles (the pavement ends after approximately 9 miles) to Watson Gap's four-way intersection and large Cohutta WMA sign.

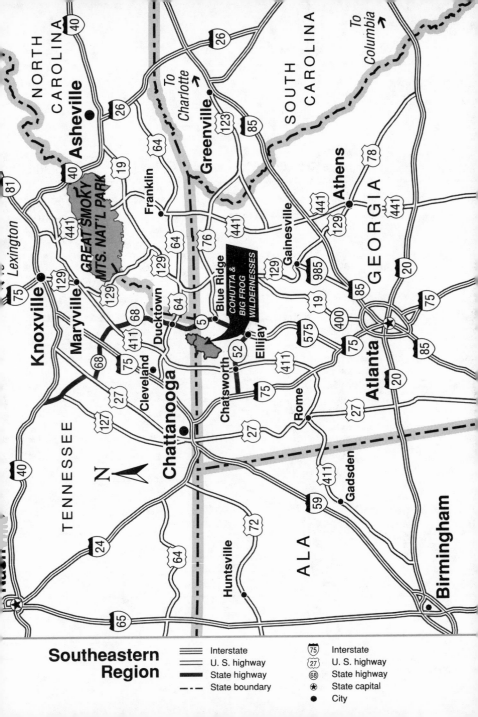

Southeastern Region

	Map Legend (lines)		Map Legend (symbols)
	Interstate	🛡75	Interstate
	U. S. highway	27	U. S. highway
	State highway	68	State highway
	State boundary	✪	State capital
		●	City

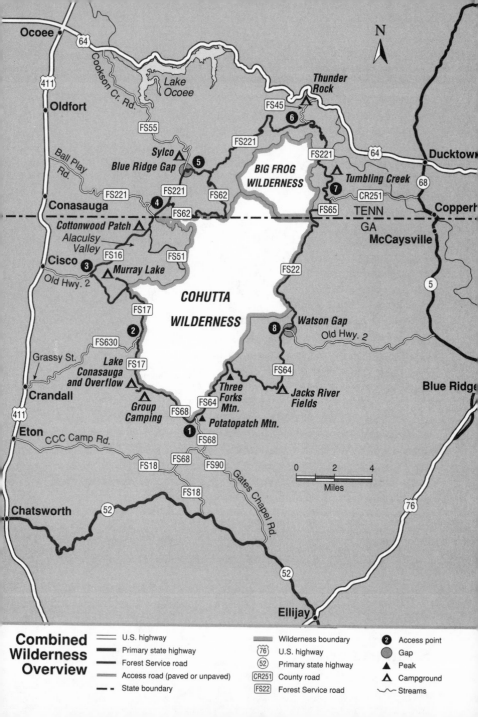

Cohutta Wilderness

I am glad I shall never be young without wild country to be young in. Of what avail are forty freedoms without a blank spot on the map?

—Aldo Leopold

Conasauga River Watershed

*Hiker fording
Conasauga River*

Trails

Conasauga River Trail
Chestnut Lead Trail
Tearbritches Trail
Hickory Creek Trail
Panther Creek Trail

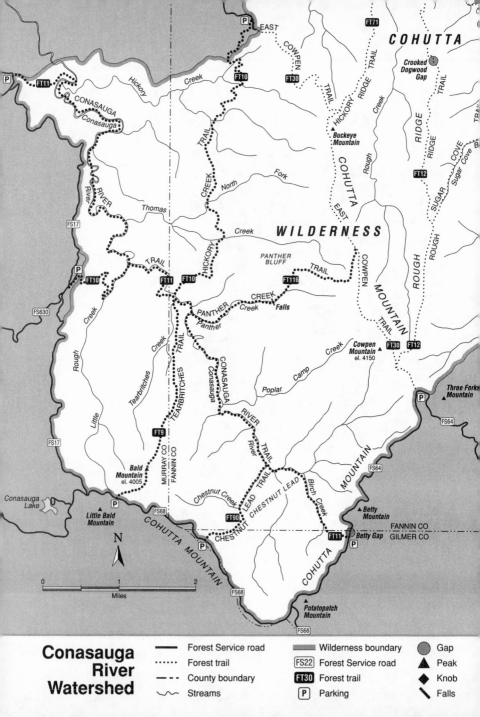

Conasauga
River
Watershed

——	Forest Service road
⋯⋯	Forest trail
—·—	County boundary
∿	Streams

▬▬	Wilderness boundary
FS22	Forest Service road
FT30	Forest trail
P	Parking

●	Gap
▲	Peak
◆	Knob
╲	Falls

Conasauga River Trail

- **Dayhiking** Easy to Moderate in either direction
- **Backpacking** (low to high) Moderate
- **Backpacking** (high to low) Easy to Moderate
- **Vehicular Access At Either End** Northwestern (low elevation) terminus off FS 17B, 1,640 feet; southeastern (high elevation) terminus at Betty Gap, 3,100 feet
- **Trail Junctions** Chestnut Lead, Panther Creek, Tearbritches, Hickory Creek
- **Topographic Quadrangles** Dyer Gap GA, Hemp Top GA-TN, Tennga GA-TN
- **Features** Giant hemlock; 38 fords; Conasauga River

FORMED FROM FEEDER STREAMS draining the southwestern corner of the Cohutta Wilderness, the Conasauga is without question one of Georgia's most beautiful rivers. The origin of its name, however, is hard to pin down. It might have come from the word *gansagi* (derivation unknown), the name of several settlements in the former Cherokee country, or from *kahnasaugh*, the Cherokee word for grass. But a more likely candidate is the Cherokee word for strong horse, which the settlers spelled *conasauga*. Perhaps a Cherokee named Strong Horse lived near the river, or maybe the Cherokee named this steep-sided mountain river for the strong horsepower of its floods.

The origin of the name for the southeastern trailhead, Betty Gap, is less mysterious. During the logging days, a widow named Betty sold meals and lodging to travelers. Her home was in a gap halfway across the Cohutta Mountains.

The Conasauga River is the usage magnet for the smaller, southwestern section of the Cohutta Wilderness. West of East Cowpen, all trails either end at, cross, or follow the river. Conasauga River is the second longest (13.0 miles) and the second wettest (thirty-eight fords) trail in the combined wilderness. The 6.3-mile stretch beyond Little Rough Creek is the longest segment of trail without a junction in the entire Cohutta–Big Frog Wilderness. This fact becomes most salient after heavy rain raises the river and forces you to decide between potentially dangerous fords or a long bushwhack out.

The Conasauga River Trail is described as it is most often walked, from southeast to northwest, from near the river's headwater springs to near its exit from the wilderness. Starting at Betty Gap, the initial 0.2 mile drops very sharply, the first of only two difficult grades on this predominantly easy trail. A sliding rivulet, a Birch Creek feeder, emerges from its spring source beneath a stand of tall white pine near the top of the descent. The rest of the forest at this high, cool end of the route is hemlock and hardwood—oaks, sweet birch, basswood, white ash, a few cucumbertrees, and yellow poplar.

Where the land slopes down to the left after the path crosses the rivulet, look for a giant hemlock (hopefully still alive) just downhill at 0.4 mile. This topped-out survivor—with a best-as-we-could measurement of 15 feet 3 inches in circumference—is the thickest trailside tree in the combined wilderness. Ringed with slowly rotting burls, the result of centuries of sapsucker pecking, this huge, hoary old tree is best described not as old growth, but as primeval growth. Eighty yards beyond the hemlock, look for the Georgia state record blackgum—measuring a modest 10 feet 5 inches in circumference —60 or 70 feet to the left of the trail.

The track proceeds on an easy downgrade parallel to the shallow, often tumbling upper run of Birch Creek. Here the treadway frequently runs along the rocky bottoms of small feeder streams. In places the path is all rock and muck, root, water, and rhododendron. Further down, the walkway descends a little steeper and angles away from the creek toward the Conasauga through forest where yellow poplar and sweet birch are abundant. At mile 1.3 the trail reaches the river and ford number one—narrow, shallow, and small rocked— easier than all the fords yet to come.

For the next 10.4 miles to the thirty-eighth ford, the trail parallels the Conasauga as it winds to the northwest, bisecting the basin almost as cleanly as the river itself. It often leads up and away or out and away from the stream, but always returns to ford. Despite these repeated rovings, the route frequently remains near the bank, where there is only a sparse screen of rhododendron between you and the rushing water. The Conasauga River Trail—like its longer twin, the Jacks River Trail—is the pleasant result of logging-rails-to-wilderness-trails succession. After the first ford, you will enter a railroad aisle promenade, a level or very easy walk down through the dark shade of rhododendron, hemlock, occasional white pine, and summer hardwoods. Beyond the first long set of cascades, the riverway arrives at its first junction, usually signed Chestnut Lead, at mile 1.9.

Its headwaters rising within the wilderness, the Conasauga flows cold and quick and clear, so clear that the shadows of trout holding in shallows have fins. The Conasauga, rippling white in the rapid water between pools, has that rhythm and magic, that inherent grace and glinting beauty of undefiled Southern Appalachian streams. The generally level treadway closely follows the crystalline Conasauga, which falls over 100 feet per mile to Bray Field. Just beyond the Chestnut Lead junction, the fords and low cascades begin again. Here the route makes seventeen river wades in 3.0 miles to the far bank of the eighteenth ford at mile 4.9. The river runs through occasional boulder-jumble dams and over high bedrock ledges pocked with water-swirl drill holes.

While the water is still squeezing through your shoes after the eighteenth ford (from right to left to the west bank), you should find the usually signed Panther Creek junction on the right edge of the trail. Panther Creek Trail fords the river immediately; the Conasauga Trail continues straight ahead toward its only dry stretch between fords. The track quickly climbs up and over a spur, descends to and crosses Tearbritches Creek, then enters what's left of Bray Field (1,920 feet) at its Tearbritches Trail connection at mile 5.4. A former cabin site and now a grassy, often congested camping area, Bray Field is the most important trail junction in the western half of the Cohutta Wilderness. Tearbritches ends here; two trails, Conasauga River and Hickory Creek, pass through the small clearing. Seventy-five yards beyond the Tearbritches junction, at the sign for the Hickory Creek ford, Conasauga River Trail turns 90 degrees to the left and follows an old road away from the river into the Bray Field floodplain.

Hickory Creek and Conasauga River Trails share the same treadway from the sharp left turn to where the fords start again at Little Rough Creek. The combined trail makes a flattened half loop away from, then back to, the river. The formerly farmed field now supports an impressive stand of second-growth trees—hemlock, sweetgum, white pine, and tall, straight yellow poplar. Christmas fern (also known as evergreen) is common beside the old wagon track. Before curling back to the river, the route passes beside an old, grassed-in beaver pond, still holding open water near the dam.

The next 0.7 mile is easy downhill walking on cobbly road above the river. The Conasauga is now wider and deeper; some of its gray, streambed boulders are as big as whalebacks. A steady whitewater cascade runs well below the grade. At mile 6.7 the trails split apart at the usually signed junction. The Conasauga River Trail angles to the right and quickly resumes its river walking ways. Only here, below the mouths of Panther, Tearbritches, and Little Rough Creeks, the lower Conasauga has more water and tougher fords than the section above Bray Field. The twentieth ford, a fast sluice above a cascade, is definitely dangerous at higher water levels and always tricky. As you make this ford from right to left, look for the railroad-cut gap in the rocks a few feet in from the bank. The railroad bed treadway heads through the cut at a right angle away from the river.

A short climb to the top of the bluff on the west bank below the twentieth ford gives you a good view of the cascade below. From this vantage point you can also see the long, straight vein of quartz running through the last third of the long plunge pool.

At the twenty-first ford, a low, broken bluff rises on the far bank. The small-leafed dwarf rhododendron blooms a light reddish purple here in late May and early June. Beyond this ford the Conasauga makes an entrenched, gorgelike bend—all slide, sluice, cascade, and short pool—between bluff and bedrock slanting back from river's edge. Two tenths mile beyond the twenty-second ford (right to left), Thomas Creek falls into the Conasauga on the far bank. Look for the narrow flash of white well above river level.

Starting with the twenty-third ford at mile 7.8, the riverway follows its usual pattern of parallel and ford—sixteen times in 3.9 miles. The woods along the lower river is a mix of conifers—white, Virginia, and loblolly pine, plus hemlock—and second-growth hardwoods. The abundance of sweetgum and the presence of sycamore and loblolly pine are proof of low elevation. The lower river is often flanked by steep, rocky slopes, the west-facing side noticeably dry, thin-soiled, and dominated by Virginia pine. The trail passes above a particularly long and scenic shoal with sparkling swimming holes at mile 10.3. The aquahiking is over after the thirty-eighth and final ford at mile 11.7.

Twenty-five yards beyond the last ford, at approximately 1,260 feet, the course turns 90 degrees to the left and climbs away from the river. An easy-to-moderate upgrade quickly leads you into a drier forest of Virginia pine, chestnut oak, mountain laurel, and deciduous heath shrubs. On the way up, a ridgecrest affords good summer and excellent winter views of Cohutta Mountain back to the left. Cohutta Mountain is a long ridgeline string of knobs and named peaks stretching away to the south, then southwest. Buckeye Mountain is almost due east; Cowpen Mountain is further south at 120 degrees.

The ascent to Conasauga River's northwestern end, no worse than moderate, winds along ridgetop and slope and around wet hardwood hollow. The track passes a wilderness sign at mile 12.7. Beyond the sign, the forest—thin yellow poplar and white pine in places—was logged a second time. With less than 0.1 mile remaining, the usually signed route turns left onto a woods road.

Nature Notes

If you walk a river-fording trail during warm weather, and especially if you wade about searching for swimming holes, you will probably see snakes on the river rocks. You can rest assured that these snakes are water snakes, not water moccasins as is commonly assumed. You will find no water moccasins (also known as cottonmouths) in the Cohutta Wilderness. None. Not a one. Nor will you encounter this poisonous reptile in the Southern Appalachians eastward and northeastward from the Cohuttas. Mountains cold enough for rhododendron, hemlock, and trout are too cold for water moccasins.

The large, banded reptile that inhabits the streams and rivers of the Southern Highlands is the northern water snake. Although the larger specimens of this species will readily strike if provoked, they are nonpoisonous. Cuts caused by a water snake's strike often bleed profusely because of an anticoagulant in the snake's saliva. If the jabs don't fend off would-be predators or human pesterers, water snakes have another little surprise waiting for their enemies. When threatened, they expel a foul-smelling musk from glands at the base of their tails.

The northern water snake (*Nerodia sipedon*) is just one of numerous species and subspecies in the *Nerodia* genus. In almost every suitable habitat throughout the eastern United States and west to the southern Great Plains, you can find one or more species of water snake. True to its name, the northern water snake is the only *Nerodia* species that ranges into Maine and across the southernmost regions of eastern Canada. This water snake can tolerate the cooler temperatures up to approximately 4,800 feet in the Southern Appalachians.

Mature northern water snakes are 22 to 53 inches long; females are generally larger than males. This species is identified by its pattern of alternating light and dark bands, most of which are highlighted with a separating line of dark brownish black. Especially along the first half of the snake's length, the darker bands widen toward the back, and the lighter bands, or blotches, widen toward the belly. The wider dark band is usually a warm orangish brown and the narrower light band is usually brownish beige.

The snake's skin darkens with age and with time elapsed since the last shed. Young snakes are more brightly colored than adults. Their dark bands are often bright orange-brown, strikingly beautiful when wet, especially in the sunlight.

Active day and night in warm weather, northern water snakes feed on fish, crayfish, frogs, salamanders, and even small mammals. They hibernate in winter. Female water snakes typically give live birth to fifteen to thirty young. Occasionally, however, they give birth to a slither of fifty—more than any other genus of North American snakes.

On the Conasauga, Jacks, and other similar Southern Appalachian rivers, I have witnessed over the years the results of numerous obligatory bludgeonings—a quick stick or rock to the head of a northern water snake presumed to be a moccasin. Even if every last one of these snakes had been a water moccasin, they should not have had their heads smashed to smithereens. If nongame species cannot live unmolested in wilderness, where then can they live free from meanness and ignorance? Spread the word. There are no water moccasins in the high mountains of North Georgia. And there are no legitimate reasons for killing water snakes in wilderness.

For nearly twenty years the Cohutta Wilderness was home to a succession of three straight state record hemlocks. In the late 1970s there was a "state record hemlock" sign near the still living (as of spring 1999), topped-out giant close to the left side of the trail at 0.4 mile. By the mid-1980s a nearby hemlock—a magnificent specimen 15 feet 2 inches in circumference and at least 150 or

eastern hemlock

more feet in height—had dethroned its very close neighbor. The same sign was moved a few hundred feet back toward Betty Gap to mark the new record holder.

The second champion died by 1990. The third state record hemlock, the larger of two towering together along that short section of treadway shared by both the Benton MacKaye and Jacks River Trails, crashed down in the mid-1990s. The current state champion hemlock, until someone finds a bigger one in the Cohuttas, is in Towns County.

While the eastern hemlock (*Tsuga canadensis*) occurs in nearly every habitat throughout the combined wilderness, this graceful conifer is most numerous and reaches its largest proportions on north-facing ridges, moist slopes, and stream margins. Where hemlock is abundant, its dense foliage darkens the forest floor. The size of its needles and cones makes the eastern hemlock one of the easiest of all trees to identify at any time of year. Its flattened needles are $\frac{1}{3}$ to $\frac{2}{3}$ of an inch long, with two whitish stripes on the undersides. Its roughly oval cones, averaging ¾ of an inch in length, are much smaller than those of any other native Southern Appalachian pine, fir, or spruce. With the lone exception of the planted firs atop Bald Mountain, the hemlock is the only small-needled evergreen along the trails in this guide.

In most parts of its large range the eastern hemlock is a medium-sized tree—60 to 80 feet in height and 2 to 3 feet in diameter. But at the rainy southern end of the Appalachians, this evergreen can grow much larger, up to 175 feet in height and 5 to 6 feet in diameter. These giant, slow-growing conifers are the oldest trees in the mountain forests of the eastern United States. The record age, rings actually counted, is nearly 1,000 years. The Conasauga River giant is at least four or five centuries old, perhaps even older.

Directions

Conasauga River has either-end vehicular access. Conasauga River's southeastern (upper-elevation) trailhead at Betty Gap can be most easily reached from Access Points 1 and 8, and its northwestern (lower-elevation) trailhead can be most easily reached from Access Points 2 and 3. (See the detailed description of the Access Points at the beginning of this guide.)

Southeastern trailhead at Betty Gap

Access Point 1: From the three-way FS 68–FS 64 intersection at Potatopatch Mountain, turn right onto FS 64 and proceed approximately 1.4 miles to the well-marked trailhead on the left side of the road.

Access Point 8: From the four-way intersection at Watson Gap, turn left onto FS 64 and follow that road for approximately 11.3 miles to the trailhead on the right side of the road.

Northwestern trailhead off Forest Service 17B

Access Point 2: From the four-way FS 630–FS 17 intersection, turn left and downhill onto FS 17, then proceed approximately 4.1 miles before turning right onto FS 17B at the Conasauga River Trail sign. Follow FS 17B for 0.3 mile to the trailhead parking area and bulletin board.

Access Point 3: From the three-way FS 16–FS 17 intersection, turn right and uphill onto FS 17, following the sign for Lake Conasauga and Conasauga River Trail. Travel approximately 3.5 miles before turning left onto FS 17B at the Conasauga River Trail sign. Continue on FS 17B for 0.3 mile to the trailhead parking area and bulletin board.

The one-way shuttle distance between trailheads is approximately 13 miles.

Notes

Chestnut Lead Trail

Foot Trail 90: 1.8 miles

- ■ **Dayhiking In** Easy to Moderate
- ■ **Dayhiking Out** Moderate
- ■ **Backpacking In** Moderate
- ■ **Backpacking Out** Moderate to Strenuous
- ■ **Start** Chestnut Lead Trailhead, 3,280 feet
- ■ **End** Conasauga River Trail, 2,290 feet
- ■ **Trail Junction** Conasauga River
- ■ **Topographic Quadrangle** Dyer Gap GA
- ■ **Features** Winter views; spring wildflower display;
  Chestnut Creek; old-growth hemlocks

MEASURING SLIGHTLY LESS THAN Big Frog's Fork Ridge Trail,
Chestnut Lead is the shortest walkway in the combined wilderness. Chestnut Lead is also the second easiest of the four Conasauga
River lead-in trails. It starts at almost 3,300 feet and, like the other
three, drops steadily to the river. But while Tearbritches and Panther
Creek Trails lose 2,085 and 1,830 feet respectively, the grades of Chestnut Lead lose only 1,000 feet and seem almost easy by comparison.

Despite its short length, this trail offers more diversity of habitat
than many of the longer paths within the Cohutta–Big Frog Wilderness. It starts out on upper slope and ridgecrest, drops into a rich,
hardwood hollow, then ends in the riparian zone of Chestnut Creek
and Conasauga River.

The geographical term "lead," which occasionally appears on
topo maps throughout the Southern Highlands, is just another word
for a prominent spur ridge that leads to a higher mountain or ridge,
in this case Cohutta Mountain.

Starting near the top of a knob on Cohutta Mountain, the trail follows and descends with Chestnut Lead to the northeast. The first 0.1 mile traverses the lead's rich, northwest-facing upper slope, where you can easily spot the distinctive, dark bark of black cherry, silverbell, and sweet birch. The track quickly angles onto the wide crest of the lead into drier forest of oak, sassafras, blackgum, and sourwood. Here you can still see slowly rotting chestnut boles to the left of the path. The trail's namesake tree is still surviving on the lead—but only as soon-to-die rootstock saplings.

The footpath drops off the crest onto southeastern slope, then begins its descent—a series of short, fairly steep downgrades on or near the ridgetop. White pine, mountain laurel, and small hardwoods are abundant in the ridgecrest forest. At 0.8 mile the route makes a short, sharp turn to the left and down into the head of a moist northwest-facing hollow. In the wake of the saw and the blight, the cove hardwood forest in the hollow has come back tall, straight, and diverse. Numerically dominant, the yellow poplars have grown perceptibly from decade to decade since I first saw them in the mid-1970s. The largest poplar, close to the trail in the upper hollow, is already slightly over 9 feet in circumference. In 100 to 125 years, if they are still healthy and protected, some of these trees from the Magnolia family will grow quite large—over 15 feet in circumference and over 140 feet tall. The treadway loses elevation steadily (easy to moderate overall) near the notch of the hollow. The stand also includes basswood, white ash, black cherry, northern red oak, sugar maple, cucumbertree, yellow buckeye, and silverbell.

Below the hollow, the path levels on slope above Chestnut Creek, rushing noisy and white through the rhododendron when the water is high. At mile 1.2, where a path continues straight ahead to a camp, the trail dips to the left and crosses the rocky creek the first of three times. The remainder of the route closely parallels the small stream through a riparian forest of hemlock and tall, still relatively thin broadleafs. At least half a dozen old-growth hemlocks remain along the creek. Between the first and second crossings, two lunkers tower on the upslope. The thicker of the two—a hoary old granddaddy of a tree—spanned 13 feet 2 inches in circumference, measured lower than the regulation 4½ feet from the ground.

The easy downhill walking continues on an old railroad grade. Occasional quartzite rocks brighten the streambed. As expected, the end of Chestnut Creek's run is a series of slides and low cascades to the cold, clear Conasauga River. Chestnut Lead Trail fords the shallow Conasauga, then ends at its usually signed junction with the Conasauga River Trail.

Chestnut Lead's first 0.7 mile offers good bare-branch views. You can see a pair of 4,000-footers near the beginning of the trail. Bald Mountain (4,005 feet) is at 310 degrees; Cowpen Mountain (4,150 feet) is at 40 degrees. Not far above the turn down into the hollow, views to the east and southeast are of the long, nearby ridgeline of Cohutta Mountain. Betty Mountain is the high point at 85 degrees, and Potatopatch Mountain is the peak at 130 degrees.

Nature Notes

On the way back from my first Chestnut Lead hike in the mid-1970s, I left the trail and followed the ridgeline of the lead for awhile before dropping down to the headwaters of the Conasauga. Along the way, on the upper southeastern slope of the lead, I came upon a hanging chestnut—suspended and loose enough to swing slightly with a shove. A chestnut snag 16 inches thick and perhaps 25 feet long hung straight down, smooth and gray, from the forked branches of a crooked old oak.

Perhaps killed by the blight, the dead tree probably stood, a stick-figure silhouette, for a decade or two before falling downslope. When it fell, the trunk wedged into the oak's fork at no more than a 30 degree angle. More time passed; the bole weakened and finally broke near its base. Because the angle of the slope was sharper than the angle of the trunk's repose, the snag swung free and caught the fork from above with its few remaining stubby branches. By the mid-1970s, the limbs of the oak had thickened just enough to hold the hanging chestnut snag snugly.

Remembering the American chestnut—the majestic tree that once dominated the virgin forest of the Southern Appalachians— always becomes a wistful eulogy. From 1904 when the blight was first detected in New York City, this accidentally introduced disease swept westward and southward on the winds with alarming speed. By the mid-1920s the fungus (*Endothia parasitica*) had already reached the Smoky Mountains. It began infecting chestnuts in the Cohutta Mountains in the early 1930s. Ten years later, most of the Cohutta's once magnificent chestnuts had been reduced to snags, bleaching gray like bones in the sun.

The American chestnut (*Castanea dentata*) was the most massive, most numerous, and most important tree—to wildlife and humans alike—in the Southern Appalachian forest. Its destruction was an ecological disaster. The species once crowned as the queen of the forest ranged from 80 to 125 feet tall, with a large, spreading crown easily recognized from a distance in winter. It grew to an incredible thickness: a maximum of 10 to 13 feet in diameter. Written reports described even larger specimens, from 14 to 17 feet in diameter.

American chestnut

Two lunkers measured in the Smoky Mountains—one of the two was even photographed —were 33 feet and 33 feet 4 inches in circumference. After both logging and blight, a Blue Ridge tree over 33 feet around is hardly imaginable, more a mythological symbol of former giantism and forest grandeur than future possibility.

The chestnut grew in a variety of habitats, from near riverside to extremely dry ridges. In some areas of the Southern Appalachians, this nut tree constituted 25 to 40 percent of the forest. It often occurred in nearly pure stands on ridgetops, such as Chestnut Lead, up to approximately 5,000 feet in elevation. Regarded as hardy and disease resistant before the blight, elderly chestnuts sometimes lived as long as 600 years.

Today, wildlife species cope as best they can with the cyclical mast productions of oaks. But before the blight, wildlife fattened upon a heavy mast crop of large, tasty chestnuts that rained to the ground. Deer, bear, raccoon, turkey, squirrel, and other animals, including free-range hogs, harvested this bonanza every year without fail. Bear and the now extinct passenger pigeon preferred the nutritious nuts above all other foods. Wildlife populations in the Southern Highlands were never the same after the disappearance of the chestnut.

Thus far the chestnut has refused to die out completely. Ever since the blight, root sprouts have grown into small saplings, only to be mowed down in turn by the fungus. Since these root sprout saplings are genetic clones, they offer no chance to develop selective resistance to the fungus. Occasionally, a sapling will reach 4 to 5 inches in diameter before being killed by the bark-ripping blight. In rare instances, one of these saplings actually produces a few nuts. But since the flowers could not be cross pollinated, the fruit provide no hope for genetic improvement. Any help, genetic or otherwise, must now come from foresters and scientists.

One more fact concerning the chestnut: it was beautiful in the spring. The great stands of chestnuts added more white to the color of spring than all the other white-flowering trees combined. In his classic book, *A Natural History of Trees*, Donald Culross Peattie observed: "In the youth of a man not yet old, native Chestnut was still to be seen in glorious array, from the upper slopes of Mount Mitchell, the great forest below waving with creamy white Chestnut blossoms in the crowns of the ancient trees, so that it looked like a sea with white combers plowing across its surface. Gone forever is that day; gone is one of our most valuable timber trees, gone the beauty of its shade, the spectacle of its enormous trunks sometimes ten to twelve feet in diameter."

Spring wildflowers abound along Chestnut Lead. Among others, Catesby's trillium, foamflower, mayapple, dwarf iris and crested dwarf iris, yellow mandarin, and giant chickweed, bloom here during the last third of April and the first half of May. Large colonies of white wake robin trillium are the best of show. Their abundant blossoms whiten the springtime woods on the moist, beginning slope, in the hollow, and along the stream. The trilliums near the river often open almost a week earlier than those near the trailhead.

The wake robin (*Trillium erectum*), also known as purple trillium and red trillium, produces deep purplish red flowers over most of its large range. But this species also bears other color morphs: pink, yellow, white, and greenish. All the wake robins I have observed thus far in the combined wilderness are white, which makes them easy to confuse with the large-flowered trilliums (*Trillium grandiflorum*).

Across the high mountains of North Georgia, trillium colonies with large white blooms are almost always composed of the large-flowered species. But that is not the case in the Cohutta Wilderness. Here there are few, if any, large-flowered trilliums, and wake robins with white flowers are often common in suitable habitat. You can distinguish these two native perennials by looking closely at the

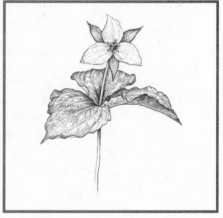

wake robin

flowers. The large-flowered trillium's white petals turn rose-pink with age; the petals of the white wake robin do not. The center of the large-flowered trillium has prominent yellow stamens; the wake robin's center has an exposed brownish maroon ovary with regular ridges similar to some cake molds.

All trilliums are characterized by plant parts—sepals, petals, leaves—that come in threes. The leaves of the wake robin are 4 to 7 inches long and so broadly ovate that they are often almost as wide as long. Usually 2¼ to 3¼ inches wide and nodding, the solitary flower rises above the whorl of leaves on an erect stalk. Unlike most wildflowers, trilliums take six years to bloom. This member of the Lily family is often 8 to 16 inches tall. Occasionally, however, very rich habitats produce jungle-sized wake robins.

A rich, moist, predominantly deciduous forest is the preferred habitat of this species. Wake robins are found at all elevations within the two-state wilderness, and they are particularly common on high north slopes and near small cove streams without rhododendron. The upper north slope of Big Frog has extensive displays that usually peak sometime between May 7 and May 21. The trillium along the lower elevation end of this trail are sometimes up and blooming before the ones near the trailhead break ground. You are likely to see the great white wake robin in bloom somewhere along this trail from April 20 to May 10.

Some wildflower guides refer to a foul odor, intended to attract carrion flies, given off by the purplish red variety of trillium. The smell accounts for this color morph's other common names—stinking Willie and stinking Benjamin. But these names seem to overstate the case. The smell of red-flowering wake robins in the Southern Appalachians is only slightly unpleasant, and not even particularly noticeable unless you sniff hard and close.

Directions

The Chestnut Lead Trailhead can be most easily reached from Access Points 1, 2, and 8. (See the detailed description of the Access Points at the beginning of this guide.)

Access Point 1: From the three-way FS 68–FS 64 intersection at Potatopatch Mountain, turn left with FS 68 and travel approximately 2.0 miles to the trailhead—complete with sign, bulletin board, and parking area—on the right side of the road.

Access Point 2: From the four-way FS 630–FS 17 intersection, turn sharply to the right and uphill onto FS 17 and travel approximately 3.3 miles to its southern end and three-way intersection with FS 68. Turn left onto FS 68 and proceed approximately 1.9 miles to the trailhead on the left side of the road.

Access Point 8: From the four-way intersection at Watson Gap, turn left onto FS 64 and follow that road straight ahead for approximately 14.8 miles—all dirt-gravel—to the Chestnut Lead Trailhead on the right side of the road. After approximately 12.8 miles on FS 64, you will arrive at the three-way FS 68–FS 64 intersection at Pota-topatch Mountain. Here, where FS 64 ends, continue straight ahead on FS 68 for the remaining 2.0 miles.

Notes

Tearbritches Trail

Foot Trail 9: 3.4 miles

- ■ **Dayhiking In** Easy to Moderate
- ■ **Dayhiking Out** Moderate to Strenuous
- ■ **Backpacking In** Moderate
- ■ **Backpacking Out** Strenuous
- ■ **Start** Tearbritches Trailhead near Little Bald Mountain, 3,606 feet
- ■ **End** Conasauga River Trail at Bray Field, 1,920 feet
- ■ **Trail Junctions** Conasauga River, Hickory Creek (see description)
- ■ **Topographic Quadrangles** Crandall GA, Dyer Gap GA, Hemp Top GA-TN
- ■ **Features** Bald Mountain; fern fields; winter views; Tearbritches Creek; Conasauga River

LIKE STIFFKNEE TRAIL in Tennessee's portion of the Joyce Kilmer–Slickrock Wilderness, Tearbritches bears one of those colorful, descriptive names—names that recall hardships of earlier times—common throughout the Southern Appalachians. Although there are plenty of brier patches on the open, upper slopes of Bald Mountain, they are not as bad as the name might suggest. The trail is usually well maintained, and the extra hikers from the group campground opposite the trailhead help keep the path open.

Tearbritches is primarily a ridgecrest and upper-slope trail with numerous winter views through the stick-figure hardwoods. It is also the most strenuous of the four Conasauga River lead-in trails. From the top of Bald Mountain, this path loses close to 2,100 feet in its final 2.9 miles. Several of its grades are among the steepest in the combined wilderness.

Beginning in the gap between Little Bald and Bald Mountains, Tearbritches climbs almost from the start—sharply at first, then moderately—to the broad crown of Bald Mountain. The upgrade, 400 feet in 0.5 mile, heads to the northeast through a largely broadleaf forest of mostly smallish trees. The occasional old oaks, low-limbed logger's culls, are noticeably thicker than the second-growth. The well-constructed path skirts the eastern edge of the wide, gently domed mountaintop.

Bald Mountain is significant for two reasons. Its broad, nearly level shoulder, Little Bald Mountain, was once an athletic field for the Cherokee, hence the name Bald (also formerly called Ball) Mountain. The peak's other claim to fame is geographical. Its high point (4,005 feet) is the westernmost landmass over 4,000 feet in elevation in the eastern United States. That is, west of Bald Mountain, no matter how far north in the United States, the land does not rise above 4,000 feet again until it reaches the Great Plains, far across the Mississippi.

This mountain is distinctive in another way. Global warming be damned, someone is trying to tinker with the glacial clock by establishing a spruce-fir forest on Bald Mountain's pate. By the late 1970s, there were already twenty-five to thirty of these highcountry conifers on the mountaintop, some 5 to 7 feet tall. They have grown well. These oldest and tallest trees are further to the left (west) of the shorter ones easily seen from the trail. Many more have been planted during the past 5 to 15 years. In the spring of 1998, he, she, or they were at it again. Someone had cleared numerous small circles, carefully planted fir and spruce saplings, then mulched them with forest duff.

The short ascent at the beginning of the trail is the only uphill grade on the way down to Bray Field and the Conasauga River. The treadway continues across the eastern side of the mountain's crest, then begins its descent on the moist, north-facing ridgeline. Especially during a wet spring, a lacy, fieldlike expanse of ferns, acres and acres of them, flanks the footpath beneath the open hardwood forest. The uppermost ridge also supports a few native yellow birches, a species extremely close to the western limit of its range that barely extends into northernmost Georgia.

Heading almost due north, the downhill walking remains fairly easy until 0.9 mile. Here the route pitches down a memorably steep, 0.3-mile long downridge run. Below this segment the descent eases to moderate, and the forest makes the transition to lower elevation and less moisture. Sassafras, yellow poplar, hemlock, and white pine saplings are all more common here than above. At mile 1.4 the track temporarily bottoms out at a headwater rivulet that probably has some flow, especially downstream, most of the year. This prong of Tearbritches Creek is often boar-wallowed upstream from the path.

Across the rivulet, the trail continues easy up or level through a drier, south-facing forest where red maple, sourwood, and blackgum are common. At mile 1.7 the hiking starts down hard again, a sharp enough descent to cause a heavy-packed, balky-kneed hiker to look for a runaway-backpacker ramp. Fraser magnolia, silverbell saplings, black cherry, and basswood shade the pitch. Beyond a very shallow gap, the footpath gently rises for a short distance, then heads down again. By mile 2.3 the forest has accomplished the transition to oak-pine. Here a shrub layer of deciduous heath has replaced the ferns, and those nearly ubiquitous indicators of drier soils—chestnut oak and Virginia pine—become increasingly abundant.

At mile 3.0, where a path continues straight ahead through pines, the treadway veers to the left and down off the ridgetop. A steep, 0.1-mile-long drop heads down into the riparian strip of rhododendron and hemlock. The remainder of the route parallels normally gentle Tearbritches Creek, crosses the stream where it is wide and shallow, then quickly ends at its usually signed tie-in with the Conasauga River Trail. This connection is located close to the Conasauga River at the upstream edge of Bray Field.

Bray Field is the most important trail junction in the western half of the Cohutta Wilderness. Tearbritches ends at the field. Two other trails—Conasauga River and Hickory Creek—pass through it, and the lower access point of a fourth trail, Panther Creek, is nearby. Hickory Creek and Conasauga River Trails share the same treadway for 1.3 miles, from Little Rough Creek's confluence with the Conasauga to Bray Field. If you turn left (northwest and downstream) from Tearbritches onto the Conasauga River Trail, you will quickly arrive (75 yards) at the wide gap where Hickory Creek Trail fords the river and diverges from the Conasauga River Trail.

Nature Notes

The dominant species of oak changes as the trail loses elevation to Tearbritches Creek. White oak predominates atop Bald Mountain and its upper slopes. Northern red oak prevails along the middle third of the ridgeline, and still lower, on the driest section of trail, the chestnut oak wears the crown.

From early to mid-June, hundreds of Indian pinks bloom along either side of the path starting at 0.9 mile. These perennial herbs, which often grow two feet tall, descend with the trail for nearly 0.1 mile. The Indian pink's unusual flower resembles a trumpet, red on the outside and bright yellow-green on the inside. At its uppermost end, the throat of the trumpet flares into five narrow, reflexed lobes.

While ferns are common beside many moist sections of trail throughout the wildernesses, they are exceptionally abundant along Tearbritches. From mile 0.6 to mile 2.2, where the forest completes the transition to drier oak-pine, fern fields often flank the path. At least seven fern species occur on Tearbritches' high, moist, north-facing ridge. New York, hay-scented, cinnamon, and interrupted ferns are all either exceedingly numerous, unusually distinctive, or both.

The most prolific species beside this section of trail, and throughout the combined wilderness, is also one of the easiest of all ferns to identify. The deciduous New York fern's mostly alternate pinnae (its leafy foliage) taper gradually to nearly nothing at either end. The lowermost pinnae of this 12- to 24-inch fern resemble tiny wings.

New York ferns frequently occur in dense monocultural beds. Growing at even intervals beneath widely spaced trees, they are similar in uniformity to an agricultural crop. There are two reasons for this appearance. First, because most ferns grow from perennial underground rhizomes, they often produce large, evenly spaced, cloned stands of a single species. New York ferns also have a competitive edge: they use herbicide to poison other plants.

"God created ferns to show what He could do with leaves." When he wrote that sentence, Henry David Thoreau could have been referring to the finely-cut, feathery fronds of the hay-scented fern. Like the New York fern, and for the same reasons, the hay-scented fern often grows in closely packed, monocultural beds. Abundant throughout the Southern Appalachians, the hay-scented is the second most common fern in the Cohutta–Big Frog Wilderness. The alternate pinnae—thin-textured, yellow-green, and delicate—have the light, sweet scent of newly mown hay. Its arching, deciduous fronds are usually 15 to 30 inches high. Because their beds are often intermixed, it would appear that New York and hay-scented ferns have developed at least some immunity to the other's poison.

The easily recognized cinnamon fern is almost always the tallest fern in the moist, nearly wet sites it requires. Throughout most of the combined wilderness, especially below 3,600 feet, this fern is usually found on the moistest slopes below ridgeline and at the heads of seeping hollows. But here on the north-facing exposure just below 4,000 feet, the cinnamon fern grows right on the ridge—often in the middle of the hay-scented and New York fern beds.

This common nonflowering plant forms clumps of 2- to 4-foot-tall fronds that arch backwards in a circular spray. During the spring several fertile stalks bearing thousands of cinnamon-colored spore cases rise from the center of the spray. Nearly as tall as the sterile fronds and completely lacking leaf tissue, these fertile fronds release their spores in late spring and early summer, then wither and die back.

The alternate pinnae, blunt tipped along the edges and deeply lobed, have distinctive, fuzzy tufts of light reddish brown hairs on their lower bases. This cinnamon-colored fuzz is also prominent along the stem, especially near the ground. Hummingbirds utilize the downy fuzz for nesting material. Pioneers, for some unknown reason, once believed that one bite of an unfolding cinnamon fern frond would prevent toothache for a full year.

On a steep downhill pitch at 0.9 mile, the path bisects one patch of interrupted fern. This colony may be the only one beside the trails in the combined wilderness. The interrupted requires cool, moist conditions, and its huge range—much of eastern North America and eastern Asia—barely extends southward into warm Georgia. So far this fern has been found in only eight Georgia counties, six of them across the northernmost section of the state. And even in the mountains, the interrupted fern is confined to rich woods at fairly high elevations.

Like the cinnamon and hay-scented, the interrupted fern has a descriptive common name helpful in identification. This fern really is interrupted. Its regular rows of green pinnae are interrupted by one to five pairs of short, fertile stalks laden with clusters of round, green-turning-to-brown spore cases. Located on the lower blade (the leafy part of the frond), these fertile stalks are noticeable because they are smaller, darker, and have no foliage whatsoever. After the spores disperse, the cases disintegrate, leaving the blade with a conspicuous gap between upper and lower pinnae.

Growing in tall clusters or clumps, the interrupted fern is usually 2½ to 4 feet high. The slightly alternate pinnae are blunt tipped and deeply divided.

Shakespeare's line, "we have the receipt of fern-seed, we walk invisible," from *King Henry IV*, expresses the myth and superstition

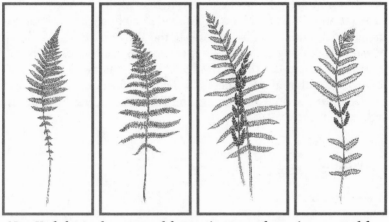

New York fern   *hay-scented fern*   *cinnamon fern*   *interrupted fern*

surrounding fern propagation. Since ferns utilize neither flowers nor seeds, fern reproduction remained a mystery until the mid-1800s. In fact, some Elizabethans believed that fern seeds were invisible, and that anyone who could obtain them would become invisible.

(Note: The bit of Elizabethan trivia is paraphrased from Field Guide to the Ferns of Georgia *by Lloyd H. Snyder Jr. and James G. Bruce.)*

Directions

The Tearbritches Trailhead can be most easily reached from Access Points 1, 2, and 8. (See the detailed description of the Access Points at the beginning of this guide.)

Access Point 1: From the three-way FS 68–FS 64 intersection at Potatopatch Mountain, turn left with FS 68 and travel approximately 3.5 miles to the trailhead bulletin board on the right side of the road. Tearbritches begins across the road from a group camping area.

Access Point 2: From the four-way FS 630–FS 17 intersection, turn sharply to the right and uphill onto FS 17 and travel approximately 3.3 miles to its southern end and three-way intersection with FS 68. Turn left onto FS 68 and continue approximately 0.4 mile to the trailhead on the left side of the road.

Access Point 8: From the four-way intersection at Watson Gap, turn left onto FS 64 and follow that road straight ahead for approximately 16.3 miles—all dirt-gravel—to the Tearbritches sign, bulletin board and parking area. After approximately 12.8 miles on FS 64, you will come to the three-way FS 68–FS 64 intersection at Potatopatch Mountain. Here, where FS 64 ends, continue straight ahead on FS 68 for the final 3.5 miles to the Tearbritches Trailhead on the right side of the road.

Notes

Hickory Creek Trail

Foot Trail 10: 8.7 miles

- ■ **Dayhiking** Easy to Moderate in either direction
- ■ **Backpacking** Moderate in either direction
- ■ **Vehicular Access At Either End** Southwestern (high elevation) terminus at FS 630 Trailhead, 2,300 feet; northeastern (low elevation) terminus near Rice Camp Trailhead, 1,800 feet
- ■ **Trail Junctions** Conasauga River (see description), Tearbritches (see description), East Cowpen
- ■ **Topographic Quadrangles** Tennga GA-TN, Hemp Top GA-TN
- ■ **Features** Winter views; Conasauga River; Little Rough Creek

HICKORY CREEK IS THE THIRD LONGEST TRAIL in the combined wilderness. Most hikers do not walk its entire length, choosing instead to hike in from either end to the scenic Conasauga River, which the trail fords. Hickory Creek's southwestern trailhead provides the shortest and easiest—and therefore the most heavily used—way to the Conasauga downstream from Bray Field. The route is described as it is most often begun, from southwest to northeast, from near the Conasauga River to East Cowpen's northern end.

This pleasant woodland walk descends gradually on the wide, rocky treadway of an old road known locally as Camp 20 Trail. It rounds several hardwood hollows full of sweetshrub before heading down on the narrow crest of a ridge at 0.5 mile. Here the second-growth forest—sourwood, blackgum, sassafras, red maple, chestnut oak, and Virginia pine—is thin and short-crowned. The rocky track soon curls to the right off the ridgecrest, crosses over a spur, then continues the easy or easy-to-moderate downgrade to mile 1.0, where it switchbacks into moister forest above Little Rough Creek. Here the trees—sweetgum, sweet birch, yellow poplar, basswood, and hemlock—are taller and thicker. Rosebay rhododendron, which starts to bloom in mid-June, adds its lustrous, year-round green to the understory.

The roadbed walkway parallels this lively brook until crossing it on piled rocks at mile 1.6. The trail continues 75 yards to the Conasauga River, where it turns right and follows the road upstream beside the river. From this turn and for the next 1.3 miles to its fording of the Conasauga at Bray Field, Hickory Creek shares its treadway with the Conasauga River Trail. The route closely parallels the western bank of the scenic, clear-watered Conasauga for 0.7 mile. This rocky segment, nearly level or easy up, provides numerous, largely unobstructed views of the river's shoals and gray, whaleback rocks.

At mile 2.4 the wide path pulls away from the river, then makes a somewhat flattened half loop back to the Conasauga at Bray Field. The course, which passes beside a long-abandoned beaver pond, often skirts the outside edge of the formerly cleared land. Bray Field has served as a family farm, a railroad switch, and a logging camp. In the 1920s the Bray family ran a boarding house for logging officials. The forest—hemlock, white pine, and tall hardwoods such as sweetgum and yellow poplar—has steadily encroached upon what was left of the grassy area over the last 25 years. Now Bray Field is a backpacking camp and a trail switch—the most important junction in the western half of the Cohutta Wilderness. Tearbritches Trail ends here. Conasauga River and Hickory Creek Trails pass through the often congested, small opening; the lower-elevation end of a fourth trail, Panther Creek, is nearby.

Hickory Creek splits apart from the Conasauga River Trail at mile 3.0 and fords (a dry-shod crossing in late summer drought) the river at the usually signed wide gap in the streamside vegetation. The remaining 5.7-mile segment is the second longest stretch without a junction in the combined wilderness. It is also the Cohutta–Big Frog's easiest long section of trail without river fords. From an elevation of 1,920 feet at Bray Field, Hickory Creek loses only 120 feet to its northeastern, East Cowpen end. This frequently undulating path has no sustained grades of even moderate difficulty. The numerous ups and downs are mostly easy, with occasional short, easy-to-moderate grades serving as reminders that this is still a mountain trail.

The undulations follow a pattern. This isolated track, used infrequently by hikers, traverses a low-elevation rough—a splay of knobs, spurs, and hollows repeatedly notched by shallow gaps and small watercourses flowing west toward the Conasauga. Thus the trail dips to a stream, rises to the upper slope or top of a ridge, dips to a gap, rises along the next spur, then drops again to water. The forest changes as quickly as the terrain. The stream margins are belts of hemlock, rhododendron, and hardwoods such as sweet birch; the spur tops and upper slopes are oak-pine—white and Virginia pine mixed in with red maple, mountain laurel, sassafras, sourwood, blackgum, and the oaks, especially chestnut and scarlet. The hollows are most often dominated by white oak and yellow poplar. Numerous stands of tall white pine flank the isolated footpath; groves of their fast-growing saplings are rising straight up to the canopy, often at 3 to 4 feet per year.

The route winds to the north after fording the Conasauga. At mile 3.7 it crosses a permanent, often mucky rivulet, the beginning of a Thomas Creek fork. The only potentially confusing point along the way occurs four-tenths of a mile further, where the track crosses rocky Thomas Creek, then turns to the right at a prominent horse camp before heading up and slightly to the left on old roadbed. The treadway rock-steps North Fork Thomas Creek, just big enough for small fish in miniature pools, at mile 4.8. After slightly more than a mile, the path steps over the first of two small branches. These two rivulets flow together just downstream to form an unnamed fork of Hickory Creek.

At mile 6.3 the route ties into a former road that was in use when the Cohutta was designated wilderness. The remainder of the walking follows the wide, very easy grades of this woods road as it crosses over culverted streams (forks of Hickory Creek) and rounds hardwood hollows. Where the hollows face north, they are moist and forested with hemlock, basswood, red maple, sweet birch, and tall yellow poplar. The trail exits the wilderness at mile 7.9. The final 0.8 mile winds through managed, sometimes sunny woods. Several of the steep-sided hollows that fall away to the left have monocultural yet aesthetically pleasing open stands of straight and symmetrical yellow poplars. A left turn onto East Cowpen Trail and 75 more yards of hiking finish the trip to the Rice Camp Trailhead.

Nature Notes

If you walk through moist, low-elevation forests during the morning or late afternoon, you will probably hear the rich and melodious voice of the wood thrush. You are not likely to spot this secretive inhabitant of the dense understory while hiking by at normal speed. But you can easily identify the bird by its distinctive song—a series of loud, flutelike phrases, each followed by a softer guttural trill. Some of the trills sound like someone shaking a large, thin sheet of metal. One of its phrases is sometimes spelled phonetically as *ee-o-lay*. Call notes include a rapidly repeated *pit-pit-pit*. Males of this species sing from the time of their arrival, usually by April 10, through July, and even into early August.

The wood thrush is a summer resident throughout almost all of the eastern half of the United States. Within the combined wilderness, it is a common breeding bird in moist deciduous or mixed forests at lower and middle elevations. Although this neotropical migrant occasionally mingles with the veery, another spotted brown thrush, on the highest mountaintops, it is much more common below 3,000 feet. By mid-October most wood thrushes have departed for their wintering grounds, mainly from Mexico down through Central America to Panama.

The wood thrush—reddish brown above and white with dark spots below—is 7½ to 8 inches long. The crown and nape are bright reddish brown; the rump and tail are brownish olive. This bird's prominent white eye ring is conspicuous against its streaked face. If you get a good look at a thrush, take note of the spots on its breast. With large dark spots on throat, breast, and sides, the wood thrush is much more heavily spotted than any other of the spotted brown thrushes. The only other summer resident thrush is the veery, which has only faint spotting on its upper breast.

The pileated woodpecker's loud call—either rising and falling both in volume and pitch or a steady ringing staccato—is one of the wildest sounds left in the Southern Highlands. Although you may catch no more than a glimpse of this wary bird in half a dozen hikes, you are almost guaranteed to hear it at least once, year round, on the longer trails in this guide.

Bird books describe this call as *kik-kik-kikkik-kik* or *cuk-cuk-cuk-cuk-cuk*. Up close, you will hear a flickerlike *wuck-a wucka-wuck* vocalization. In spring, these big woodpeckers drum to establish territory. They find just the right, resonant spot of dead wood, then tattoo an amazingly quick drumroll for 3 to 5 seconds.

While pileateds are wary, these large crested birds are not as cautious as many accounts suggest, especially in the deep woods of wilderness. If you sit quietly while taking a break, especially in an open hardwood hollow, they will occasionally forage in plain view 30 to 40 yards away. Pairs often feed in the same vicinity, and frequently communicate back and forth. Their antics and interactions are interesting to observe. And their feeding pattern, which includes a series of stiff, quick hitches—like a windup toy—is comical.

With the default by extinction of the ivory-billed woodpecker, the crow-sized (16½ to 17½ inches) pileated becomes not only the largest but also the only crested woodpecker north of Mexico. Perched birds are almost entirely black on their backs and folded wings. Black and white stripes lead up the neck before bending toward the bill. Male and female differ in the amount of red on their heads. The dapper male has a red moustache back from his bill and below his eyes. And his crest, from the upper bill all the way back across the crown, is bright crimson. The female lacks the mustache, and her forehead is black above the bill. Only the rear half of her topknot peak is scarlet.

Like many other large birds, this woodpecker has a black-and-white flash pattern on the underwings. The pileated can be readily identified at considerable distances—from one slope of a wide creek valley all the way across to the other for instance—by its sweeping wing beats and undulating flight.

This woodpecker's large size, its ability to rip apart a rotten log quickly, and its habit of startling daydreaming walkers with its loud call inspired frontier names such as log cock, cock of the woods, wood Kate, Indian hen, good God, and Lord-a-mighty. Coming from Greek, its genus name (*Dryocopus*) means tree cleaver or woodcutter. The species name (*pileatus*) means capped or crested. Translated as the crested tree cleaver, its scientific name gives you a good idea of its power.

Although they prefer low-elevation hardwoods, pileateds can be found in all habitats and elevations of the combined wilderness. These woodpeckers thrive in mature forests with plenty of trees large enough for nesting and roosting cavities—and large enough to support colonies of black carpenter ants, their favorite food. They hammer out large oval holes for nests and roosts, and they often excavate long, shallow, rectangular holes in rotting wood as they search for food. Abandoned cavities provide shelter for numerous other wildlife species.

Crested tree cleavers eat insects and berries from plants such as American holly, poison ivy, and pokeberry. In winter their major food source is the large black carpenter ant. They locate a colonized tree, jackhammer into the tunnel system, then lap up ants with their long tongues, which are both barbed and sticky.

Naturalists have long wondered how these woodpeckers recognize ant-infested trees. Most authorities still maintain that these big birds hear the ants inside the tree. Recently, however, others have proposed that the woodpeckers can smell the distinctively tangy formic acid the ants excrete as waste. If this is true, pileateds are not the only creatures who home in on this scent: formic acid is an ingredient used in making the popular snack called Pop-Tarts.

Directions

Hickory Creek has either-end vehicular access. Hickory Creek's southwestern (upper-elevation) trailhead at the end of FS 630 can be most easily reached from Access Point 2, and its northeastern (lower-elevation) terminus near the end of FS 51 can be most easily reached from Access Points 3, 4, and 5. (See the detailed description of the Access Points at the beginning of this guide.)

Southwestern trailhead off FS 630

Access Point 2: From the four-way FS 630–FS 17 intersection, travel straight ahead through the junction on FS 630 and continue

0.3 mile to the large trailhead parking area. The trail is the old road on the other side of the gate.

Northeastern terminus near the end of FS 51

Hickory Creek's northeastern end is 75 yards beyond the gate at the Rice Camp–East Cowpen Trailhead. Follow the directions to Rice Camp Trail to the Rice Camp–East Cowpen Trailhead. East Cowpen is the gated trail that continues straight ahead from the dead end. The signed, Hickory Creek–East Cowpen junction is located on the right side of East Cowpen 75 yards past the gate. (See Rice Camp Trail, page 128, for further information.)

The one-way shuttle distance between trailheads is approximately 17 miles.

Notes

Panther Creek Trail

Foot Trail 116: 3.4 miles

- ■ **Dayhiking (low to high)** Moderate
- ■ **Dayhiking (high to low)** Easy to Moderate
- ■ **Backpacking (low to high)** Moderate to Strenuous
- ■ **Backpacking (high to low)** Moderate
- ■ **Interior Trail** Western (low elevation) terminus on Conasauga River Trail, 1,940 feet; eastern (high elevation) terminus on East Cowpen Trail, 3,770 feet
- ■ **Trail Junctions** Conasauga River, East Cowpen
- ■ **Topographic Quadrangle** Hemp Top GA-TN
- ■ **Features** Panther Creek; boulder field; pocket of old growth; Panther Creek Falls; bluff; overlook

EAST-WEST RUNNING **PANTHER CREEK** is probably the most heavily used interior trail in the combined wilderness. The reasons for its popularity are obvious to all who have stood at Sunset Point. This trail has one of the three open views in the combined wilderness, one of two accessible waterfalls, a cascade, a boulder field, a bluff, and even some big trees.

Most hikers do not walk the entire trail; they walk from the upper or lower end to the overlook above the falls. Panther Creek gains, or loses, 1,830 feet of elevation. The route is primarily a series of easy or easy-to-moderate grades interrupted by three steep pitches—one below the falls, the other two above. Although relatively short, these three grunts are moderate to strenuous when walked uphill with a backpack.

This trail is described from low to high, from the Conasauga River to Cohutta Mountain. Starting at its usually signed junction with the Conasauga River Trail, Panther Creek Trail immediately fords the Conasauga from west to east, across a miniature island, straight to the small mouth of its namesake stream. The track, an old railroad grade, quickly crosses to the left side of the creek, then closely parallels the small stream through rhododendron thickets between crossings. Although the creek is only branch-sized, its deepest pools are plenty deep enough for trout, probably browns. The second-growth forest is predominantly hardwood—sweet birch, red maple, sweetgum, sourwood, yellow poplar—and white pine. Here, as is often the case in once-cut Southern Appalachian forests, tall, skinny sweet birch thrive beside the steep-sided, rhododendron-lined stream.

After the sixth crossing at 0.5 mile, the route follows the easy, aislelike railroad grade up and away from the creek. At 0.8 mile it angles further uphill onto cut-in path high above the stream. The forest, now on northwest slope, exhibits larger specimens and more diversity than below. American holly, silverbell, Fraser magnolia, black cherry, basswood, cucumbertree, hemlock, and several species of oak can be seen at a single glance. Striped maples are often abundant in the understory. The uphill walking becomes easy to moderate before dipping to and crossing the creek for the final time below the falls at mile 1.1. The crossing is at the bottom of a long, narrow, boulder-jumble cascade—much more lively after spring rain than during summer drought.

The rocky climb to the falls, easily the most rugged and memorable stretch of trail in the combined wilderness, begins immediately across the stream. Here, where the contour lines are bunched tight and brown on the topo sheet, rock from Panther Bluff has rolled down the west slope to form a boulder field. This field was created during the last ice age, during the Pleistocene epoch 15,000 to 20,000 years ago. During this period of widespread glaciation to the north, extremely cold temperatures regularly reached the Southern Appalachians. Many of the higher peaks were above tree line. With the added moisture of the falls nearby, water seeped into the bedrock cracks in the bluff, and the intense freezing and thawing action broke off the now rounded boulders.

For the most part, the forest in the block field was spared because it was just too hard to snake the logs out through the boulders. The loggers may have selectively cut (high graded) the high-dollar black cherry with great effort, but they certainly left most of the rest. Today this tiny pocket of old-growth forest consists of hemlock and diverse hardwoods—including mature silverbells and several large sugar maples and yellow buckeyes. The majority of the larger trees are eastern hemlocks. Like the other old-growth trees scattered throughout the wilderness, the hemlocks took a severe pounding from the storms of the 1990s. A trail crew cut a cross section out of a hemlock deadfall 30 to 35 feet up from its base, and even though it was not particularly large, perhaps 10 feet in circumference near the bottom, there were still at least 175 rings at the cut.

Once across the creek, the route rises past the first grove of old-growth hemlock, dips toward the creek, then enters the boulders. No blazes or bare-dirt treadways guide you over the rock, but you will see slightly worn and scuffed spots here and there. The over-the-boulder track remains fairly close to the creek until it reaches a lunker hemlock (approximately 12 feet in circumference), still anchored in rock near the base of the falls. Panther Creek Falls, the tall spill of a small-volume stream, is approximately 75 to 85 feet high to its uppermost ledge. The fall is at its splashing and surging best—foaming white under the noon sun—after heavy late winter or early spring rains. By late in a typical summer, however, the waterfall dribbles up high before sliding in a thin veneer down the wide, smooth rock face.

The rock-hopping course turns left and up at the hemlock, climbs over and between bigger boulders, then switchbacks to Panther Bluff. The trail closely follows the base of the 20- to 25-foot-high rock wall to the flat bedrock perch, open to the west, atop the falls. Sunset Rock offers one of only three open vistas in the combined wilderness. The highest peaks are two unnamed knobs (260 and 265 degrees) on a spur descending northward from Bald Mountain. When the air is clear, you can see the lines of long parallel ridges—the Ridge and Valley Physiographic Province—fading to the horizon between 280 and 290 degrees.

Continuing northeastward from the falls, the footpath crosses two small forks of Panther Creek before entering a nearly level area with a diverse, predominantly deciduous forest. Next the walking rises steadily on an easy grade up a cove past several prominent clumps of Fraser magnolia. At mile 1.9 the second ascent—a moderate-to-strenuous climb through a drier oak-pine forest—leads 0.1 mile to a ridge, where it turns 90 degrees to the right and follows the crest. The upgrade eases after the turn, one short, steep pitch then easy to moderate. Chinkapin shrubs are common in the understory; several old-growth blackgums—one approximately 8 feet in circumference—show off their square-blocked bark near the path.

The treadway turns right again at mile 2.3 and continues the easy walking up the Cohutta Mountain spur. The oaks are now noticeably larger than below; some of the northern red oaks are 2 to 3 feet in diameter. The upridge run becomes more difficult, easy to moderate or harder, before the route angles onto moist, north-facing slope and rises gently to a slight gap at mile 2.7.

Beyond the gap, the remainder of the trail follows the wide walkway of an old road. Clumps of arching witch-hazel become increasingly common. After rounding a moist, open hollow with yellow poplar, basswood, and cucumbertree, the final stretch heads north on the drier west-facing slope to its usually signed junction with East Cowpen Trail.

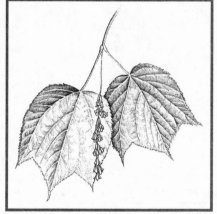

striped maple

Nature Notes

Panther Creek Trail leads through a diverse mixture of exposures, elevations, habitats, and intergrading forest types. During wet springs, the north-facing slope along the uppermost mile is lush with herbaceous wildflowers, shrubs, and ferns. Sweetshrub and flame azalea are abundant. Tearbritches, East Cowpen, and this segment of Panther Creek have the most extensive fern fields—large dense patches of primarily New York and hay-scented (a slight, sweet scent) ferns—in the combined wilderness.

Hiking from river to ridge, you will pass numerous striped maples (*Acer pensylvanicum*) on the north-facing slope before the final creek crossing below the falls. Well-known in New England as moosewood, this small, widespread maple is also called goosefoot where its range fingers down the mountains of the Southern Blue Ridge. This aptly named tree is easily identified even in winter by its conspicuously striped bark. The bark of a young trunk is yellowish olive green and is streaked with chalky white to pale green vertical lines. As the tree matures the lower trunk loses its distinctive coloration, but the white-on-green striping remains on the upper trunk and on small and medium-sized branches.

Essentially a northern hardwood, this small maple requires cool, moist soils beneath a largely broadleaf canopy. This understory tree

sweet birch

grows from shrub size to 30 or 40 feet in height. Its large, three-lobed leaves are 4 to 6 inches long and 3 to 5 inches wide. The margins are doubly saw-toothed.

Within its preferred habitat—high ridges, rich slopes, and riparian zones above steep-sided streams—the sweet birch (*Betula lenta*) flourishes in the combined wilderness. While it is often numerous on moist slopes, this succession species is most plentiful along the once-logged stream corridors like Panther Creek, especially above 1,800 feet. There you can frequently find stands of sweet birch poking up through the rhododendron thickets.

The bark on young sweet birch trunks resembles that of immature black cherry. Dark brown tinged with red or sometimes nearly black, the bark on these young boles has prominent horizontal stripes (lenticels) and very small vertical peels, nothing at all like the wide, papery curls of yellow birch. On older trees the almost black bark is fissured into large, irregularly scaled plates. In winter, the dark bark and the long, drooping male catkins near the tips of the twigs make this birch easy to identify.

Sweet birch leaves, paired at the end of short branchlets, turn bright yellow in autumn. The crushed leaves and cracked twigs of this species have the spicy scent of wintergreen. In the past, birch beer was fermented from its sap, and oil of wintergreen was obtained from the bark and wood of saplings. Yellow birch has the same scent, but not as strong.

A medium-sized tree, sweet birch is usually 50 to 80 feet in height and 1 to 2½ feet in diameter. Its maximum measurements are 110 feet in height and 5 feet in diameter. This tree, also known as black birch, reaches maturity in 150 years, and old trees may attain the three-century mark.

Directions

Panther Creek is an interior trail that has its eastern (upper-elevation) end on East Cowpen Trail and its western (lower-elevation) end on Conasauga River Trail.

To reach Panther Creek's eastern end, walk 2.4 miles on East Cowpen Trail, starting from its southern (upper-elevation) trailhead at Three Forks Mountain. Panther Creek's sign and beginning treadway are to the left in a level, open area. (See East Cowpen Trail, on page 81, for further information.)

To reach Panther Creek's western end, walk 5.0 miles on Conasauga River Trail starting from its southeastern (upper-elevation) trailhead at Betty Gap. You will find the usually signed Panther Creek junction approximately 50 yards beyond the eighteenth ford (right side to left facing downstream, nineteenth ford at mile 6.8). Panther Creek Trail's lower-elevation end immediately fords the Conasauga River. (See Conasauga River Trail, page 41, for further information.)

The shortest route to Panther Creek's Conasauga River junction is Hickory Creek Trail from its southwestern, FS 630 trailhead. Follow Hickory Creek Trail for 3.0 miles (it shares the same treadway with the Conasauga River Trail from mile 1.7 to mile 3.0) to its usually signed junction with the Conasauga River Trail in Bray Field. Here, just before Hickory Creek Trail fords the Conasauga River, turn right with the Conasauga River Trail and continue to head upstream. Follow the Conasauga River Trail for 0.4 mile (cross Tearbritches Creek, then walk up and over a spur away from the river) to Panther Creek's usually signed junction. (See Hickory Creek, the preceding trail, for further information.)

In intercourse with Nature you are dealing with things at first hand, and you get a rule, a standard, that serves you through life. You are dealing with primal sanities, primal honesties, primal attraction; you are touching at least the hem of the garment with which the infinite is clothed.

—John Burroughs

Cohutta Mountain

*Wilderness sign on
Three Forks Mountain*

Trail

East Cowpen Trail

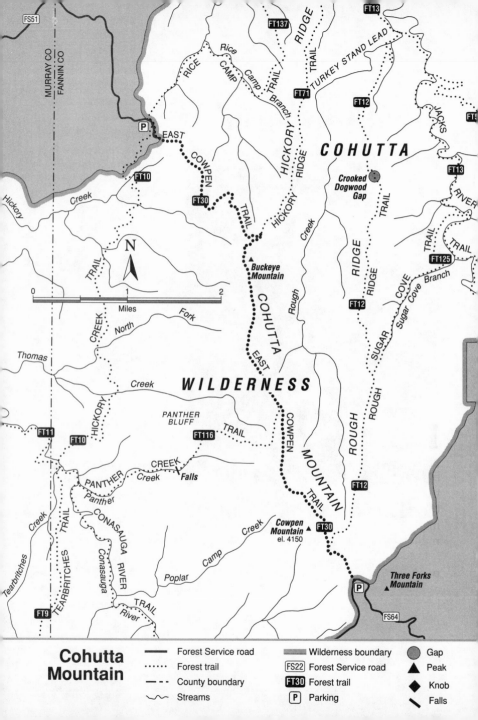

FS51

MURRAY CO
FANNIN CO

FS13

FT137

RICE

Rice

CAMP

Camp

Branch

TURKEY STAND LEAD

RIDGE

TRAIL

FT71

FT12

JACKS

FT13

P

EAST

COWPEN

TRAIL

FT10

FT30

HICKORY

RIDGE

Hickory

Creek

Creek

COHUTTA

Crooked
Dogwood
Gap

FT13

RIVER

TRAIL

TRAIL

FT125

N

Buckeye
Mountain

COHUTTA

Rough

RIDGE

FT12

RIDGE

SUGAR

COVE

Sugar Cove Branch

0   1   2
Miles

TRAIL

CREEK

North   Fork

EAST

Creek

Thomas

WILDERNESS

COWPEN

ROUGH

ROUGH

FT11

FT10

HICKORY

PANTHER
BLUFF

TRAIL

FT116

Creek

CREEK

Falls

MOUNTAIN

TRAIL

FT12

PANTHER

Panther

Creek

Camp   Creek

Cowpen
Mountain
el. 4150

FT30

Three Forks
Mountain

CONASAUGA

Conasauga

RIVER

Poplar

P

Tearbritches

Creek

TEARBRITCHES

TRAIL

TRAIL

River

FS64

FT9

Cohutta
Mountain

——— Forest Service road

·········· Forest trail

— · — County boundary

〜〜 Streams

▨▨▨ Wilderness boundary

FS22 Forest Service road

FT30 Forest trail

P Parking

● Gap

▲ Peak

◆ Knob

╲ Falls

East Cowpen Trail

■ **Dayhiking (low to high)** Easy to Moderate
■ **Dayhiking (high to low)** Easy
■ **Backpacking (low to high)** Moderate
■ **Backpacking (high to low)** Easy to Moderate
■ **Vehicular Access at Either End** Southern (high elevation) terminus at Three Forks Mountain Trailhead, 3,500 feet; northern (low elevation) terminus at Rice Camp Trailhead, 1,760 feet
■ **Trail Junctions** Rough Ridge, Panther Creek, Hickory Ridge, Hickory Creek, Rice Camp (at trailhead)
■ **Topographic Quadrangle** Hemp Top GA-TN
■ **Features** Winter views; state highway turned into wilderness path

EAST COWPEN TRAIL IS THE FORMER ROUTE of old Georgia Highway 2. This state road remained open even after Congress designated the Cohutta as wilderness in 1975. During a legal dispute between the Forest Service and the state, the East Cowpen section of the road was not maintained. Ruts quickly grew into gullies, making the roadbed increasingly dangerous for conventional vehicles and increasingly challenging for four-wheel drive vehicles. Beer cans and mufflers littered the dirt highway.

After long negotiations, the oxymoronic wilderness highway was permanently closed to vehicular traffic in September 1987. Today, as a legal and biological part of the wilderness, the old roadbed becomes more trail-like every year. Already long sections of it have narrowed to path through new growth.

East Cowpen and Hemp Top are the only two trails within Georgia's much larger share of the Cohutta Wilderness that do not lead to either the Jacks or Conasauga Rivers. Because of East Cowpen's orientation and location—north-south along the ridge that divides watersheds to the east and west—relatively few hikers walk this entire trail at one time. Most walk it as a means to an end, to reach the three interior trails that drop down to the wilderness rivers. This usage pattern has made the section of East Cowpen between its Panther Creek and Hickory Ridge junctions one of the least traveled segments in the Cohutta Wilderness.

This trail remains on or near the ridgecrest of Cohutta Mountain for most of its length. As a ridgetop and upper-slope route, it provides excellent winter views and more partial summer views than most of the other ridge-running trails in the combined wilderness. Even walking north to south, you can negotiate East Cowpen's low-to-high elevation difference of over 2,300 feet with a minimum of leg strain. The sustained grades of the old roadway are no worse than easy to moderate.

East Cowpen is described as it is most often walked, from south to north, from high to low. Starting at its southern trailhead at Three Forks Mountain, the route rises easily on its first and only sustained upgrade along the high east slope of Cowpen Mountain. The state highway turned bear path begins atop the ridgecrest, but soon slips onto the sunrise slope where the ridge climbs harder than the road builders wanted to follow. Here the fairly moist forest—northern red oak, yellow poplar, hemlock, black cherry, red maple, and sweet birch—is largely broadleaf and second growth. Dense fern colonies, primarily hay-scented and New York, often flank the path. After 0.4 mile, East Cowpen reaches its Rough Ridge Trail junction to the right (northeast) at a prominent sign.

Easy up or nearly level, the gradual ascent continues on or near ridge keel. This segment has two small, wet-weather springs, one at 0.8 mile and the other 0.1 mile further. Both are probably unreliable not long after leaf-out in early May. Multiboled clumps of witch-hazel often arch over the old highway. At mile 1.3 the trail tops out at approximately 4,100 feet on the crest of the ridge north of Cowpen Mountain's peak (4,150 feet).

In its final 5.8 miles, East Cowpen loses 2,340 feet—the most from high point to low point in the Cohutta Wilderness. With the exception of occasional upgrades not worth mentioning, the remainder of the trail is nearly level or a steady, mild downhill. Once the treadway straightens out and heads north, the forest becomes moister and more open. Hemlock and white pine are minor components in the largely hardwood forest. Occasional old-growth oaks—mostly northern reds in bad shape—were bypassed by loggers as too crooked and low-limbed. The footpath descends with the ridgeline to a level, loafing area (3,770 feet) at mile 2.4. The usually signed, upper-elevation end of Panther Creek Trail is to the left (west) in the opening.

Beyond the Panther Creek connection, the light gap of the former road becomes more brushy and briery. The track continues, for the most part nearly level or easy down, on the ridge or upper west slope. When the route swings around the northwest side of a low knob, the second-growth forest—black cherry, yellow poplar, northern red oak, white ash, and sweet birch—is tall, straight, and open. White pines and their saplings become increasingly common on the ridge. A sign on a tree at mile 4.4 marks the upper-elevation end (3,180 feet) of Hickory Ridge Trail to the right (north). Before the wilderness reclaimed the road, Hickory Ridge was often hard to find, and you couldn't miss East Cowpen, which curls sharply to the left and down at the intersection. Now, if the sign at the open resting spot were down, it would be very easy to continue straight ahead on the wrong trail.

After completing the horseshoe-shaped switchback over a Buck-eye Mountain spur, the walkway winds around two rich hardwood hollows dominated by yellow poplar. This section of East Cowpen affords winter views of Big Frog to the right (40 degrees). As East Cowpen loses elevation, the ridge and upper western slope become drier and drier. By mile 5.1, where the trail crosses over a slight spur, the forest has changed to oak-pine. The most common oaks are chestnut and scarlet. Short-needled Virginia pines are abundant; their saplings often flank the trail.

In places the easily followed path is eroded and rocky where the grade heads down a little harder (easy to moderate). Following a pattern, the treadway usually switches slopes soon after arriving on the exact spine of the ridge. A look back to the left (190 degrees) at mile 6.2 rewards you with a good, bare-branch view of Bald Mountain's broad dome. A short distance beyond the winter view, the walking rounds the final steep-sided, hardwood hollow, this one with tall red maple and a colony of sweetshrub on the near downslope. The usually posted Hickory Creek junction is to the left (southwest) 75 yards before East Cowpen's northern end.

Nature Notes

Starting from the southern end at Three Forks Mountain, East Cowpen's first mile frequently passes beneath large clumps of witch-

witch-hazel

hazel (*Hamamelis virginiana*) arching over the old road. The witch-hazel, a stooped understory tree usually 10 to 30 feet high, obviously found the moisture of this high slope and the light gap of the former road favorable. Growing at all elevations throughout the wilderness, this slightly aromatic broadleaf is most common and noticeable on moist, hardwood slopes and along stream banks free from rhododendron. Most everything about this tree is unique, unusual, or distinctive. Its easily recognized alternate leaves—3 to 5 inches long and 2 to 3 inches wide, widest beyond midpoint—have lopsided bases and round-toothed, wavy-edged margins.

The witch-hazel blooms later than any other tree, perhaps even any other plant, in the Southern Appalachians. It starts flowering in late October and continues blooming through most of November. Winterbloom was once another common name. Each small, bright yellow blossom has four twisted, hairlike petals. When the flowers are in clusters, as they often are, they resemble tufts of teased yellow hair.

Witch-hazel disperses its seeds in an unusual way. About the same time the blooms appear in the fall, the seedpods that developed from the previous year's flowers shoot their black, shiny seeds up to 30 feet from the tree.

The hardwood cove forest is well known for its tall, straight trees and spring wildflowers. But come the cloudless blue skies of autumn, the hardwood cove's foliage is rather drab. If you are looking for fall color, walk in the dry, low-elevation oak-pine forest, like the one along the northernmost several miles of this trail. Here the blackgum, scarlet oak, red maple, sassafras, and sourwood show off their newly turned shades of red against the conifer green of the pines.

Also known as sorrel tree and lily-of-the-valley tree, the sourwood (*Oxydendrum arboreum*) is the largest member of the Heath family. This family includes the azaleas, the rhododendrons, mountain laurel, and even that strange little plant without chlorophyll—the Indian pipe. Both the genus name, *Oxydendrum,* and the common name refer to the sour-smelling and sour-tasting sap in the twigs and leaves.

This hardwood is easily recognized by the graceful sprays of white flowers that are borne terminally on the outer edge of the

sourwood

crown. Starting in mid-June and often lasting into early August, the 4- to 10-inch-long drooping flower clusters, thin and fingerlike, can be seen at a distance. The individual blossoms look like tiny lily-of-the-valley flowers—upside down urns only a quarter of an inch across. In early summer short sections of trail are sprinkled with the spent blossoms. Bees swarm the fragrant flowers and produce a honey famous for its taste and light color.

The sourwood's alternate leaves—4 to 7 inches long and 1½ to 2½ inches wide—are pointed at the tip and sometimes finely saw-toothed toward the apex. The brilliant red to purplish red fall foliage is most common in the second-growth oak-pine forest. Before the leaves drop, they often fade to a washed out pinkish red color.

The brownish gray bark of a mature tree is deeply furrowed into narrow ridges, which are in turn fissured horizontally. Older boles are noticeably divided into roughly rectangular blocks. Small branches are red.

Usually 40 to 60 feet in height and 1 to 1½ feet in diameter, the sourwood is a small- to medium-sized tree whose crown often bends downward to one side. A recent Georgia state record was 95 feet tall and had a girth of 8 feet. As a moderately intolerant species, which means it doesn't tolerate shade particularly well, the sourwood is most numerous on disturbed sites. This hardwood grows best in fertile, well-drained soils, but it competes best and is most common on sunny ridges and dry slopes up to about 4,800 feet in the Southern Highlands.

Directions

East Cowpen has either-end vehicular access. East Cowpen's southern (upper-elevation) trailhead at Three Forks Mountain can be most easily reached from Access Points 1 and 8, and its northern (lower-elevation) trailhead can be most easily reached from Access Points 3, 4, and 5. (See the detailed description of the Access Points at the beginning of this guide.)

Southern trailhead at Three Forks Mountain

Access Point 1: From the three-way FS 68–FS 64 intersection at Potatopatch Mountain, turn right onto FS 64 and travel approximately 4.3 miles to the large, graveled, trailhead parking area to the left of the road in the middle of a sharp curve.

Access Point 8: From the four-way intersection at Watson Gap, turn left onto FS 64 and proceed on that road for approximately 8.5 miles to the large trailhead parking area to the right of the road in the middle of a sharp curve.

Northern trailhead at the end of FS 51

East Cowpen's northern trailhead is located at the turn-around/parking area at the end of FS 51. Both East Cowpen and Rice Camp begin where the road ends. East Cowpen is the gated trail that continues straight ahead from the dead end. Rice Camp begins to the left of the turnaround, next to its sign and trailhead bulletin board. (See Rice Camp Trail, page 128, for directions to East Cowpen's northern trailhead from Access Points 3, 4, and 5.)

The one-way shuttle distance between trailheads—around the southwestern perimeter of the Cohutta Wilderness—is approximately 28.5 dirt-road miles.

Notes

It is imperative to maintain portions of the wilderness untouched so that a tree will rot where it falls, a waterfall will pour its curve without generating electricity, a trumpeter swan may float on uncontaminated water—and moderns may at least see what their ancestors knew in their nerves and blood.

—Bernard De Voto

Jacks River Watershed

Jacks River Falls

Trails

Jacks River Trail
Benton MacKaye Trail
Rough Ridge Trail
Sugar Cove Trail
Hickory Ridge Trail

Rice Camp Trail
Horseshoe Bend Trail
Penitentiary Branch Trail
Beech Bottom Trail

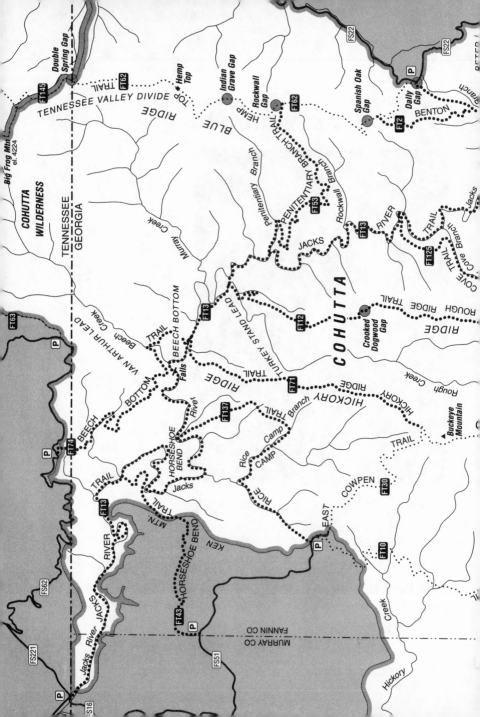

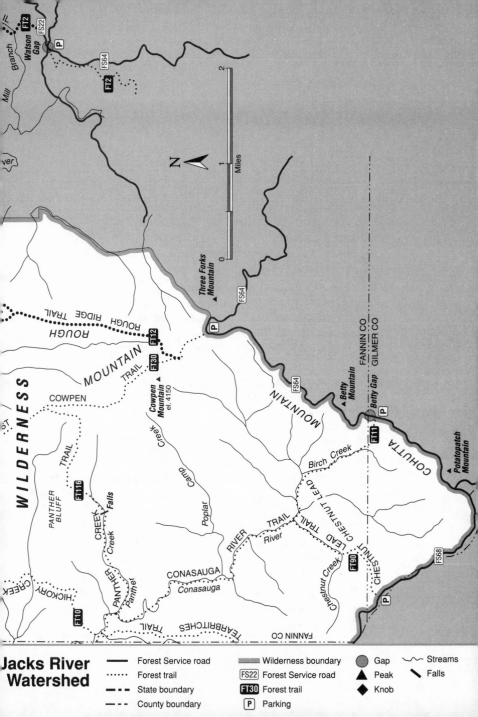

Jacks River Watershed

—— Forest Service road	▓▓▓ Wilderness boundary
·········· Forest trail	FS22 Forest Service road
—·—·— State boundary	FT30 Forest trail
—··—··— County boundary	P Parking

Gap ● | Streams 〰
Peak ▲ | Falls ╲
Knob ◆

WILDERNESS

ROUGH RIDGE TRAIL
ROUGH MOUNTAIN TRAIL

FT2
FS22
Watson Gap
FS64
FT2
Mill Branch

Three Forks Mountain ▲
FS64
N
Miles

FT12
FT30
COWPEN
Cowpen Mountain ▲ el. 4150

Camp Creek
Poplar

PANTHER BLUFF
FT116
CREEK Creek Falls
PANTHER TRAIL
Panther

HICKORY CREEK
FT10

CONASAUGA
Conasauga
TEARBRITCHES TRAIL

RIVER TRAIL
River

Birch Creek

COHUTTA MOUNTAIN

Betty Mountain ▲
FANNIN CO
GILMER CO
Betty Gap ●
P
FT11
COHUTTA

Potatopatch Mountain ▲

CHESTNUT LEAD TRAIL
Chestnut Creek
FT90
CHESTNUT LEAD TRAIL
P

FANNIN CO

FS68

Jacks River Trail

Foot Trail 13: 16.5 miles

- ■ **Dayhiking** Easy in either direction
- ■ **Backpacking** Easy to Moderate in either direction
- ■ **Vehicular Access At Either End** Southeastern (high elevation) terminus at Dally Gap Trailhead, 2,578 feet; northwestern (low elevation) terminus at Alaculsy Valley Trailhead, 966 feet
- ■ **Trail Junctions** Hemp Top (at Dally Gap Trailhead), Benton MacKaye, Sugar Cove, Penitentiary Branch, Rough Ridge, Hickory Ridge, Beech Bottom, Rice Camp, Horseshoe Bend
- ■ **Topographic Quadrangles** Hemp Top GA-TN, Tennga GA-TN
- ■ **Features** Old-growth hemlocks; Jacks River Gorge; Jacks River Falls; 42 fords; bluffs

A N EARLY SETTLER GAVE THE ALACULSY VALLEY its name, borrowing a Native American word and anglicizing it in sound and spelling. This valley was home to a stout Cherokee called Jack who, for a small fee, carried travelers across the river on his back. The river now bears his name.

The Jacks River is the linear focus of the larger, northeastern section of the Cohutta Wilderness. The Jacks River Trail (JRT) is the longest and wettest (forty-two fords) in the combined wilderness. The river it follows and fords is also the most popular destination in the combined wilderness. A network of eight trails leads dayhikers and backpackers directly to this trail and its river, so expect plenty of company on weekends and crowds on three-day holidays. The Jacks River Trail can be walked as the first or last leg of a Jacks River–Penitentiary Branch–Hemp Top loop (no backtrack, 13.0 miles), beginning and ending at Dally Gap.

Jacks River Trail has changed over the last three decades. Even as late as the mid-1970s, the treadway still had the appearance of a recent rails-to-trails conversion project. The route was wide, often aisle straight, and generally free of deadfalls and encroaching vegetation. Railroad spikes were still easily found, and the corduroy ripples of old railroad ties were still obvious along much of the former track.

Since then, time, resentment, and nature have steadily altered the character of this trail. Nearly half a century after the last train hauled timber, hemlock saplings finally began to reclaim the heavily compacted soils of the former grade. In November of 1981, an arsonist walked down the Jacks River Trail from Sugar Cove Branch to Rough Creek, setting sixteen fires that resulted in numerous deadfalls. Floods have washed away short sections of the old railroad grade and have considerably narrowed others. In the 1990s, a blizzard, a hurricane, and a tornado piled deadfalls and windthrows atop the trail, further narrowing and twisting the route. A hearty thanks and pat on the back goes to all the Forest Service personnel and volunteers who helped clear the trail after the extensive tornado damage in the spring of 1998. A hard job well done.

The trail is described as the river flows, from high to low, from southeast Dally Gap to northwest Alaculsy Valley. The riverway begins by following the easy grades of a wide old road downhill from Dally Gap. Here the forest, made up of white pine, hemlock, rhododendron, and mountain laurel mixed with hardwoods, is green year-round. The tall white pines are impressive for second-growth. At 0.7 mile the Benton MacKaye Trail shares the treadway for 90 yards. To the left of this shared segment stands (hopefully) the most impressive tree along the Jacks River Trail—an old-growth hemlock 12 feet 9 inches in circumference and probably 130 to 135 feet in height. In the mid-1990s, this conifer was the smaller of a pair of giant hemlocks growing almost crown to crown. The larger of the two, a state record before it fell, is slowly rotting 30 to 35 feet to the left of the other.

Although it parallels Bear Branch from the gap, the path does not venture close enough for a view until mile 1.7. Bear Branch is a small brook, shallow shoaled and quiet by the time of year most people hike the Jacks River Trail. Three-tenths of a mile further, the walkway switches streams and swings parallel to the Jacks as it winds to the north. Only two or three old-growth hemlocks, many fewer than just 20 years ago, still survive near the trail. At mile 2.3 you arrive at your first ford. Beyond this easy, warm-up wade through cool mountain water, the walking closely follows the Jacks for 0.6 mile to the next ford. This segment passes above a series of high shoals—loud, white cascades cutting down through rock ledges.

The second ford is just upriver from a low falls or high cascade. If there has been recent heavy rain and if this ford looks tough—the water high, fast, and powerful—bail out and backtrack to Dally Gap. The most difficult fords, much wider and deeper than the beginning ones, are below Jacks River Falls, after all the major tributaries have added their volume. If number two causes concern, the downriver fords will be even more difficult and potentially dangerous.

After the second ford, the route makes a short, uphill scramble, then continues to rise up and away from the river on a rocky, hardwood slope that includes silverbell, basswood, and Fraser magnolia. Below, the steep-sided river rushes through its most turbulent stretch: Jacks River Gorge. Here the Jacks exhibits the V-shaped profile of a youthful river cutting back into mountain. The gorge river is a continuous cascading run of chutes, sluices, slides, swirlholes, and short pools for nearly a mile. During high water the river is one long, loud thread of foaming white.

Where the Jacks descends, so does the trail. It may climb a hillside first, but it always drops back down to the river. After the treadway descends to bank level near the end of the gorge, it picks up the old railroad grade. Sugar Cove Trail fords the river to its usually signed junction with JRT at mile 3.9.

Beyond several boulder-jumble runs, the riverwalk makes its fourth ford at mile 4.6. Now the wades come in quick succession, most only 0.1 to 0.3 mile apart. Counting the fourth ford, this aquahiking trail crosses the river sixteen times in 2.7 miles. The track remains nearly level and parallel to the river between fords. The riverine forest along this segment is the usual evergreen-deciduous mix. Stands of tall white pine are common in the narrow floodplain near the now gentler Jacks. Green tunnels of rhododendron and hemlock heighten the sense of linear traveling.

Immediately after the eighteenth ford (left to right facing downstream), the JRT arrives at its usually signed Penitentiary Branch Trail junction at a large, often messy campsite at mile 7.1. Beyond the nineteenth ford at mile 7.3, the path appears to pull away from the river. Actually, the river makes a meander, a flattened half-circle to the east, and the course continues across the opening of the horseshoe. Here the route rises up and away from the stream, crosses a shallow notch in the spur that forced the river eastward, then descends to and crosses Rough Creek at mile 7.9. On the bank across the creek, Rough Ridge Trail ends at its usually signed connection with the JRT.

The trail turns to the right from this junction and closely parallels the creek downstream before swinging to the left, above and then away from the river. From here it ascends on an easy grade higher and further away from the green river pools, up to and over another ridge forcing the Jacks into another eastward meander. Once over the spur, it rounds a ravine with moist-site hardwoods and hemlock on its way down to the twentieth and final ford before the falls at mile 8.4. Hickory Ridge Trail fords the river before tying into JRT at mile 8.5. Forty yards further, Beech Bottom Trail joins in from the right.

Beyond the second junction, the trail closely parallels the Jacks on rocky, eroded footpath, often on bank edge almost right above the water. This portion, from the Beech Bottom tie-in to several tenths of a mile beyond the falls, suffers from chronic overuse. The track reaches the high, railroad-cut overlook above the falls at mile 9.2. It is easy to see why so many feet beat their way to this waterfall. Dropping in stages at the head of a gorgelike amphitheater of rock, Jacks River Falls—wide, powerful, and approximately 80 feet high— is easily the most scenic and most visited single feature in the combined wilderness.

If you would like to see and hear the falls at its frothing, roaring best, wait until winter or early spring, after several days of heavy rains. Then, on a sunny afternoon when the unnamed laws of light and reflection hold sway, the white leap becomes one long crashing, upwelling run of spray-throwing foam. In contrast, the falls often shrivels to three separate streaks of listless whitewater during the dry dog days of July and August.

Beyond the falls, the route follows the obvious railroad grade back down to river's edge. It reaches the twenty-first ford, the first in 1.8 miles, at mile 10.2. Coming in back to the left (60 degrees), Rice Camp Trail ties into JRT a tenth of a mile further. Now the familiar pattern of crossing and paralleling the river begins again. Only this time the treadway remains level or slightly downhill between fords. Low-elevation tree species such as loblolly pine, sycamore, and red-bud become increasingly common in the riverside forest.

Downstream from the start of the twenty-eighth ford, you will see the first of several tall bluffs along the lower Jacks. The gap at the top of this bluff is Horseshoe Bend Overlook. Downriver from the thirtieth ford, you will notice a particularly craggy bluff—100 to 120 feet high, pine-capped and picturesque—along the left bank.

Horseshoe Bend Trail joins JRT at its usually signed junction on the left side of the river at mile 12.9. This is the last easy place to bail out during high water. From here on, the fords just keep coming, and even when shallow, the lower ones are knee- to midthigh-deep. The last nine fords occur, often only 0.1 mile apart, in 1.8 miles. You can catch the best views of the steep-sided, pine-capped ridges that hem in the river from the middle of the fords.

After the forty-second and final ford at mile 14.7, the last section of the trail closely parallels the north bank, occasionally close enough for long up and downstream views. Here, as it flows toward its end at the Conasauga River just outside the wilderness boundary, the Jacks becomes wider and slower, its swimming holes deeper, longer, and greener. Near the Alaculsy Valley Trailhead, you will notice layers of upthrust rock in the riverbed and above the railroad cut. Some of the finlike, water-worn layers in the river stand almost straight up.

Nature Notes

The Jacks River Trail offers a more diverse forest, more tree species, than any other route in the combined wilderness. Here you can find over forty-five kinds of trees without making a concerted effort to pad the count. Good botanists could easily identify fifty-five or more. In addition to the obvious benefit of length, this trail has the added advantage of running along a river valley. Trees extend their ranges along rivers. Those species requiring cool, moist conditions finger down lower in the moist, sheltered river valley. And conversely, trees that thrive at the lowest elevations lengthen their reach farthest into the mountains along rivers.

The elevation differential of the Jacks River Trail is modest—only about 1,610 feet. But the trail's particular high point and low point are favorable for maximum diversity. The trail begins just high enough to include all high-elevation species found in the wilderness except the yellow birch. But its lowermost reaches, the only place elevation dips below the 1,000-foot contour in the combined wilderness, provide habitat for a number of low-elevation species. A partial list of these trees includes pawpaw, loblolly pine, sycamore, winged elm, redbud, and ironwood (American hornbeam).

More umbrella magnolias (*Magnolia tripetala*) grow along the banks of the Jacks River than anywhere else in the combined wilderness. This is not a testament to its abundance along the Jacks, but rather to its scarcity or absence from most of the wilderness. Although it occurs only occasionally along the Jacks, this deciduous magnolia—with the largest flowers and noncompound leaves of any tree in the Southern Blue Ridge—is distinctive and easily identified. The tropical-sized leaves—10 to 20 inches long, 5 to 10 inches wide, and broadest beyond the midpoint—are whorled in umbrella fashion near the end of the branch stems. Like most broadleafs, the saplings have significantly larger leaves than mature trees. A 6-foot-high specimen next to the Jacks River had a leaf 18½ inches long.

Unlike the Fraser magnolia, which has the second largest leaf and flower of any tree in the wilderness, the umbrella magnolia bears leaves that are pointed at both ends. Occasional to common throughout the two-state wilderness, the Fraser magnolia (see description on page 225) has whorled leaves with noticeably eared bases.

From mid-April through mid-May, when the Jacks is often still running full and cold, the umbrella magnolia produces creamy white flowers that are 7 to 10 inches across and somewhat stinky. The fruits—2½ to 4 inches long, green in spring and red by fall—

are typical of the Magnolia family. Also typical are the shiny red seeds that hang and twist in the wind from thin white threads.

Although it ranks first in flower and leaf size, the umbrella magnolia is a small tree. It is by far the smallest of the three deciduous magnolias (the third one, the cucumbertree, is described on page 116) that inhabit the Cohutta–Big Frog. This magnolia's maximum height, which it attains in the rainy Southern Appalachians, is listed as 30 to 40 feet. Usually, however, this hardwood is much shorter and often has several shrubby trunks. I have not seen one taller than 20 feet along the Jacks River. Most seem too small to bloom.

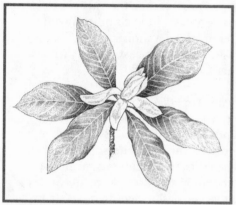

umbrella magnolia

Rare or occasional over large parts of its range, the umbrella magnolia prefers rich soils, primarily along mountain valley streams below 2,500 feet.

Because of its length, its low elevation, and numerous springs and seeps, the Jacks River Trail passes through more cardinal flower habitat than any other trail in the combined wilderness. *Lobelia cardinalis* is not only the largest lobelia but also the only one with red flowers. Its common name refers to its coloration, the bright red of the robes worn by Roman Catholic cardinals. This plant's size, blooming period, and vibrantly beautiful scarlet blossoms make it impossible to miss or misidentify. No other 2- to 4-foot-high, brilliant red wildflowers bloom in the wilderness during late August and throughout September.

The numerous leaves are alternate, toothed along the margins, and lance-shaped. Up to 6 inches long at the bottom, the leaves are progressively smaller toward the top of the stem. In late summer and early fall, you can easily spot the many tubular flowers clustered on a terminal raceme 8 to 12 inches in length. Rather than blooming all at once, the buds open in sequence, starting at the bottom and ending at the top of the raceme. The intensely colored corollas are about 1½ inches long, five petaled, and strongly two lipped. The lower lip is spreading and cleft into three lobes; the upper lip has two long, thin lobes. The individual flowers look like they could fly right off the stem.

This member of the Bluebell family needs constant moisture and at least some sun. Within the wilderness it is most often found along the margins of the larger streams, at the edges of spring runs, and beside mucky seeps. Unfortunately, wild hogs love to wallow in and around the boggy seeps. This species is much less common above approximately 2,600 feet in the Southern Appalachians.

In its own way, the cardinal flower heard the birds and bees lecture geologic ages ago. And it chose the birds. This species of lobelia is almost exclusively pollinated by the ruby-throated hummingbird. Its long, tubular blossoms—brightly colored and scentless—are highly characteristic of plants that desire to attract hummers. Hummingbird-pollinated flowers are red or orange—wavelengths of the light spectrum that attract birds but not bees.

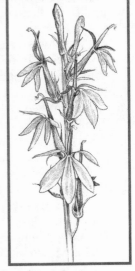

cardinal flower

Directions

Jacks River has either-end vehicular access. Its southeastern (upper-elevation) trailhead at Dally Gap can be most easily reached from Access Points 7 and 8, and its northwestern (lower-elevation) trailhead in Alaculsy Valley can be most easily reached from Access Points 3, 4, and 5. (See the detailed description of the Access Points at the beginning of this guide.)

Southeastern trailhead at Dally Gap

Access Point 7: From the paved three-way intersection of FS 221, FS 65, and County Road 251, continue across the bridge over Tumbling Creek and proceed straight ahead (south) on FS 65—then

FS 22—for approximately 8.0 miles to the Dally Gap Trailhead. Forest Service 65 turns to dirt-gravel after 0.5 mile, enters Georgia, then becomes FS 22. Two signed and gated trails begin to the right side of the road at Dally Gap. Jacks River heads downhill past the bulletin board; Hemp Top starts up and to the right.

Access Point 8: From the four-way intersection at Watson Gap, turn right and uphill onto FS 22, then travel approximately 3.4 miles to the obvious (bulletin board, trail signs, pull-off parking to the left and right) trailhead at Dally Gap. Two signed and gated trails begin to the left side of the road at Dally Gap. Jacks River heads downhill past the bulletin board.

Northwestern trailhead in Alaculsy Valley

Access Point 3: From the three-way FS 16–FS 17 intersection, continue straight ahead on FS 16 for approximately 5.5 miles to its intersection with FS 221, which is located on the Georgia-Tennessee border immediately across the big iron bridge over the Jacks River. The Jacks River Trailhead, with bulletin board and pull-off parking, is to the right of the FS 16–FS 221 intersection.

Access Point 4: The Jacks River Trailhead is located at the FS 16– FS 221 intersection, a stone's throw from the big iron bridge over the Jacks River. This intersection is Access Point 4.

Access Point 5: From the three-way, FS 55–FS 221 intersection, turn right onto FS 221 and travel approximately 3.0 miles to the Jacks River Trailhead, which is to the left just before the iron bridge over the Jacks River.

Even if you go back out to the paved highways, setting a shuttle between the Jacks River Trailheads is very time consuming. The shortest distance along the dirt-road loop between trailheads—the northern route that half-circles the Big Frog Wilderness on FS 221— is approximately 31.0 miles in length. The southern route, which winds around the southern end of the Cohutta Wilderness, is approximately 36.0 miles long. Either way you go, there are sections of sharply curving or rough road.

Benton MacKaye Trail

Total distance will be approximately 250 miles in length
when completed (See history on page 12.). This
narrative details a 4.1-mile segment of Section 10.

- **Dayhiking** Easy to Moderate walked in either direction
for the 4.1-mile segment
- **Backpacking** Moderate walked in either direction
for the 4.1-mile segment
- **Start** Watson Gap Trailhead (the southern end
of Section 10), 2,700 feet
- **End of 4.1-Mile Narrative** Hemp Top Trail
(see description), 2,920 feet
- **Trail Junctions** Jacks River (see description), Hemp Top
- **Topographic Quadrangle** Hemp Top GA-TN for the
4.1-mile segment
- **Features** Small streams; beaver ponds;
stands of large white pine

HEADING NORTH TOWARD TENNESSEE, Georgia's last BMT section is
its first to traverse wilderness. Beyond mile 1.4 to Double Spring
Gap, Section 10 remains within the 36,977-acre Cohutta Wilderness.

Beginning at its southern end at Watson Gap, Section 10 continues
across the four-way intersection and proceeds up FS 22 (east-north-
east) toward Dally Gap. After 0.3 mile of easy uphill road walking, the
route bends back hard left onto path through recently cut-over forest.
Wide wooden steps, a trail sign, and Benton MacKaye's increasingly
familiar white diamond blaze make this sharp turn impossible to miss
for all but the most determined daydreamers.

Once in the woods, the trail quickly rises on an easy grade to the
crest of a low, oak-pine ridge. Here the trees—thin trunked second or

third growth—are nevertheless much thicker than those near the road. The track drops below the crest, comes back to ridgeline, levels, then angles to the right and down off the keel onto dry, southeastern slope. Following a descent with several very short, steep dips, the treadway reaches a slight gap, where it curls to the right and down off ridgeline again. From here the walking heads down a shallow hollow to a floodplain beside Mill Branch. The moldering remains of an old home place can still be found to the right of the trail before it crosses the branch at 0.8 mile.

Across the narrow stream, the BMT rises gradually on the old lane, still remarkably open, that once led to the homesite. Fence wire once used to corral the bottomland is plainly visible to the right. The easy strolling occasionally tunnels through the heavy shade of overarching rhododendron, mountain laurel, and hemlock. At mile 1.0 the route dips to and crosses a step-over rivulet, then switchbacks to the left with the old roadbed. The effortless walking continues as the wide treadway parallels hollows and slowly gains elevation to where it crosses a ridgecrest—the Cohutta Wilderness boundary—at mile 1.4.

Over the ridge and now in wilderness, the track makes a winding, 0.6-mile descent to a fork of Bear Branch. The downgrade, easy hiking interspersed with a few short moderate stretches, often parallels hollows before half-circling around their heads. These hollows are generally north facing and moist for their relatively low (2,720 to 2,520 feet) elevation. Ferns, especially the densely colonial New York fern, are abundant in most of the hollows and occasionally flank the trail for hundreds of feet. As is usual in low elevation, second-growth hollows, white pines and yellow poplars are the tallest trees.

Section 10 turns to the right off the old road, then heads downslope through hemlock on another, narrower roadbed. It crosses a shallow, 10- to 12-foot-wide tributary of Bear Branch in Peter Cove at mile 2.0. Once across, the course bends to the west and parallels the brook downstream well above the water. The fork soon stills as it flows through a string of old beaver ponds. Some of the dams are grassed over, and most of the gray snags have fallen. The path drops with the stream toward its meeting with Bear Branch. As it approaches the confluence, the treadway curls to the north and crosses larger Bear Branch—20 feet wide and usually rock-step shallow by mid-June—at mile 2.4.

Just to the left of the trail across the stream stands an old-growth hemlock with a girth of approximately 11½ feet. The route ascends a short, easy-to-moderate grade before gaining elevation more gradually through a forest with numerous tall white pine, many in the 8- to 10-foot circumference range. At mile 2.6 the BMT, guided with a sign, turns to the right onto the wide, well-worn Jacks River Trail. It shares the JRT's treadway for 90 yards, then turns to the left (northwest) onto path at another sign.

Traveling solo again, Section 10 climbs an easy-to-moderate grade (starting at 2,480 feet) through a forest with some of the largest trailside white pines in North Georgia. Many of the largest specimens—second growth, 10 to 11 feet in girth and still holding onto their lower limbs—appear to have grown in the open for a few decades. Steadily rising, the footpath parallels a hollow filled with New York fern, curls around its dry notch at mile 2.8, then continues easy up or level through oak-pine forest with mountain laurel and deciduous heath in the understory. A little more than a tenth of mile beyond the hollow's furrow, the track swings onto the top of a spur. Here the BMT makes a 0.2-mile upridge run (easy to moderate overall) to the top of the first in a series of unnamed knobs.

With one exception, the mile before the Hemp Top junction follows a north-south trending ridgeline that undulates through shallow gaps and rises over nearly identical knobs. Wooden arrows in the gap at mile 3.4 point left to water. Just beyond the wooden-arrow gap, the route ascends (easy to moderate) toward the next high point before slabbing to the left off the ridgecrest. Here the break in the pattern parallels the notch of an upper hollow that has a dense, almost solid colony of New York fern covering the forest floor. At mile 3.6 the trail curls onto a spur leading back to the main ridge.

After coasting over the last two knobs (the highest of the bunch at 3,040 and 3,030 feet), the BMT descends 0.2 mile on an old roadbed to its tie-in with the Hemp Top Trail at the south end of Spanish Oak Gap. The downgrade is moderate overall and passes beside some unusually thick Virginia pine. Here the Benton MacKaye turns left (300 degrees) onto the Hemp Top Trail.

Section 10 of the Benton MacKaye Trail combined with Section 11 to its crossing of FS 221 offers a 15.6-mile hike, all but 3.0 miles of it within the Cohutta–Big Frog Wilderness. Heading north from Section 10's southern end at Watson Gap, the BMT is on its own; it follows its own treadway (with a 90-yard exception) for the first 4.1 miles to its connection with Hemp Top Trail. Beyond that junction, however, the remainder of Section 10 and all of Section 11 south of FS 221 share treadways with well-established trails.

If you want to complete Section 10 and much of Section 11 through the wilderness, turn left onto Hemp Top Trail (page 155) and follow it northward for 5.2 miles to its end at Licklog Ridge Trail. (Section 11 begins north of Double Spring Gap on Hemp Top Trail.) Turn left (west) onto Licklog Ridge (page 221) and proceed 0.5 mile to its end at the three-way junction with Big Frog and Wolf Ridge Trails atop Big Frog Mountain. Head downhill and to the north for 1.2 miles on Big Frog Trail (page 199) to its connection with Fork Ridge Trail. Switch paths and continue downhill to the northeast on Fork Ridge Trail (page 211) for 1.8 miles to its tie-in with Rough Creek Trail. Turn left (northwest) onto Rough Creek (page 206) and walk that path for 0.6 mile to its junction with West Fork Trail near West Fork Rough Creek. Finish the route by hiking all 2.2 miles of the West Fork Trail (page 216) generally northeastward to its FS 221 trailhead.

Nature Notes

Over the past thirty years, the two most noticeable changes in forest composition within the wilderness have been the dramatic decrease in flowering dogwoods due to disease (see page 137 for more information) and the rapid increase in the numbers of eastern white pine. White pine saplings are much more abundant and widespread than in the 1970s. The reason for this conifer's recent proliferation is twofold: fire suppression and shade tolerance. White pines cannot tolerate fire, but unlike most other eastern pines, they can tolerate shade and readily grow up through a hardwood canopy. Unless there is a series of extensive fires, the white pine will be a major component in the climax forest to come.

There is no mistaking an eastern white pine in the Southern Blue Ridge. Everything about this conifer—its growth rate, its height, its needles, cones, branches, and bark—is distinctive. It is the only five-needled pine in eastern North America. The slender needles, soft bluish green and 3 to 5 inches long, spray out five to a bundle or sheath. Its slender cones are 4 to 8 inches long, tapering, and often slightly curved. The branches spoke from the trunk in definite whorls, one whorl per year, a useful aid in estimating age.

The fast-growing and long-living white pine is the tallest tree east of the Rockies. Mature trees can be recognized from a distance by the graceful, upward sweeping tiers of branches that tower, pagodalike, above the hardwoods. In America's now-gone virgin forests, many of these giants once ranged from 200 to 220 feet in height and 4 to 6 feet in diameter. The current Georgia state champion (an old-growth tree in Rabun County) is 12 feet 7 inches in circumference and 193 feet high. The largest of the second-growth white pines in this wilderness,

eastern white pine

most less than seventy-five years old, are already 9 to 11 feet in circumference and 100 to 130 feet in height. Barring the southward spread of an exotic fungal disease, they will grow much more.

A very old white pine has drawn water skyward for 450 to 500 years. No doubt some of the largest specimens cut in the early logging days of New England were even older.

Although little remembered today, England's proprietary use of the white pine was one of the most important economic and emotional issues for the early settlers in the northern colonies. In fact, the dispute over the white pine eventually contributed to the unrest that led to the Revolutionary War.

In the early 1600s, when their ships first cruised the piney coasts of Maine, the wood-starved English had been piecing together masts of Scotch pine for years. British shipbuilders quickly discovered that North America's incredibly tall and arrow-straight white pine, also light and strong, made the best masts in the world.

At first the supply of prime white pine seemed endless. But by the 1700s settlers began moving northward and westward, clearing land and cutting the Crown's valuable mast pines for profit. In 1761 an angry King George III declared all white pines over 24 inches in diameter as property of the Crown. All of these large white pines were blazed with three hatchet chops forming an upward-pointing arrow.

The settlers resented the King's law. Believing that they had a God-given right to harvest all the white pine they wanted, the cash-poor frontiersmen ignored the edict and continued to fell the big pines, their most valuable export. They cut away the King's "broad-arrow" blazes, sawed the boles into shorter lengths, then floated them down rivers for sale and export—sometimes to England's enemies.

Promised the land of violators as a reward, the Crown's spies attempted to bring the illegal loggers to justice, but American officers and judges would neither arrest nor sentence them. When British agents drove them from their homes and burned their sawmills, the loggers disguised themselves as Indians and cut pines at night.

Tensions between the colonists and their overseas landlords increased, and in 1774 the Colonial Congress stopped the export of all goods, mast wood included, to England. The Revolutionary War's first flag, the banner that flew over the Battle of Bunker Hill, bore the image of the white pine.

Directions

Vehicular access to this segment of the Benton MacKaye Trail is at Watson Gap: the gap's four-way intersection is Access Point 8. This section's first 0.3 mile follows FS 22, which is uphill and to the right as you approach the intersection from Old Highway 2 out of Blue Ridge. (See the detailed description of the Access Points at the beginning of this guide.)

The Benton MacKaye's only other vehicular access near the combined wilderness is at the West Fork Trailhead, on FS 221 north of the Big Frog Wilderness. (See West Fork Trail, page 216, for further information.)

Notes

Rough Ridge Trail

Foot Trail 12: 7.0 miles

- **Dayhiking (low to high)** Moderate
- **Dayhiking (high to low)** Easy to Moderate
- **Backpacking (low to high)** Moderate to Strenuous
- **Backpacking (high to low)** Moderate
- **Interior Trail** Southern (high elevation) terminus on East Cowpen Trail, 3,760 feet; northern (low elevation) terminus on Jacks River Trail, 1,620 feet
- **Trail Junctions** East Cowpen, Sugar Cove, Jacks River
- **Topographic Quadrangle** Hemp Top GA-TN
- **Features** High ridgeline; winter views; Rough Creek

R OUGH RIDGE, THE LONGEST OF THE SEVEN Jacks River approaches, is also the longest interior trail in the combined wilderness. Its length and location—a 7.0-mile interior trail totally within just one of the area's two main watersheds—attest to the size of the Cohutta Wilderness. With the exception of its final 0.7 mile, Rough Ridge is a ridgecrest and upper-slope trail that offers diversity of elevation, exposure, and forest type. It provides occasional framed summer views and frequent winter vistas, which include Big Frog to the north-northeast. Beyond the Sugar Cove connection, this route is lightly used and enters remote forest where bear sign is often hard to miss, especially in the fall.

This trail's namesake ridge is a major, north-south spur of Cowpen Mountain, the second highest peak in the combined wilderness at 4,150 feet. The distinctive, steep-sided slopes of Rough Ridge—separated and defined by entrenched Rough Creek to the west and Sugar Cove Branch and Jacks River to the east—are easily recognized from many vantage points in the Cohutta Wilderness from East Cowpen Trail to Big Frog Mountain.

How rough is the Rough Ridge Trail? Not that bad really. Its upper-elevation half is a cake walk on old road. Its top-to-bottom elevation loss—2,140 feet—is a tame, manageable 306 feet per mile. The elevation change, however, is not at all steady. Walked high to low, the route loses only 160 feet to the Sugar Cove junction at mile 2.1, and the first sharp descent occurs at mile 3.4. Additionally, there are occasional short, easy upgrades and a few somewhat harder short ascents on the way down to the Jacks River.

This wilderness walkway is described from south to north, from high to low, from Cowpen Mountain to Jacks River. Following a wide, often grassy roadbed, the trail begins on a largely deciduous slope below ridgeline. Here, at its uppermost end, colonies of hay-scented and New York fern are common. After 0.3 mile the route crosses a spring run—the first of only two water sources down to Rough Creek—that usually flows except during dog-day drought. The treadway gains the exact crest of Rough Ridge in a slight saddle at 0.4 mile.

From this gap to the Sugar Cove junction, the trail gently undulates on or very close to the keel. Conifers—hemlock, white and Virginia pine—are minor components of the largely broadleaf forest. Most of the larger boles are oaks: chestnut, northern red, or white. Below the oaks are sweet birch, red maple, sourwood and blackgum. Witch-hazel, sassafras, and a deciduous, red-berried holly are regulars in the understory.

After dipping to its usually signed Sugar Cove junction at mile 2.1, the track continues its easy descent on or near the top of Rough Ridge. The crest line forest becomes steadily drier below the Sugar Cove connection. Stands of white pine saplings are common; mountain laurel and deciduous heath, including the deservedly famous flame azalea (usually in peak bloom from May 20–June 10), are abundant. At mile 2.6 the old roadbed slabs onto the moister eastern slope for the first time. As it angles back toward the ridge, it passes through an open, northeast-facing forest—tall, straight yellow poplar, black cherry, sweet birch, basswood, and white ash. This open hardwood forest affords good winter and partial summer views of Big Frog Mountain, just east (20 degrees) of due north.

Back on the ridge, the trail passes an open hollow to the left and continues the easy walking through a forest where green-branched sassafras saplings—evenly spaced from root suckers—are abundant. At mile 3.4 the route makes its first downridge pitch, not as steep as those on Tearbritches and only 0.1 mile long. After descending to a shallow gap at mile 3.7, the course rises on an easy-to-moderate grade 0.2 mile to the top of a knob (3,090 feet). Here, as it loses elevation toward Crooked Dogwood Gap, the treadway deviates from its usual pattern. Instead of following the spine, the footpath drops onto western slope well below ridgeline.

The trail crosses the smaller of a pair of seepage runs at mile 4.3. (Horses drink this water; wild hogs wallow in it upstream.) Two wildflowers that need to keep their feet wet—grass-of-Parnassus and turtleheads—bloom at one or both of the gravelly springs from the middle of September to early October. Some years back in the last millennium, a fellow hiker and I took a lunch break by the wider of the two rivulets. To our amazement, a doe and two unspotted fawns approached closely, drank from the stream, then walked slowly downstream right in front of us, grazing as they went.

Beyond the second streamlet, the track (now a wilderness path for hikers only) starts its second and final climb—a sharp 0.1 mile ascent back up to a spur, then ridgetop. From here, Rough Ridge becomes a downhill roller coaster, alternating level stretches or easy downgrades with short steep plunges to mile 6.3. The ridgeline supports an increasingly drier oak-pine forest. Where the walking slips onto the sunset slope, the forest becomes more and more hardwood the further you drop below ridgeline. At mile 5.3 the trail rounds a yellow poplar hollow with a sweetshrub thicket just below the treadway. This shrub often flanks the route from the Sugar Cove junction down to the rhododendron.

After angling down off the ridge, the footpath enters the riverine belt of hemlock and rhododendron at mile 6.3. It then parallels a small feeder stream before curling parallel to Rough Creek and descending upstream to the crossing. Once across, the remainder of the route follows an old railroad bed above the small pools and rocky runs of this Jacks River tributary. Saplings continue to reclaim the former railroad grade, forcing the path to wind much more than it did in years past.

Rough Ridge Trail ties into the Jacks River Trail on the western bank of Rough Creek. Rough Ridge Trail does not cross the creek a second time; it ends where the Jacks River Trail crosses the creek. If you continue straight ahead from the usually signed junction, downstream beside the creek, you will be walking the Jacks River Trail toward its low-elevation end at Alaculsy Valley.

Beyond mile 5.0 the western slope provides good winter views through the stick-figure hardwoods. Back to the left across the Rough Creek valley, you can see Buckeye Mountain and the 3,600-foot knob just south of Buckeye to the southwest. The highest mountain in the combined wilderness—4,224-foot Big Frog—is visible through the leafless trees to the north-northeast (20 to 30 degrees). Turkey Stand Lead, a spur off Hickory Ridge, lies nearby, just across the Rough Creek valley at 315 degrees.

sweetshrub

Nature Notes

Sweetshrub abounds along the lower-elevation, northern half of this trail. Spreading by underground root stalks, this deciduous shrub forms dense, almost monocultural colonies that often flank both sides of the path. Normally 3 to 7 feet tall, sweetshrub is easy to identify even when not in bloom. Both the branches and the 2- to 4-inch-long leaves are opposite. Paired opposite leaves at branch ends are diagnostic, especially along this trail. The leaves, which turn clear yellow in the fall, are somewhat aromatic when crushed.

When the distinctive brownish-maroon flowers are seen in combination with the paired leaves, there is no mistaking this shrub for any other. The unusual 1- to 1½-inch-wide corollas are composed of numerous thin, undifferentiated sepals and petals that form an erect, shaggy cup. Sweetshrub starts blooming at the lower elevations by mid-April and continues at the middle and higher elevations throughout May and into early June.

Most wildflower guides emphasize the spicy scent of this shrub's blossoms. Although the plant also earned the names sweet Betsy and Carolina allspice, the fragrance of its flowers varies widely in intensity from colony to colony. Most often, they are only faintly fragrant. Occasionally, when the sun is warm on the fresh flowers from the right colony, they have a definite spicy, applelike aroma.

mountain winterberry

Except in the driest habitats, sweetshrub is common throughout much of the combined wilderness below 3,500 feet. It is particularly at home beneath the canopy of cove hardwoods at lower elevations, and among mixed hardwoods on middle-elevation slopes and ridges. Above the 3,600- to 3,800-foot level it becomes increasingly scarce.

A fairly common shrub or small tree, the mountain winterberry (*Ilex montana*), also known as mountain holly, prefers moist hardwood forests up to 6,100 feet in the highcountry of the Southern Appalachians. Within the combined Cohutta–Big Frog Wilderness, this deciduous holly is much more frequent above 3,200 feet than below. It is especially abundant along the moist, upper-elevation ends of Panther Creek, East Cowpen, and Rough Ridge Trails. These three sections are not only high and hardwood, but they also were all once roads, so it is likely that the slight light gaps have encouraged this shrub's growth.

Throughout much of the year, this holly's dull-green foliage and tiny white flowers make it easy to overlook. It is especially inconspicuous in spring, when flame azalea, mountain laurel, and sweetshrub bloom on Rough Ridge. But mountain winterberry's fall fruits are bigger, brighter, and much more noticeable than its spring flowers. During the last half of September, and through October, November, December, and perhaps even into January, this shrub's large red drupes (berrylike fruits) make it an eye-catcher.

The dull-green alternate leaves—finely saw-toothed, abruptly pointed at the tip, 2½ to 5 inches long and 1 to 2¼ inches wide—are usually bunched near the ends of short spur twigs. Summer's green fades to pale yellow in late autumn. Clusters of the quarter-inch-wide flowers bloom white on the ends of twigs in May and early June. As its common name suggests, the showy, bright-red drupes, often clustered two or three together, persist into winter.

Even though mountain winterberry can attain its maximum size in the Southern Appalachians, most often you will see smaller specimens—large, spreading shrubs or occasionally small trees up to 25 feet in height.

Directions

Rough Ridge, an interior trail, has its southern (upper-elevation) end on East Cowpen Trail and its northern (lower-elevation) end on Jacks River Trail.

To reach Rough Ridge's southern end, walk 0.4 mile on East Cowpen starting from its southern (upper-elevation) trailhead at Three Forks Mountain. Look for Rough Ridge's sign and beginning treadway to the right. (See East Cowpen Trail, page 81, for further information.)

To reach Rough Ridge's northern end, walk 7.9 miles on the Jacks River Trail starting from its southeastern (upper-elevation) trailhead at Dally Gap. After the nineteenth ford (right side to left facing downstream), the Jacks River Trail angles up and away from the river before descending to and crossing Rough Creek. The usually signed Jacks River–Rough Ridge junction is immediately across Rough Creek. Rough Ridge ends there on the northern bank of Rough Creek; Jacks River Trail turns right and heads back toward its namesake river. (See Jacks River Trail, page 92, for further information.)

The shortest distance to Rough Ridge Trail's northern end junction with the Jacks River Trail is 4.6 miles—4.0 miles on Beech Bottom Trail and 0.6 mile and one upstream ford on the Jacks River Trail. (See Beech Bottom Trail, page 145, for further information.)

Sugar Cove Trail

Foot Trail 125: 2.3 miles

- **Dayhiking (low to high)** Moderate to Strenuous
- **Dayhiking (high to low)** Easy to Moderate
- **Backpacking (low to high)** Strenuous
- **Backpacking (high to low)** Moderate
- **Interior Trail** Southern (high elevation) terminus on Rough Ridge Trail, 3,600 feet; northern (low elevation) terminus on Jacks River Trail, 1,900 feet
- **Trail Junctions** Rough Ridge, Jacks River
- **Topographic Quadrangle** Hemp Top GA-TN
- **Features** Spring wildflower display; rich hardwood cove; Sugar Cove Branch; Jacks River

SUGAR COVE, AN INTERIOR TRAIL that leads hikers through rich hardwood cove and riparian habitat, remains lightly used because it requires a 2.5-mile walk to reach its upper end, and because it is the steepest of the seven Jacks River lead-in routes. Its 730 feet of elevation change per mile (not including the short climb beyond the last crossing of Sugar Cove Branch walked high to low) ranks it as the steepest trail in the combined wilderness. Sugar Cove is described as it is most often walked, from high to low, from Rough Ridge to the Jacks River.

The trail immediately curls to the left and plunges into the obviously moist upper reaches of Sugar Cove. With a tall, straight, parklike stand of cove hardwoods and an understory of ferns, wildflowers, and sweetshrub, the steep-sided upper cove is especially scenic in spring and allows largely unobstructed views of 50 to 60 yards. As you descend, the forest becomes denser and the individual trees grow taller and thicker. Here, beside the normally dry headwater streambed of Sugar Cove Branch, the second-growth forest—

black cherry, white ash, yellow poplar, northern red oak, sugar maple, basswood, yellow buckeye, and cucumbertree—has grown to larger dimensions than any other once-cut forest in the Cohutta Wilderness. Sugar Cove's largest tree, a yellow poplar about 40 feet to the left of the path at 0.6 mile, already has a circumference of over 11 feet.

This footpath loses nearly 1,100 feet in its first 1.2 miles. The first 0.3 mile is one of the steepest grades in the combined wilderness. Below that initial pitch, the downhill run becomes progressively easier as the trail slopes down to its first crossing of Sugar Cove Branch.

During the spring of 1998, a tornado ripped through Sugar Cove and smashed portions of its forest nearly flat. The uppermost cove escaped the twister, but sections of the middle and lower cove were hammered. As a result, the treadway will probably be rerouted around some of the worst snarls. Luckily, the old sugar maple just to the right of the track at 0.8 mile survived the storm. At 10 feet 8 inches in circumference and possibly 110 to 120 feet tall, this tree is the largest trailside sugar maple in the mountains of North Georgia.

Continuing to the northeast, the route crosses Sugar Cove Branch for the first of seven times at mile 1.1. (The number of crossings, formerly five and always an odd number, varies depending on deadfalls, floods, and hiker preference.) The evergreen of rhododendron and hemlock flanks the small stream, which rushes noisily through mossy rocks after substantial rain. Between crossings the path parallels the branch, often following the easy downgrade of the old railroad bed.

At mile 1.6 the trail angles up and to the left through a rocky notch away from the stream. It then climbs for nearly 0.2 mile, steep at first then progressively easier, to the top of a spur running east from Rough Ridge to the Jacks River. The dry, sunny forest along the upgrade—Virginia and white pine, sourwood, and blackgum above, mountain laurel and deciduous heath in the understory —is an abrupt change from both the cove and the moister slope on the other side of the spur.

As soon as the track rounds the spur, the final descent—500 feet in 0.5 mile—begins. Here the walking on cut-in path is occasionally steep, often at least easy to moderate, as it winds around several rich hollows on the way down to the river. The route fords the Jacks on a downstream angle then ends at its usually signed junction with the Jacks River Trail.

Nature Notes

High, steep-sided, and northeast-facing, the upper end of Sugar Cove has the most diverse spring wildflower display in the Cohutta Wilderness. From April 10 through early June at least twenty-five kinds of wildflowers take their turn blooming in this rich habitat. The Lily family is represented by Catesby's trillium, white wake robin, Vasey's trillium, yellow mandarin, Solomon's seal, and false Solomon's seal. Other easily identified species include blue cohosh, rue anemone, bloodroot, dwarf crested iris, mayapple, sweet cicely, foamflower, and meadow rue.

As I picked my way down through the tornado wreckage in Sugar Cove, I was surprised to see so many cucumbertree boles and branches on the ground. The cucumbertree (*Magnolia acuminata*) is a deciduous magnolia, one of three found in the combined wilderness. Overall, this tree is occasional throughout the wilderness and the Southern Appalachians. Even in the hardwood cove, where the cucumbertree is most numerous and grows best, it is still only a minor component of the forest. But the evidence underfoot strongly suggested that this species is more common, at least in some coves, than one would think at first glance.

Some of Sugar Cove's hardwoods—black cherry, basswood, sugar maple, yellow buckeye, and Northern red oak for example—are relatively easy to differentiate by bark alone. The cucumbertree, however, is similar in both bark and growth habit to the most common cove hardwood in the wilderness—the yellow poplar, also in the Magnolia family. Obviously, some of those tall, straight, gray-barked trees in the distance are cucumbertrees, and not all yellow poplars as is often assumed.

Six to 10 inches long and 3 to 6 inches wide, the large, oblong- to oval-shaped leaves have smooth margins that are either straight or wavy. The abruptly tipped leaves are yellowish-green above, paler beneath. The silver-colored terminal buds are noticeably long. The twigs are somewhat aromatic.

The flowers are not nearly as large, showy, or fragrant as those of the other two magnolias, Fraser and umbrella. Occurring singly at twig end, the erect, bell-shaped blossoms are most often 2½ to 3½ inches long and 1½ to 2½ inches wide. The six large petals are green to greenish yellow with orange streaks. Depending on elevation and the progress of the season, the cucumbertree can start blooming anytime from mid-April through early May.

The common name of this species stems from the cucumberlike shape of its fruit. The irregularly shaped fruits—green at first, then dark red at maturity—are 2 to 3 inches long. Like other magnolias, the cucumbertree's shiny red seeds hang from slender white threads when ripe. These seeds, dispersed by birds, twist and sway in the breeze.

cucumbertree

Although it grows on drier sites, the cucumbertree requires the moist, deep, fertile soils of coves and lower slopes to compete successfully for the canopy. This member of the cove hardwood forest is found from the lowest elevations up to 5,000 feet in the Southern Highlands. It occurs less and less frequently above 4,000 feet.

Although it is a distant third in leaf and flower size, this species is by far the largest of the three magnolias within the combined wilderness. Mature trees often grow 60 to 90 feet in height and 2 to 3 feet in diameter. In rich, old-growth coves some specimens become large trees: 3 to 5 feet in diameter and 110 to 145 feet in height. Georgia's state record cucumbertree is less than stellar, but Tennessee's record tree is a lunker—an impressive 13 feet 3 inches in circumference and 137 feet in height.

In 1802 the famous botanist and explorer Francois Michaux made a wry observation concerning pioneer usage of cucumbertree fruits: "The inhabitants of the remotest parts of Pennsylvania and Virginia and even the western countries, pick the cones when green, to infuse in whiskey, which gives it a pleasant bitter. This bitter is very much esteemed in this country as a preventative against intermittent fevers, but I have my doubts whether it would be so generally used if it had the same qualities when mixed with water."

The abundance of sugar maple—a tree at the southern limit of its range—is the cove's most distinctive feature and the obvious reason for its name. These maples occur less and less frequently from west to east across the Georgia mountains. Although fairly common from the Cohuttas westward, sugar maples are rare in the trailside forests of north-central and northeastern Georgia.

sugar maple

Classified as a northern hardwood, the sugar maple was the dominant tree in the cove's climax forest before logging. After logging, however, the yellow poplar—a quick-growing, prolific, succession species—became numerically dominant. Although the yellow poplar often persists in climax stands, it is intolerant; it cannot regenerate itself in shady forests. But the sugar maple can regenerate without disturbance, and its saplings are abundant throughout the cove. The tornado that ripped through the cove in the spring of 1998, however, opened the canopy enough in several places for yellow poplar regeneration. Thus the subtle war for dominance continues.

The leaf of the sugar maple (*Acer saccharum*) is distinctive—its silhouette graces the Canadian flag. It has long, pointed lobes and smooth margins, whereas the red maple leaf has much shorter lobes and toothed, serrated margins. Generally recognized as the most brilliant leaf display in North America, its fall foliage is multicolored—red, yellow, and orange often occur on the same tree, on the same branch.

The sugar maple is one of the largest hardwoods of the eastern forest. In the rainy Southern Appalachians, mature, forest-grown trees have clear, straight boles and average 75 to 100 feet in height and 2 to 4 feet in diameter. The maximum size of this species is 135 feet in height and 7 feet in diameter. Mature trunks have moderately furrowed, light gray bark, often with a flaky or shaggy appearance. The sugar maple is long-lived, from 300 to 450 years.

It is not the slightest bit anthropomorphic to state that the sugar maple is a chemically sentient being. The tree has evolved a strategy to cope with the inherent problem of monoculture—the monoculture of like-tasting leaves. It employs the same strategy that many agricultural experts advise farmers to use: diversification. When insects start munching, the sugar maple diversifies by varying the chemistry, and thus the palatability, of its leaves. This chemical defense forces the insects to move elsewhere in search of good forage, which may become undesirable shortly after they arrive. And even worse for the insects, while the little buggers are playing the sugar maple's version of the shell game, they expose themselves to predation.

The sugar maple's defense system is both internal and external. When attacked, these trees get on the horn and send airborne chemical signals to neighboring maples, thereby triggering their defense systems. Not bad for a dumb tree.

Directions

Sugar Cove is an interior trail that has its southwestern (upper-elevation) end on Rough Ridge Trail and its northeastern (lower-elevation) end on Jacks River Trail. Sugar Cove is one of only two trails in the combined wilderness (the other is Fork Ridge in the Big Frog) that requires walking segments of two other trails to reach one of its ends.

To gain Sugar Cove's upper-elevation end, you must first walk 0.4 mile on East Cowpen Trail starting at its upper-elevation, southern trailhead at Three Forks Mountain, then walk 2.1 miles on Rough Ridge Trail. After hiking the easily walked 2.1 miles on Rough Ridge, you will come to the prominent, usually signed Sugar Cove junction to the right (northeast). This junction is further marked by a flat rock large enough to sit on, a worn resting spot around the sign, and Sugar Cove's descending treadway. (See East Cowpen Trail, page 81, and Rough Ridge, page 108, for further information.)

To reach Sugar Cove's lower-elevation end, walk 3.9 miles on the Jacks River Trail starting from its Dally Gap Trailhead. The usually signed junction is on the east side (right side facing downstream) of the Jacks River; the lower-elevation end of Sugar Cove fords the Jacks River immediately before its connection with the Jacks River Trail. The Sugar Cove–Jacks River junction is between fords two (mile 2.9) and three (mile 4.1) hiking the Jacks River Trail from Dally Gap. (See Jacks River Trail, page 92, for further information.)

Notes

Hickory Ridge Trail

Foot Trail 71: 3.5 miles

- ▪ **Dayhiking (low to high)** Moderate
- ▪ **Dayhiking (high to low)** Easy to Moderate
- ▪ **Backpacking (low to high)** Moderate to Strenuous
- ▪ **Backpacking (high to low)** Moderate
- ▪ **Interior Trail** Southern (high elevation) terminus on East Cowpen Trail near Buckeye Mountain, 3,180 feet; northern (low elevation) terminus on Jacks River Trail, 1,550 feet
- ▪ **Trail Junctions** East Cowpen, Jacks River, Beech Bottom (see description)
- ▪ **Topographic Quadrangle** Hemp Top GA-TN
- ▪ **Features** Winter views; Jacks River; occasional old-growth chestnut oaks

HICKORY **R**IDGE **IS PRIMARILY A RIDGETOP** and upper-slope trail, affording nearly continuous winter vistas and numerous partial summer views. This path can be walked as the second or third leg of a no-backtrack loop beginning and ending at the East Cowpen–Rice Camp Trailhead. Linking East Cowpen, Hickory Ridge, Jacks River, and Rice Camp Trails together makes a good one- or two-day hike of 11.8 miles. The grades are somewhat easier if Hickory Ridge is walked downhill as the second leg of a counterclockwise circuit. There is no water on East Cowpen and none on Hickory Ridge until it reaches the Jacks River.

Hickory Ridge is one of the few trails in the Cohutta Wilderness that did not evolve in some measure from railroad or logging road. It is a wilderness footpath from top to bottom. This lightly used interior trail is described as it is most often walked, from high to low, from south to north, from the shoulder of Buckeye Mountain to the Jacks

River. The narrow track starts out as easy walking on the exact crest of its namesake ridge. It quickly makes a short, easy downgrade, then another a little sharper through a predominantly hardwood forest where sassafras and white pine saplings flourish in the understory. The fast-growing white pines will not remain below the canopy for long.

At 0.5 mile the treadway begins a short, steep downridge run of less than 0.1 mile to a shallow gap. This is the toughest grade on the trail. From this saddle to mile 3.1, the route repeats the same pattern as it continues northward toward the Jacks River. It rises easily from each gap, levels, then heads down with the ridge on a series of short descents, most ranging from easy through moderate, to the next shallow gap. These saddles, some more obvious than others, are at mile 1.9, 2.3, 2.7 and 3.0.

Especially along its upper half, the path parallels deeply entrenched Rough Creek, way down and to the right (east). Rough Creek's long, narrow watershed is hemmed in between Hickory Ridge and nearby Rough Ridge. Its steep-sided valley is V-shaped—the shape geographers classify as a "youthful valley."

Dry-site species such as Virginia pine become increasingly common as the rainfall decreases with elevation. The ridgecrest's lower reaches support several stands of shortleaf pine, and the abundant white pine saplings continue their race toward the canopy. The dry end of the oak-pine forest displays the best reds of autumn. Blackgum, red maple, sourwood, and scarlet oak blend their various shades of red against conifer green.

At mile 3.1 the walkway breaks the pattern. It slants down and to the right off the ridgeline and drops steadily to the riparian zone of rhododendron and hemlock above the river. From here the route descends parallel to a tributary branch, crosses it, then heads upstream along the Jacks River over a rocky flood channel. The track continues close beside the river for nearly 0.2 mile before fording at a normally shallow and always rocky place. Hickory Ridge Trail ends at its usually signed junction with the Jacks River Trail just up the river bank. Turning left, west and downstream, onto the Jacks River Trail leads you to the Beech Bottom–Jacks River intersection in 40 yards and Jacks River Falls in 0.7 mile.

As you descend the upper half of the trail, bare-branch views to the right are of Rough Ridge, the next ridge over at 150 degrees, and the high peak of Big Frog at 35 degrees. From the lower half, the long ridge to the left, nearly due west, is Ken Mountain. To the right, the lower end of Rough Ridge is at 100 to 110 degrees. The Blue Ridge, climbing from Double Spring Gap to the top of Big Frog, is 60 to 30 degrees on your compass.

Nature Notes

Hickory Ridge traverses an oak-pine forest that exhibits an elevation-dependent transition from moist to dry. Although hickories—mockernut and pig-nut—are more common than usual on North Georgia ridges, the oaks—northern red, scarlet, black, white, and chestnut—still dominate the trailside forest for most of its length. Chestnut oaks (*Quercus montana—Quercus* is Latin for beautiful tree), prefer-ring the dry, rocky soils of ridges and mountainsides, are especially common along the upper por-

chestnut oak

tion of the trail. As is usual in this type of forest, a shrub layer of mountain laurel, flame azalea, and deciduous heath—blueberries and huckleberries—dominates the oak-pine forest understory.

Old-growth chestnut oaks—crooked, low-limbed loggers' culls—are still the thickest trees on Hickory Ridge. When I first hiked this trail in the late 1970s, a fair number of them were still alive. Even then, though, most of these ridgetop survivors were either topped out or hollowed out. Now, after more years and more storms, especially Hurricane Opal in the summer of 1995, many of these old-timers are down, standing dead, or dying. Probably only a half dozen or so of these large oaks remain in relatively good condition.

The chestnut oak—mainly a mountain tree of the Appalachians—is one of the most abundant ridge and dry-slope hardwoods in the wilderness. It greatly increased its share of the canopy after the chestnut blight and is now a major component of the oak-pine forest. Another common name for this species is mountain oak. In fact, Boy Scouts and other children are taught to remember this name by folding a leaf's width in half along the midrib to see the silhouette of the mountains.

This oak received its accepted common name because its leaves somewhat resemble those of the American chestnut, no longer able to survive in most of its range beyond sapling stage. The leaves, however, are easy to tell apart. Much narrower than the chestnut oak leaves, American chestnut leaves have numerous sharp-pointed teeth. The leaves of the chestnut oak—4 to 9 inches long—have margins with noticeably rounded, wavy lobes, no points and no bristles. No other large Southern Appalachian hardwood has this type of leaf.

Quercus montana, often the thickest tree on low- and middle-elevation ridges, averages 60 to 85 feet in height and 2 to 4 feet in diameter. Its maximum size—130 feet in height and 7 feet in diameter—represents the record, or near record, for both dimensions. Like many other broadleafs in eastern North America, the chestnut oak attains its largest dimensions in the Southern Appalachians, in the highlands of Tennessee, North Carolina, and Georgia. The current Georgia state record is 95 feet tall and slightly over 15 feet in circumference. Slow-growing even on good sites, this member of the white oak group is also long-lived—up to half a millennium.

Like many of the other trails traversing similar habitat in the combined wilderness, Hickory Ridge passes through several colonies of sassafras saplings. The sassafras (*Sassafras albidum*), a tenacious tree that can survive fire, is a common pioneer on disturbed sites in the oak-pine forest. And although this successional species cannot tolerate heavy shade, obviously enough light filters through the open canopies of dry ridges to support numerous saplings. These evenly spaced sapling stands are the result of root-suckering, a type of vegetative propagation.

The sassafras is the northernmost New World representative of the Laurel family, an important and very large group (approximately 2,500 species) of tropical trees and shrubs. There are two other sassafras species—one in China, the other in Taiwan. The word sassafras stems from the Native American name for this hardwood, which was adopted and adapted by the early French in Florida. This hardwood is a highly aromatic tree; the leafstalks, twigs, bark, and especially the roots have a pleasant, spicy scent.

The deciduous leaves are variable in size and shape on the same tree, even the same small branch. The alternate, smooth-margined leaves—3 to 6 inches in length and 1½ to 3½ inches wide—come in three different shapes: unlobed (entire), two lobed or mitten shaped (the thumb on the left or right), and three lobed. In autumn the leaves are variable in color—orange, red-orange, and a salmon pink spotted with bright red. When crushed, sassafras leaves produce a mucilaginous slime. Pioneer

sassafras

children loved to chew them for the spicy taste. Tender young leaves are still used to thicken and flavor Creole dishes. The filé in real filé gumbo consists of powdered and dried sassafras leaves.

Mature bark is dark orangish-brown and deeply furrowed with rough, broken ridges. Twigs and branches of saplings and first-year twigs on older trees are green.

Small yellow flowers (⅜ of an inch long) bloom in clusters at the ends of leafless twigs in early spring. The dark blue, berrylike drupes ripen at the ends of bright red stalks in September and October. Eaten and dispersed by songbirds, the fruits are also consumed by deer, bear, and turkey. Bears are so fond of the small fruits that they break branches and occasionally even smash down small trees to obtain them.

Throughout most of its range, and especially in the North, the sassafras remains a small- to medium-sized tree—from 1 to 2 feet in diameter and 30 to 60 feet in height at most. But when this hardwood matures in the Southern Appalachian canopy, it can grow 70 to 90 feet tall. A few specimens from uncut areas within the Great Smoky Mountains National Park are over 30 inches in diameter. Its maximum size is approximately 5 feet in diameter and 100 feet in height.

Found in a variety of habitats, this broadleaf is usually uncommon to rare above 4,200 feet in the Southern Highlands. The contours from 5,000 to 5,200 feet appear to be its uppermost limit.

The sassafras played an important role in early colonial exploration and commerce. Early on, Native Americans taught several ailing Spaniards how to make medicine from the highly aromatic oil derived from the root bark. The sick Spaniards must have recovered and lived to tell the tale, because the news quickly reached Europe. In 1574 a Spanish physician from Seville wrote a tract entitled *Joyfull Newes Out of the Newe Founde Worlde*, in which he extolled the virtues of sassafras as a miraculous cure-all. As you can imagine, disease-ridden Europe was desperate for the next panacea—especially a wonderful tasting one from the fabulous Newe Worlde.

The rush to supply demand was soon in full swing. English merchants sailed to the New World to fill their holds full of sassafras bark. If their ships struck the coast too far north for sassafras, they headed south until they found it. Sassafras was one of the first exports sent by Captain John Smith from Jamestown. As late as 1610, it was still shipped from Virginia, as a condition of that colony's charter. But as usual, credibility faded to gullibility, followed closely by disillusionment.

The belief in sassafras as an effective medicament stemmed from its aromatic properties. A plant with a strong pleasant smell was supposed to ward off evil—the cause of disease—and cure the illness. Donald Culross Peattie discussed the origins of this notion in his book *A Natural History of Trees*: "This conception of the curative, since evil dispelling, nature of an odor is very ancient; it goes back to Egyptian and druidical ceremonies, and was strongly believed in by Europeans during the bubonic plague, when doctors wore great nose-beaks filled with spices."

Directions

Hickory Ridge is an interior trail that has its southern (upper-elevation) end on East Cowpen Trail and has its northern (lower-elevation) end on Jacks River Trail.

To reach Hickory Ridge Trail's southern end, walk 2.7 miles on East Cowpen Trail starting from its northern (lower-elevation) trailhead at the end of FS 51. You will find the usually signed junction to the left (due north) in the middle of a sharp, horseshoe-shaped switchback that curls up and to the right. The junction is marked further by a small, open, loafing area. (See East Cowpen Trail, page 81, for further information.)

The northern end of Hickory Ridge Trail is located on the north side (right side facing downstream) of the Jacks River, 8.5 miles from Jacks River Trail's Dally Gap Trailhead and 8.0 miles from its Alaculsy Valley Trailhead. Hickory Ridge Trail fords the Jacks River before reaching its usually signed junction with the Jacks River Trail at a heavily used camping area. (See Jacks River Trail, page 92, for further information.)

The shortest-distance route to the Hickory Ridge–Jacks River junction is the Beech Bottom Trail. Walk Beech Bottom's 4.0 miles to its junction with the Jacks River Trail, then turn left (east and upstream) onto Jacks River Trail and continue 40 yards to its junction with Hickory Ridge Trail. (See Beech Bottom Trail, page 145, for further information.)

Notes

Rice Camp Trail

Foot Trail 137: 3.9 miles

- ■ **Dayhiking In** Easy
- ■ **Dayhiking Out** Easy to Moderate
- ■ **Backpacking In** Easy to Moderate
- ■ **Backpacking Out** Moderate
- ■ **Start** Rice Camp Trailhead, 1,760 feet
- ■ **End** Jacks River Trail, 1,350 feet
- ■ **Trail Junctions** Jacks River, East Cowpen (at trailhead)
- ■ **Topographic Quadrangle** Hemp Top GA-TN
- ■ **Features** Rice Camp Branch and tributary;
  riparian habitat; cascade; Jacks River

THIS TRAIL AND THE BRANCH IT CROSSES were named for the logging camp that once housed laborers on the flat ridgecrest at mile 2.4. The two people I asked about the origin of the Rice Camp name had different answers. The first person, from the Forest Service, said the camp's name came from the former owners of the land—the Rice family. The second source, a young man I met on the trail, claimed to know the real reason for the name.

He told me that his family has lived near and hunted in the Cohuttas for generations. They make hunt camp near Rice Camp Trail every fall. His grandfather, who had worked at Rice Camp, told him the name came about one winter when heavy snows prevented supplies from reaching the loggers. Finally, after considerable worry and wait, someone managed to lead in a few mules during a cold snap. The mules foundered in drifts from time to time. The drover jettisoned canned goods to lighten the load. By the time the mules made it to the hungry camp, all they carried was bags of frozen rice.

His story lost credibility, however, when he launched quickly into another Rice Camp tale. He recounted the time, not long past, when a big old bear nosed into a failed cocaine shipment, then ran around crazed—an animal gone seriously amuck—until he died of a drug overdose. Maybe the Forest Service should start a new anti-drug campaign: Coky the bear.

Rice Camp is a moderately to heavily used Jacks River approach, popular because it doesn't lose much elevation and because it ties into the Jacks River Trail near the falls. Rice Camp has two very dissimilar halves, a wet one and a dry one. The first half is easy walking that parallels, then crosses, the clear, cold, often sliding water of small streams. Traversing a succession of low, dry spurs, the second half is harder ridgecrest and upper-slope hiking through a predominantly oak-pine forest.

Descending to the northeast on an old roadbed, wide and always mucky, the trail soon parallels a quickly growing unnamed tributary of Rice Camp Branch. Here the moist, second-growth forest—especially the fast-growing white pines, yellow poplars, and sweetgums—are tall and straight. At 0.8 mile the route crosses the 6- to 12-foot-wide branch for the first of five times (the number of crossings changes with floods and deadfalls).

After the fifth crossing at mile 1.1, the track curls to the southeast, switching streams and direction of travel. It now heads upstream, closely paralleling and crossing larger Rice Camp Branch. Immediately after the switch, the treadway swings close beside a sliding cascade, perhaps 8 to 10 feet high and 15 to 20 feet long. The crossings, slaloming from one side to the other, come in quick succession. Although relatively tranquil for a mountain brook, Rice Camp still has its share of narrow raceways, sluices, and long slides over solid bedrock. Small brown trout dart for cover as you approach their pools near the crossings.

Beyond the ninth and final crossing, Rice Camp Trail switchbacks up and to the left away from its namesake branch. Here the walking, to the north again and still on old roadbed, rises on an easy grade above a small Rice Camp tributary. After stepping across the feeder stream, the footpath continues its gradual elevation gain to a level area atop a Hickory Ridge spur at mile 2.4. The flat terrain, the nearby springs, several large double-trunked white oaks, and the bed frame to the right of the trail all indicate the site of the former logging camp.

The route dips from camp, crosses two step-over spring runs, then heads up through drier woods numerically dominated by sourwood, sweetgum, sassafras, blackgum, and several oak species. At mile 2.7 the track makes a short, sharp drop to a muddy rivulet. Once across, it ascends an easy-to-moderate grade to a cut-up rough of forking spur ridges and ravines splayed in every direction. The trailside terrain often slopes away slowly on dry spurs, or falls away suddenly into moister hollows on either side of the ridgeline. Once the treadway reaches ridgetop, it roller-coasters on the exact crest or upper slope to a slight gap at mile 3.2. Chestnut oak and several species of red oak along with Virginia and shortleaf pines account for the majority of the larger boles.

The drop to Jacks River, sharp in places but moderate overall, begins at mile 3.4. On the way down, you will pass a magnificent pignut hickory less than 10 feet to the left of the trail. With a girth of nearly 10 feet and perhaps 120 to 125 feet tall, this old-growth hickory—wide crowned and seemingly still healthy—is easily the largest hickory beside the trails of North Georgia. The end of this wilderness path dips through a belt of rosebay rhododendron and eastern hemlock. Rice Camp ties into the Jacks River Trail on the south side of the river. Jacks River Falls is one ford and 1.1 miles to the right, east and upstream, on the Jacks River Trail.

Nature Notes

At mile 2.9, on a dry, low-elevation ridgetop, Rice Camp passes through a small, scattered stand of shortleaf pine. Four pine species are found at least occasionally beside some of the trails in this guide. While white and Virginia pines are exceedingly common within the combined wilderness, the shortleaf, sporadic or occasional at best, is a very distant third in overall abundance. The loblolly grows in small numbers only at the lowest elevations. Most common on the drier upland soils of low-elevation ridges, shortleaf pine (*Pinus echinata*) seldom occurs at elevations above 3,200 feet. Here in the Cohutta–Big Frog, it is found much more frequently below 2,400 feet than above.

A mature shortleaf pine is easily recognized by its relatively short needles, growth habit, and distinctive bark. The shortleaf's dull orange-brown bark is broken into large—often roughly 2 inches wide by 3 inches long—irregularly rectangular plates with thin, flat scales. These scales are very brittle; even a squirrel can knock a few of them off while hitching up a tree. The surface exposed when a scale falls is a colorful, light orange-brown.

While their 2¾- to 5-inch-long needles are relatively short, they are noticeably longer than the very short, twisted needles of the Virginia pine (description on page 165), which also inhabits the area's dry ridges. The shortleaf's dark yellow-green needles come in bundles of two or three to the sheath.

This conifer's clean, telephone-pole-straight trunk remains clear of branches for much of its height. Its pyramidal crown, short and somewhat narrow, is sparsely branched.

shortleaf pine

On the best sites, such as well-drained alluvial soils along streams, shortleaf pine can grow 90 to 120 feet tall and 2 to 3 feet in diameter. On dry ridges, however, it is slow-growing and usually remains less than 85 feet tall and 26 inches thick. Very old specimens may live 400 years.

Eaten by turkey, squirrels, and some songbirds, the seeds from the 1½- to 2½-inch-long cones are an important food source where the tree is common.

The easily recognized foamflower is fairly common along the first half of this trail. Also known as false miterwort, this spring wildflower is yet another perennial that spreads by underground rhizomes. Its common name comes from the feathery, foamlike appearance of the blossoms. This member of the Saxifrage family is common in moist, rich woods, especially near small streams that flow through hardwoods.

Withstanding all but the coldest winter weather before withering, this herbaceous plant's basal-stalked leaves come close to being ever-

green. The shape, the pointed lobes, and the toothed margins of the 2- to 4-inch-long leaves closely resemble red maple foliage.

Like most wildflowers that possess spikes of numerous, small corollas, the foamflower breaks bud from bottom to top along the spike, and blooms for a much longer time than most single-flowered plants. The foamflower is usually in bloom, at least somewhere along its spike, from the middle of April at low elevations through early July up higher. The flower stalks are usually 6 to 13 inches tall with 1½- to 3-inch-long racemes of numerous, five-petaled, white blossoms at the top. Sprays of stamens capped in dull orange emerge from the centers of the tiny (¼ inch wide) star-shaped corollas.

foamflower

Directions

The Rice Camp Trailhead can be most easily reached from Access Points 3, 4, and 5. (See the detailed description of the Access Points at the beginning of this guide.)

Access Point 3: From the three-way FS 16–FS 17 intersection, continue straight ahead on FS 16 for approximately 4.6 miles to its signed junction with FS 51. Turn uphill and to the right onto FS 51, then travel approximately 4.7 miles (there are two fords across normally shallow Jigger Creek) to the end of the road at the turnaround/

parking area. Two trails—East Cowpen and Rice Camp—begin where FS 51 ends. Rice Camp begins to the left, next to its trailhead bulletin board. (East Cowpen is the gated trail that continues straight ahead from the dead end.)

Access Point 4: From the three-way FS 221–FS 16 intersection, turn right onto FS 16, immediately cross the big iron bridge over the Jacks River, then continue approximately 0.8 mile to the signed left turn onto FS 51.

Access Point 5: From the three-way FS 55–FS 221 intersection, turn right onto FS 221 and travel approximately 3.0 miles to its junction with FS 16 at the big iron bridge over the Jacks River. Cross the bridge, continue on FS 16 approximately 0.8 mile, then turn uphill and left onto signed FS 51.

Notes

Horseshoe Bend Trail

Foot Trail 43: 3.0 miles

- ■ **Dayhiking In** Easy to Moderate
- ■ **Dayhiking Out** Moderate
- ■ **Backpacking In** Moderate
- ■ **Backpacking Out** Moderate to Strenuous
- ■ **Start** Horseshoe Bend Trailhead, 1,540 feet
- ■ **End** Jacks River Trail, 1,160 feet
- ■ **Trail Junction** Jacks River
- ■ **Topographic Quadrangle** Hemp Top GA-TN
- ■ **Features** Year-round view; Jacks River

HORSESHOE BEND TRAIL IS KNOWN PRIMARILY for three things: its heavily managed beginning, its great vista, and its steep ending. Named for a small portion of its view—a winding bend in the Jacks River that almost doubles back on itself—this trail begins in the Chattahoochee National Forest 1.8 miles from the wilderness boundary. Signs of recent management are noticeable for most of the first mile. The ending, a sharp, 0.3 mile downgrade to the Jacks, is particularly memorable after carrying a heavy pack up from the river on a hot day. This short segment is steep enough to raise the difficulty ratings a notch.

Most of Horseshoe Bend's first mile is easy walking on a woods road. The managed forest along this stretch, a mosaic of merchantable timber mixed with plots of saplings regenerating from past cuts, has looked different on every hike since my first in the late 1970s. If not brushed out, the sun gap of the road can be densely vegetated by late summer.

At 0.5 mile and again at 0.9 mile, the track crosses a fork of an unnamed tributary branch of Jacks River. After crossing the usually mucky second fork (less than 0.1 mile beyond a rivulet), the treadway rises easily on washed-out road, then makes a short climb to another road at mile 1.1. Here, at the small "trail" sign, the route turns right and follows the grassy road for 65 yards before angling left and somewhat up onto a narrower woods road. This wide, open walkway provides easy, pleasant hiking through a dry oak-pine forest on or near a Ken Mountain spur. Shortleaf, Virginia, and white pine comprise the conifer component; chestnut, scarlet, black, and northern red account for the bulk of the oak boles. As usual, red maple, blackgum, sassafras, and sourwood are common in the subcanopy.

At mile 1.8 the old-road trail enters the Cohutta Wilderness at a large wooden sign. Now the track heads generally northward—easy up for a short distance, then easy down—on or close to Ken Mountain's ridgeline. The walking remains on old road through dry, second-growth oak-pine forest. The treadway angles to the right and down off the main ridge at mile 2.2, then dips slightly harder (easy to moderate) to the east on slope below another spur. You soon hear the deeply entrenched river to the right.

The old road descends to a small open spot at the top edge of a precipitous bluff at mile 2.6. This is Horseshoe Bend Overlook, open to the southeast. The canopied landscape of mountains timbered to their tops, the ridgelines overlapping into haze, the bend of shining river below the only break in the forest, the solitude—all are characteristic of the Cohutta Wilderness. The highest peaks in the near view—Cohutta Mountain and two of its major spurs, Hickory Ridge and Rough Ridge beyond Hickory—span the horizon from 160 to 180 degrees.

Continuing toward the Jacks River, the route rises from the bluff on a narrow Virginia pine ridge, then curls to the left onto the side-hill. Here, at approximately 1,600 feet, the path begins a sharp pitch of 440 feet in a little over 0.3 mile. (Whenever a trail changes elevation 100 or more feet per 0.1 mile—basically a 20 percent grade—it is tough hiking.) The trail winds and works its way down the abrupt slope through a moister and more sheltered forest. The oaks here are bigger than those above. Tall, straight sweet birch, yellow poplar, basswood, and white pine shade silverbells in the understory. The final grade becomes mild as it angles upstream toward the river and its usually signed junction with the Jacks River Trail.

Nature Notes

The scarlet oak (*Quercus coccinea*) plays a significant role in the low- and middle-elevation climax forests of the Southern Appalachians. And it is also distinctive enough that non-botanists can distinguish it from the other red oaks.

The numerous oak species are usually divided into two groups—

scarlet oak

the white oaks and the red oaks. The lobes of red oak leaves are generally pointed and bristled on the tips, while the lobes of the white oak leaves are generally rounded and lacking bristles. Especially on young trees, the red oaks have long, smooth, vertical streaks dividing their bark. These easily recognized, slick-looking streaks disappear from more and more of the trunk as a tree reaches maturity. White oak bark lacks these smooth streaks. Northern red, southern red, black, scarlet, and pin oaks are all included in the red oak group. The white oak group contains chestnut, post, and of course, white oaks.

Scarlet oak leaves—4 to 8 inches long and 2½ to 5 inches wide— have 5 to 9 (usually 7, rarely 9) bristle-tipped lobes. These lobes are deeply separated by wide, rounded sinuses that extend almost to the midvein. The sinuses in the middle of the leaf are so deeply scalloped that they often form more than half of a slightly flattened circle. True to its name, the scarlet oak's fall foliage is a glossy dark red. Its leaf display is considered the most colorful of the oaks, red or white.

Beyond the smooth streaks, which are characteristic of the red oak group, the bark of this species offers no obvious clues to aid in further clarification. Like that of other reds, the thick bark becomes darker with age and is broken into irregular ridges separated by shallow fissures. If you find some acorns beneath a suspected scarlet oak, however, you can make a positive identification. The exposed ends of the ½- to 1-inch-long acorns are ringed with concentric circles.

Even though it is only a medium-sized oak, the scarlet—often 60 to 90 feet tall and 2 to 3½ feet thick at maturity—is still a fairly substantial tree. Large specimens on good sites can reach 130 feet in height and 5½ feet in diameter. The current Georgia state record is 128 feet tall and 13 feet 3 inches in circumference. Maximum lifespan is approximately 400 years.

Although it occurs up to 5,000 feet, the scarlet oak is most common on dry upland sites below 3,600 feet. Its ability to achieve rapid growth on the dry, often poor soils of ridges and upper slopes makes it an important component of the oak-hickory and oak-pine forests. Because this species is quite intolerant of heavy shade, it is usually excluded from good sites by more tolerant and faster growing trees.

As I hiked the trails within the combined wilderness in 1990, I noticed something strange, something I had not seen only a few years before. In many areas throughout the wilderness, flowering dogwoods appeared stressed and diseased. In the moistest, coolest pockets of habitat—high coves, steep-sided stream valleys, high elevation north-facing slopes and ridges—many were already dead. "Dead and dying dogwoods" became an oft repeated notation. I was witnessing the southward spread of a disease, dogwood anthracnose, across the mountains of North Georgia.

Like the much more deadly chestnut blight, the pathogenic culprit is an accidentally introduced fungus. Thought to have entered the New York City area in the late 1970s or early 1980s, this fungus was confirmed in the Southern Appalachians by 1987. Unlike the fungus that wiped out the chestnut, however, this fungus, *Discula*, has two requirements that limit its virulence. *Discula* needs extended periods of wetness or high humidity on a daily basis. It also does not spread once the temperature reaches 78 to 80 degrees.

These two necessities insure that the distribution of the *Discula* fungus in lethal doses will remain spotty. The mortality rates of flowering dogwoods in the cooler, wetter Southern Appalachians have been much higher than in the surrounding Ridge and Valley or Piedmont physiographic provinces. And even within the mountains, total or near total devastation occurs only within the coolest, moistest pockets.

When I walked these same trails again in 1998, this disease had all but eliminated the dogwood from the most vulnerable sites. And it didn't take long. Anthracnose can kill a dogwood from the ground up in only three to five years. Dead twigs, ragged leaf edges, and twigs sprouting from the trunks are all signs of infection.

At present plenty of flowering dogwoods still grace the sunnier, drier forests, like those along most of this trail, within the combined wilderness. And although it is still too early to tell, researchers are hopeful that the dogwood will reinvade the blighted areas, albeit in lower population levels than before.

Directions

The directions for Horseshoe Bend Trail are exactly the same as those for Rice Camp Trail to the FS 16–FS 51 intersection. After turning onto FS 51 from the FS 16–FS 51 junction, continue approximately 2.7 miles (there are two fords across normally shallow Jigger Creek) before turning left into the primitive camping area at the Horseshoe Bend sign. A bulletin board 30 yards in from the road marks the beginning treadway. (See Rice Camp, the preceding trail, for Access Point directions to the FS 16–FS 51 intersection.)

Notes

Penitentiary Branch Trail

Foot Trail 53: 3.6 miles

- **Dayhiking (low to high)** Easy to Moderate
- **Dayhiking (high to low)** Easy
- **Backpacking (low to high)** Moderate
- **Backpacking (high to low)** Easy to Moderate
- **Interior Trail** Eastern (high elevation) terminus on Hemp Top Trail, 3,080 feet; western (low elevation) terminus on Jacks River Trail, 1,700 feet
- **Trail Junctions** Hemp Top, Jacks River
- **Topographic Quadrangle** Hemp Top GA-TN
- **Features** Winter views; hardwood hollows; Penitentiary Branch; Jacks River

IN THE EARLY DECADES OF THE **1900s,** loggers worked long hours six days a week in a remote camp near a small stream deep in the Cohuttas. They were so far back in the woods that there was no place they could go on Saturday night and still make it back for work bright and early Monday morning. So on Sundays, their only day off, the men were forced to stay in camp—stuck in what felt like prison. The creek near their isolated camp is now known as Penitentiary Branch.

Most of what is now Hemp Top Trail was once a Forest Service road all the way to the high point of Hemp Top Mountain. That road provided vehicular access to the Penitentiary Branch Trailhead. The Georgia Wilderness Bill of 1986 added 2,900 acres to the Cohutta Wilderness, all within the Chattahoochee National Forest. As a result, FS 73 was gated at Dally Gap, and Penitentiary Branch became an interior trail. Now both trails, especially Hemp Top, have more of what geographers refer to as "the friction of distance."

Moderately used Penitentiary Branch is primarily a ridgecrest–upper slope–upper hollow trail. Rather than descending a single ridge to the Jacks River, it follows and traverses a series of ridges, often dropping far enough below ridgeline to wind around the upper ends of hardwood hollows. Winter views through hibernating hardwoods are frequent; partial between-branch summer views are fairly common.

This route is frequently walked as the second leg of a Hemp Top–Penitentiary Branch–Jacks River loop—no backtrack, 13.0 miles—beginning and ending at Dally Gap. Steadily losing a mere 1,380 feet to the Jacks River, Penitentiary Branch has no sustained grades more difficult than easy to moderate.

This interior trail is described as it is most often walked, from high to low, from east to west, from near Rockwall Gap on the Blue Ridge to the Jacks River. The first mile is a cakewalk, all level or easy down on a wide, well-defined treadway. The track follows an old roadbed into a dry, south-slope oak-pine forest. Red maple, blackgum, sourwood, sassafras, and the oaks—chestnut, scarlet, and black—compose the bulk of the deciduous species. The conifer component consists of white and Virginia pine, the latter more common. The understory is shrubby with mountain laurel and deciduous heath, including flame azalea, which blooms throughout most of May and early June.

After winding around several moister hollows, the path passes through a shallow gap at 0.5 mile. Beyond the gap, the trail skirts the southeastern flank of an unnamed knob (3,060 feet) and winds around more hollows before reaching the next ridgecrest gap at mile 1.2. It quickly slabs onto slope again, rounds another hardwood hollow, then heads down harder (easy to moderate) for the first time on ridgetop at mile 1.6. Following a second downridge dip, the wide walkway slants onto sidehill and winds around a series of west- and northwest-facing hardwood hollows. Here the second-growth forest—black cherry, yellow poplar, and several species of red oak, among others—is taller and straighter than on the ridge. Sweetshrub is often abundant in the upper portions of the hollows.

From mile 2.2, where the walking is easy on a Virginia pine ridge, to mile 2.8, the footpath remains on or near a succession of spurs. Shortly after you hear the river good and loud, the route swings to the east onto the moist, north-facing slope above the Jacks. As soon as the treadway turns, the composition of the forest abruptly changes. Here rhododendron and tall hemlock, beech, white pine, basswood, sweet birch, and yellow poplar shade the path. The course rock-steps across normally shallow Penitentiary Branch at mile 3.2, then closely follows the sliding, pooling stream toward the river. Penitentiary Branch Trail ties into the Jacks River Trail at a large permanent campsite close to the Jacks. To the right (downstream) it is two fords and 2.1 miles to Jacks River Falls.

Most of the wintertime views from Penitentiary Branch are to the left of the trail. A look to the southeast (150 degrees) at 0.8 mile affords views of unnamed Blue Ridge knobs, 3,000-footers rising beside Hemp Top Trail near Spanish Oak Gap. Further along, bare-limb outlooks to the south, across the Rockwall Branch valley, provide a peek at the spur ridge descending to the southwest toward the Jacks River. Once the trail turns to the northwest, prospects to the southwest and nearly west are of Rough Ridge.

Nature Notes

Many mountain hikers develop a certain fondness for box turtles. It's not because they want to eat them or pet them. And it's not because of the turtles' grace or power or beauty. It is simply because they are what they are—slow, plodding, easily seen, unwary creatures millions of years beyond their epoch of origin. Box turtle sightings have bailed out many a mountain hike from being a wildlife shutout beyond the occasional songbird and boar rootings.

Easily identified by its high-domed, brightly patterned carapace (yellow to orange), the eastern box turtle is the only terrestrial turtle in the Southern Appalachians as well as throughout much of its range, which stretches from southernmost Maine to southern Florida and westward to the Great Plains. Native Americans living in what is now New York were responsible for wiping out this turtle from much of its territory between Ohio and New England. They ate box turtle meat, used the shells for ceremonial rattles, and buried turtles with their dead.

Eastern box turtles eat, among other things, slugs, earthworms, wild strawberries, and mushrooms. They can even consume the highly toxic amanitas without ill effect. Native Americans and early settlers who ate box turtle meat soon after the reptile had an amanita meal, however, quickly dropped dead from secondhand mushroom poisoning.

The sexes of these 4- to 8½-inch-long tortoises are easily distinguished. Males usually have red eyes and always have concave depressions in the hind ends of their plastrons (the bottom hinged parts of their shells). These concavities, the result of natural selection completed several geological ages ago, keep the male from sliding off the female's shell during mating. The yellowish-brown–eyed females are capable of storing sperm and producing fertile eggs for several years after a single mating.

Eastern box turtles hibernate during winter and estivate during the prolonged hot, dry spells of summer. They are most often encountered early in the day after dewfall or anytime during the day after rain. A heavy thunderstorm brings them out of summer estivation. At that time they move about eagerly, and you can easily see them from trail or road, even while it is still raining.

If environmental conditions remain constant, a box turtle may spend its entire long life (its maximum lifespan has been documented at 100 years and more) in an area not much larger than a football field.

As you walk from Dally Gap toward the Penitentiary Branch junction, you have an opportunity to observe running ground pine—the short, stiff, evergreen plant that occurs in dense colonies on the upper banks of Hemp Top's old roadbed. Commonly called running cedar, this plant belongs to a genus (*Lycopodium*) known as the club mosses. Despite their name, club mosses are not mosses. These nonflowering vascular plants are intermediate between higher plants (flowers and trees) and those without conductive tissue (lichens, mosses, liverworts, and fungi).

Often a pioneer on disturbed sites, running ground pine is abundant for much of the first mile of Hemp Top Trail. This betweener plant creeps slowly along the ground by means of long horizontal stems. If conditions are right and if it has been spreading for years, a colony occasionally covers large areas of the forest floor.

What we see above ground are essentially branches growing up at intervals from the horizontal stems. These branches, which reach a height of 5 to 10 inches, have erect stems composed of scalelike leaves flattened and fanned out in one plane.

Club mosses produce spores on slender, erect cones called strobiles. Each of the running ground pine's fruiting stems forks, then forks again to create four cones. The twin pairs of cones resemble double tuning forks or candelabrum arms. These cones are the "clubs" that give this group of plants the first part of their confusing common name.

Once collected commercially, the tiny dry spores were used as ignition powder for fireworks and the flash for early cameras.

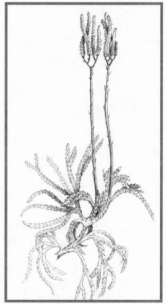

running ground pine

Directions

Penitentiary Branch is an interior trail that has its eastern (upper-elevation) end on Hemp Top Trail and its western (lower-elevation) end on Jacks River Trail.

To reach the upper-elevation end of Penitentiary Branch, walk 2.3 miles on Hemp Top Trail starting from its Dally Gap Trailhead. The hiking to the Penitentiary Branch junction is easy—it gains approximately 465 feet on the gentle grades of a former Forest Service road, now Hemp Top Trail. The Penitentiary Branch–Hemp Top junction is impossible to miss. Penitentiary Branch angles down and to the left onto an old woods road at its large sign and well-worn resting spot. (See Hemp Top Trail, page 155, for further information.)

The lower-elevation end of Penitentiary Branch is located on the east side (right side facing downstream) of the Jacks River, 7.1 miles from Jacks River Trail's Dally Gap Trailhead. Immediately after fording the river for the eighteenth time (left bank to right facing downstream), look for the Penitentiary Branch Trail sign at a large permanent campsite too close to the river. (See Jacks River Trail, page 92, for further information.)

Notes

Beech Bottom Trail

Foot Trail 74: 4.0 miles

- ■ **Dayhiking** Easy to Moderate in either direction
- ■ **Backpacking** Easy to Moderate in either direction
- ■ **Start** Beech Bottom Trailhead, 1,570 feet
- ■ **End** Jacks River Trail, 1,540 feet
- ■ **Trail Junctions** Jacks River, Hickory Ridge
  (see description)
- ■ **Topographic Quadrangle** Hemp Top GA-TN
- ■ **Features** Old-growth trees; winter views; Jacks River;
  Jacks River Falls (see description)

B EECH BOTTOM, THE FLOODPLAIN where Beech Creek enters the Jacks River, is now wilder than it has been for over a hundred years. The Forest Service has a photograph taken in the early 1890s of Tasker's sawmill, operating in the bottomland on a small scale with oxen. In the 1920s and early 1930s, when cut-everything-and-run logging came to the Cohuttas, Beech Bottom was the site of a logging camp. After logging came farming; the bottom was cleared, settled, fenced, and plowed.

When the Cohutta was designated wilderness in 1975, a large hunting cabin and two old houses stood at the edge of the bottom near Beech Creek. The small houses were torn down shortly after designation. Jacks River Game and Fish Preserve, Inc. owned the hunting lodge. The company's rights to the property expired in 1981, and that structure was removed in the early 1980s.

Relatively short at 4.0 miles, Beech Bottom is the second easiest trail in the combined wilderness. It is also the only trail that leads to the most scenic single feature in the combined wilderness—Jacks

River Falls—without forcing hikers to walk at least 5 miles and ford the Jacks at least once. This route's easy accessibility to the falls accounts for the fact that Beech Bottom is the most heavily used trail per mile in the combined wilderness. Suffering from overuse and misuse, the area from the end of Beech Bottom Trail to Jacks River Falls is marred by hacked trees, bare dirt, and trash. The Forest Service may have to take steps, however unpopular and unpleasant, to prevent further degradation.

Starting in Tennessee's Cherokee National Forest, Beech Bottom winds to the southeast on the wide walkway of the former road. The hiking, level or barely downhill, rounds a series of hollows where the forest—hemlock, hardwoods, and white pine—is taller and straighter than the dry, somewhat scraggly oak-pine woods on the upper slopes. The trail enters the Cohutta Wilderness and Georgia's Chattahoochee National Forest in quick succession. At 0.6 mile the route begins a steady, easy downgrade that soon parallels an entrenched branch headed for the Jacks River.

Beech Bottom rock-steps across a fork of that branch at mile 1.0, then gradually rises parallel to the southeastern fork. In the ravine to the right you can still see some old-growth trees—a few beech, hemlock, and sugar maple—that escaped the logging early in the last century. The thickest trailside tree, an old hemlock just to the right of the former road, measured 11 feet 10 inches in circumference.

The track ascends easily up and away from the small stream. At mile 1.6, where it crosses over a Van Arthur Lead spur, the old road starts to follow a pattern that holds until it reaches the trail's high point at mile 2.4. Slowly rising from one contour line to the next, the wide footpath crosses over a spur then rounds a hollow, again and again. The dry oak-pine forest—scarlet and chestnut oak, Virginia and shortleaf pine, red maple, sourwood, and blackgum—is all second-growth.

After crossing the ridge of Van Arthur Lead, the walkway is usually level or easy down all the way to the bottom. You hear the river now, and see cheater trails running straight down the sidehill toward the loudest white noise. If you can find downed wood nearby, do your best to block off the entrances of these highly erodable cheaters. The hollow-spur pattern continues as the tread-way follows the contour around upper hardwood hollows. At mile 2.9, to the right of the trail, there is a good winter vista and a par-tial summer view of two high ridges—the Blue Ridge (Hemp Top) to the east and slightly southeast, and Rough Ridge almost to the south.

The path curls down and to the right into Beech Bottom at mile 3.3. It continues straight ahead through a camping area (thin trees mark the site of the former hunt-ing cabin), crosses rocky Beech Creek, then follows the cobbly old road into the relatively flat bottom. Beech Creek varies widely from season to season. One April it was fast, wide, and midcalf deep; one September it was completely dry. Back on smooth treadway, the route passes the old home place site, now most prominently marked by a few exotic royal paulownia trees (huge leaves in summer, large nut clusters in winter), just to the left of the trail. Pawpaw, sycamore, and American horn-beam (also known as blue beech or water beech), species that do not occur at the middle and upper elevations of the combined wilderness, are common in the fertile soils of the bottom.

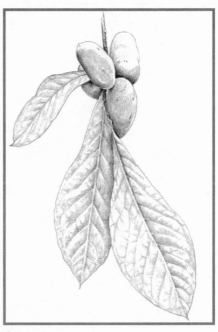

pawpaw

Beech Bottom ties into the Jacks River Trail on the northern bank of its stream. The Jacks River–Hickory Ridge junction is 40 yards to the left and upstream from the Jacks River– Beech Bottom intersection. To the right, downstream, it is a little more than 0.6 mile to the cliffside overlook above Jacks River Falls.

Nature Notes

Near its end, where it skirts the eastern edge of the bottom, the old road passes through the largest trailside colony of pawpaw (*Asimina triloba*) in the combined wilderness. Elsewhere in the wilderness this species occurs in small scattered colonies, the individual specimens arching and usually no taller than five feet. But here in this low-elevation floodplain—its preferred habitat—the pawpaw is not only much more abundant but also larger, some 20 to 25 feet tall. A few may be large enough to bloom and bear fruit.

pawpaw blooms

Also known as custard apple, wild banana, and fetid shrub, the pawpaw is the northern-most member of the chiefly tropical Custard-apple family. The pawpaw seeks rich soils, especially floodplain bottomlands beneath hardwoods. It is most common and reaches its best growth—40 feet in height and slightly over a foot in diameter—in the lower Mississippi Valley. Large colonies are rare to occasional at best throughout the Southern Appalachians for two reasons, both having to do with elevation: humans long ago cleared the largest, lowest bottomlands for agriculture, and the pawpaw's upper-elevation limit is approximately 2,500 feet. A skinny, 25-footer is big in the mountains.

Asimina triloba is easily recognized by its stooped growth habit and its large, alternate, short-stemmed leaves, which turn butter yellow in the fall. The dark green leaves—sharp pointed at the tip, tapered at both ends, and broadest beyond the midpoint—are usually 7 to 10 inches long and 3 to 5 inches wide. Some saplings have leaves up to 15 inches in length. If it looks like a pawpaw, and smells like a pawpaw—it's a pawpaw. Just for verification purposes, rub a leaf's underside and note the smell—not the aroma, but the foul smell. This odor is obviously the reason for the name fetid bush.

Appearing in April before the leaves, the dark brown to brownish maroon flowers, with three prominent outward curling petals, are approximately 1½ inches wide. The resulting kidney-shaped, cylindrical fruits are 3 to 5 inches long and 1 to 1½ inches in diameter. When they ripen in September and October, the innards of the yellow-green to brownish fruits are soft, custardy, and quite edible. Native Americans liked them so much they planted pawpaw orchards. Early settlers harvested basketfuls of the wild fruits for making pawpaw jelly.

lobelia

The combined wilderness is home to at least four native lobelia species, not counting the cardinal flower. (See description on page 98.) These lobelias are fairly similar, and some are obscure enough to lack common names. They occur in a variety of habitats, from seeps to dry oak-pine forest, at the lower and middle elevations of the wilderness. In general, those lobelias that are found in the moistest environments are taller and have larger, showier flowers than those in drier habitats.

Usually 1 to 3½ feet tall, these members of the Bluebell family have blossoms that range in color from light to dark lavender-blue to pinkish blue. The lobelia common along this trail is a relatively short species with small, light blue or light lavender-blue flowers. It is usually in bloom from mid-August into October.

The narrow, pointed leaves of these herbaceous perennials, usually 2 to 4 inches long near the base of the plant, become progressively smaller up the stem. Near the top, on the flowering parts of the stems, the leaves are reduced to bracts.

Lobelia flowers break bud from bottom to top along terminal, spikelike racemes. Depending upon the species, three or four to over a dozen flowers are often open at once on a single plant. The corollas of the various lobelias, varying from ⅓ to ¾ of an inch long, are five petaled and two lipped. Three partly fused petals form the spreading lower lip, and two small, narrow petals constitute the upper lip. The white streaks at the base of the lower lip are honey guides, little landing strips designed to help insects find their way to what they want, nectar, and to what the plant wants, pollination.

The common name of *Lobelia inflata,* one of the lobelia species found in the wilderness, is Indian tobacco. Pioneers observed the Cherokee and other tribes pipe-smoking this lobelia's dried leaves, which contain an alkaloid similar to the nicotine in regular leaf tobacco. This alkaloid, lobeline, is used in products that help people stop smoking.

Directions

The Beech Bottom Trailhead can be most easily reached from Access Points 3, 4, and 5. (See the detailed description of the Access Points at the beginning of this guide.)

Access Point 3: From the three-way FS 16–FS 17 intersection, continue straight ahead on FS 16 (then FS 221 beyond the big iron bridge over the Jacks River) for approximately 6.5 miles to the sharp right turn uphill onto FS 62. Once on FS 62, Big Frog Loop Road, proceed approximately 4.5 miles to the Beech Bottom Trailhead— large gravel parking area to the left, bulletin board and gated trail on the right.

Access Point 4: From the three-way FS 221–FS 16 intersection at the Jacks River Trailhead, curl left with FS 221 and continue approximately 1.1 miles to the sharp right turn onto FS 62. Follow FS 62 (Big Frog Loop Road) for approximately 4.5 miles to the well-marked Beech Bottom Trailhead.

Access Point 5: From the three-way FS 55–FS 221 intersection, turn right onto FS 221, travel that road for approximately 1.9 miles, then turn left onto FS 62. Follow FS 62 (Big Frog Loop Road) for approximately 4.5 miles to Beech Bottom's unmistakable trailhead.

Notes

For me, and for thousands with similar inclinations, the most important passion of life is the overpowering desire to escape periodically from the clutches of a mechanistic civilization. To us the enjoyment of solitude, complete independence, and the beauty of undefiled panoramas is absolutely essential to happiness.

—Bob Marshall

Big Frog Mountain

*Early spring along
Hemp Top Trail*

Trails

Hemp Top Trail
Chestnut Mountain Trail

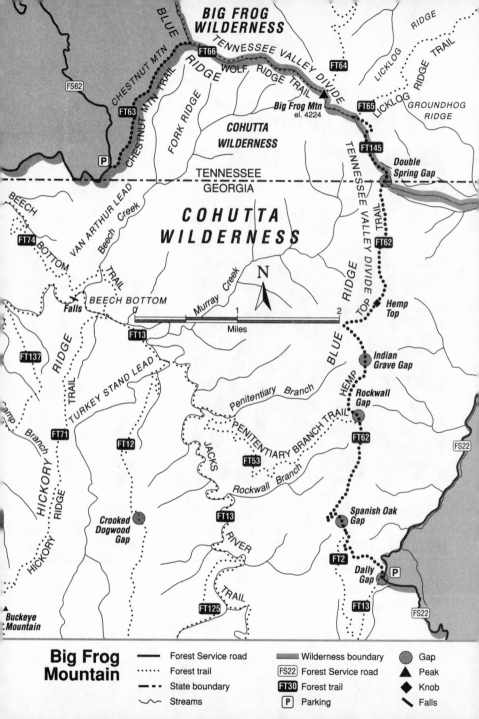

Big Frog Mountain

Legend	
Forest Service road	———
Forest trail	········
State boundary	— ·· — ··
Streams	～～～
Wilderness boundary	▓▓▓▓
FS22 Forest Service road	
FT30 Forest trail	
P Parking	
● Gap	
▲ Peak	
◆ Knob	
＼ Falls	

BIG FROG WILDERNESS

TENNESSEE VALLEY DIVIDE

WOLF RIDGE TRAIL

BLUE RIDGE

CHESTNUT MTN TRAIL

FORK RIDGE

CHESTNUT MTN

FS62

FT66

FT63

P

FT64

LICKLOG RIDGE

LICKLOG RIDGE TRAIL

GROUNDHOG RIDGE

Big Frog Mtn
el. 4224

FT65

FT145

Double Spring Gap

COHUTTA WILDERNESS

TENNESSEE
GEORGIA

COHUTTA WILDERNESS

BEECH BOTTOM

FT74

VAN ARTHUR LEAD

Beech Creek

BEECH BOTTOM TRAIL

Falls

FT13

FT137

RIDGE

TURKEY STAND LEAD

Murray Creek

N

0   1   2
Miles

TENNESSEE VALLEY DIVIDE

BLUE RIDGE

FT62

Hemp Top

HEMP TOP TRAIL

Indian Grave Gap

Rockwall Gap

FT62

Camp Branch

FT71

HICKORY RIDGE

HICKORY RIDGE

FT12

JACKS

Penitentiary Branch

PENITENTIARY BRANCH TRAIL

FT53

Rockwall Branch

Crooked Dogwood Gap

FT13

RIVER

TRAIL

FT125

Spanish Oak Gap

FS22

FT2

Dally Gap

P

FT13

FS22

Buckeye Mountain

Hemp Top Trail

Foot Trail 62 in GA, 145 in TN: 6.1 miles

- ■ **Dayhiking In** Moderate
- ■ **Dayhiking Out** Easy to Moderate
- ■ **Backpacking In** Moderate to Strenuous
- ■ **Backpacking Out** Moderate
- ■ **Start** Dally Gap Trailhead, 2,585 feet
- ■ **End** Licklog Ridge Trail at Big Frog Mountain, 4,030 feet
- ■ **Trail Junctions** Jacks River (at trailhead),
  Benton MacKaye, Penitentiary Branch, Licklog Ridge
- ■ **Topographic Quadrangle** Hemp Top GA-TN
- ■ **Features** Winter views; Double Spring Gap;
  Big Frog Mountain

HEMP TOP TRAIL AND THE MOUNTAIN it rises over were named for a crop that was once important to the Cherokee as well as to the Europeans who settled in the area. Cherokee women wove hemp into rope, fishnets, and cloth. The local settlers used it for making rope. Hemp was listed as one of Fannin County's major cash crops in 1860.

The old Hemp Top Trail, which began at the former trailhead atop Hemp Top Mountain, was 2.1 miles long. The Georgia Wilderness Bill of 1986 added 2,900 acres to the Cohutta Wilderness, all within the Chattahoochee National Forest. This addition extended the Cohutta to the northeast, from Dally Gap along FS 22 to the Tennessee line. Today, Hemp Top's first 4.1 miles follow the easy grades of former FS 73. The route is quickly succeeding from dirt-gravel road to wilderness path.

Hemp Top, primarily a ridgecrest and upper-slope trail, offers numerous winter vistas and occasional, partial summer views. The ridge it follows is not just any ridge: it is the Blue Ridge, which also serves as the Tennessee Valley Divide in this area. And Hemp Top is not just one trail. The Benton MacKaye Trail—its best days still in the future—shares Hemp Top's treadway from mile 0.9 all the way to Hemp Top's ending junction at Licklog Ridge Trail.

Beyond the Penitentiary Branch junction, Hemp Top–Benton MacKaye becomes the least-walked section of trail in the Cohutta Wilderness. Without the Benton MacKaye Trail Association's excellent maintenance, this little-used section would be overgrown by midsummer. The last time I walked this trail, in late August, the Benton MacKaye volunteers had just brushed out the trail so well and so wide that I was able to see a bear run across the path in front of me.

Hemp Top is frequently walked as the first or final leg of a Hemp Top–Penitentiary Branch–Jacks River loop—no backtrack, 13.0 miles—beginning and ending at Dally Gap.

Starting behind its gate in Dally Gap, Hemp Top heads north on the upper sunrise slope of the Blue Ridge. Here the trail, rising on the steady easy grades of the former road, is through a predominantly second-growth hardwood forest with numerous early succession species flanking the former light gap. Mountain laurel is common in the understory, especially on the upslope above the road bank. The route rounds several moist, hardwood hollows, open and full of ferns in their upper ends. At 0.9 mile Section 10 of the Benton MacKaye Trail, marked with a white diamond blaze and a sign to the left, joins Hemp Top's treadway at Spanish Oak Gap (2,920 feet).

Beyond this first gap, the footpath switches sides and remains on the ridgecrest or upper sunset slope as it continues toward Hemp Top Mountain. The grades, including one downhill, are even milder than before. The pines—white and Virginia—are minor components of the largely deciduous forest. The saplings of a short-lived succession species, the black locust, are often common along the edges of the former road. At mile 2.3 the track arrives at its prominently signed junction with Penitentiary Branch Trail just south of Rockwall Gap (3,100 feet at gap).

Beyond the Penitentiary Branch connection, the treadway becomes narrower and more pathlike. As the trail skirts the western flank from gap to gap, the effects of elevation and exposure become more noticeable. The drier southwest slope supports an oak-pine forest. But as the path curves onto northwest-facing slope, a difference of only 90 degrees, it passes through an open forest of tall hardwoods with an increasing number of fern fields below the canopy. Species requiring moist conditions for good growth—black cherry, white ash, basswood, and sweet birch—are now common on the northwest sidehill. The course runs through Indian Grave Gap (3,220 feet) at mile 3.1 and continues to rise gradually on the upper-west slope.

After curling over a Hemp Top spur at mile 3.6, the wilderness walkway works its way back to the ridge, then gradually ascends to the crown of Hemp Top (3,580 feet) at mile 4.1. Along the way it passes an open grove of shagbark hickory to the left. A fire tower once stood on top of the mountain to the right, and the former Forest Service road ended here at a turnaround loop. Saplings have already reclaimed the site.

Still heading northward, the path veers to the left and down off the mountaintop, then makes a short, sharp pitch to an old woods road. The descent continues on easier grades (alternating easy with easy to moderate) through a west-slope oak-pine forest to mile 4.7. Here the route roller-coasters with the ridgeline—rising over low knobs, dipping to the shallow gaps—before dropping on steeper grades to the belt of white pine in Double Spring Gap (3,220 feet) at mile 5.4.

True to its name, the gap has two springs, one to the right and the other to the left. What its name doesn't tell you, however, is that the water from these two springs, starting only a few rods apart, takes vastly different journeys to the sea. Double Spring Gap is located at the intersection of an east-west running man-made boundary and a north-south running natural barrier. The political border separates states, national forests, counties, and WMAs. The geographical boundary is the Tennessee Valley Divide, which separates major watersheds.

The spring to the left (west) of the gap feeds one of Murray Creek's headwater prongs. Its flow chart is a list of Native American names: Jacks River, Conasauga River, the Oostanaula, the Coosa, the

Alabama, and the Tensaw River to the Gulf of Mexico at Mobile Bay. The spring to the east of the gap takes a slightly less direct route to the gulf: Silvermine Creek, Tumbling Creek, Ocoee River, the Hiwassee, the Tennessee, the Ohio, and finally down the Mississippi with Huck and Jim.

These two springs are your last and only chance at water on Hemp Top Trail. The spring to the right (east) has a wider path and more water; therefore it receives more use, including the watering of stock. It is probably a good idea to drink the Mobile Bay–bound water to the left. Come dry weather, the springs are often nothing but ooze mud and wet rock at their sources. When this happens, wrestle rhododendron downstream until you find a catch basin.

Double Spring Gap is the southern end of Section 11 of the Benton MacKaye Trail. It is also the beginning of a climb that gains 810 feet of elevation in Hemp Top's last 0.8 mile. This grunt, moderate to strenuous overall, raised the difficulty rating of this trail one notch. It is definitely not a good idea to carry a heavy pack up this pitch on a hot day unless you are young or ready.

Closely following the boundary between the two wildernesses beyond the gap, Hemp Top is the only route that connects the trail systems of the Big Frog and the Cohutta. Just above the gap, a usually battered sign welcomes hikers to the Cherokee National Forest. The upgrade, mostly on old road, heads up through the swath of white pine into a predominantly deciduous, south-facing forest of oaks and other dry-site (for this elevation) hardwoods. As the track nears the 4,000-foot level, sugar maple and increasing numbers of black cherry thrive in the moister woods. The ascent angles to the right of the wide ridgeline before easing up to its tie-in with Licklog Ridge Trail. A cairn usually marks the intersection; hopefully a sign will be added soon. If you want to finish the walk to the top of Big Frog (4,224 feet), turn left (west) with the Benton MacKaye onto Licklog Ridge Trail and follow that path for 0.5 mile to its end near the exact high point of the mountain.

Nature Notes

Starting at mile 3.7 Hemp Top passes by an open grove of shagbark hickory (*Carya ovata*) on the west side of the trail. This distinctive species becomes gradually more common from east to west across the mountains of North Georgia; it is rare in northeasternmost Georgia and increases its numbers to occasional in northwesternmost Georgia. So even though there are probably no more than fifty to a hundred of these trees scattered through the forest here, that relatively small number is still many more than you would find along any other trail in the combined wilderness. In fact there are more shagbark hickories beside Hemp Top than near any other North Georgia trail from the Cohutta Wilderness eastward across the mountains.

Mature shagbark hickories are easy to identify both in summer and winter. As the common name so aptly suggests, the curling, smoke gray bark—unique in the forests of eastern North America—is rough and shaggy. The bark of a mature tree has large vertical strips (plates), often a foot or more long, that curl away from the trunk at either end. The older the tree, the more pronounced the curl, the deeper the pile of shag. The hickories beside Hemp Top are still fairly young and small, so they have not yet developed their full snarl of curling plates.

shagbark hickory

Like all hickories, this species has alternate, pinnately compound leaves. The shagbark's leaves are usually 9 to 15 inches long, with five (occasionally seven) oval, finely toothed, stalkless (or nearly so) leaflets per leaf. The terminal leaflet—5 to 7 inches long and 2 to 3 inches wide—is the largest. The foliage turns golden brown in the fall.

Commonly 70 to 90 feet in height and 2 to 3 feet in diameter, this hickory is a medium- to large-sized tree. In rich bottomland soil, its favored habitat in the South, the shagbark occasionally grows 100 to 120 feet tall and over 3 feet in diameter. Its maximum, record-sized dimensions are approximately 150 feet in height and 4 feet in diameter. Even though fast growing for a hickory, the shagbark still grows slowly, but it grows slowly for a long time—up to 300 to 350 years.

This species occurs in a variety of sites and soils, from well-drained lowlands to dry mountain slopes up to approximately 3,600 feet in the Southern Highlands. (This grove is at and slightly above 3,400 feet.) The nutmeat of this hickory's fruit is sweet, delicious, and highly esteemed. Early settlers relished the tasty kernels so much that they formed nut-gathering parties called "nutcracks," where they often cut the trees down rather than wait for the nuts to fall a few at a time.

Native Americans used shagbark hickory nuts as a staple food item for thousands of years. Our word "hickory" was derived from *pawcohiccora*, the Native American word for hickory milk. William Bartram, the eighteenth-century botanist and explorer, described the Native American's use of shagbark hickory nuts in his book, *Travels*, first published in 1791:

> The fruit is in great estimation with the Indians. The Creeks store shagbark hickory nuts in their towns. I have seen above a hundred bushels of these nuts belonging to one family. They pound them to pieces and then cast them into boiling water, which, after passing through fine strainers, preserves the most oily part of the liquid; this they call by a name which signifies hickory milk; it is as sweet and rich as fresh cream, and is an ingredient in most of their cookery, especially hominy and corn cakes.

Settlers used everything but the leaves (and they probably had an occasional use for them too) of the shagbark hickory for one purpose or another. They fashioned primitive door hinges from the curling strips of bark, ate the tasty nuts, smoked hams over smoldering hickory fires, and produced yellow dye from its inner bark. And even though it was hard to split and rotted quickly, settlers often roughed out fence rails from this wood, probably because they had already cut the trees down for nuts and firewood. Over much of the eastern half of the country, this tree was the favorite fuel of settlers and townspeople alike because of its very high BTU value. Millions of cords of this heavy wood were pitched into fireplaces, wood-burning stoves, and on campfires.

The last two times (both in June) I hiked Hemp Top, I was stopped dead in my tracks by the Southern Appalachian's most striking butterfly—the Diana. The two butterflies I saw—the only ones of this species I have ever seen in Georgia—were the unmistakable males. The Diana is one of only two eastern butterflies that exhibit dramatic sexual dimorphism. The blue-black female Diana is larger and much longer lived than the male. The female is also a pipevine swallowtail impersonator; it mimics this bad-tasting butterfly to gain protection from predators. Natural selection has made it almost impossible for all but butterfly experts to identify the female Diana.

But not the male. The male is wow-look-at-that-butterfly beautiful. Its unique pattern and coloration would stand out even in the tropics. The inner two-thirds of the upper wings are black; the outer one-third is brilliant orange with a few small black spots. The underside is tan-orange. When a male springs up from a closed-wing position on a nearby flower, the unexpected burst of color is startling.

This species has only one brood, or flight, per year. In Georgia, they first fly in early June, and even the relatively long-lived females are but tattered fragments on the forest floor by mid-September. Most adults feed avidly on nectar, sap, scat, and even carrion. Milkweed flowers, which usually start blooming in late May and early June, are the Diana's preferred nectar source. This fact explains the timing of their flight, and also explains their occurrence along the Hemp Top Trail. Sun-loving, early succession species like milkweed, briers, and asters have reclaimed the light gap of the former roadbed.

At 3 to 3⅞ inches across, the Diana is one of the largest fritillaries, a large and colorful family of butterflies. It is regarded by lepidopterists (butterfly experts) as the most striking member of that family.

The Diana's stringent habitat requirements, shrinking range, and relative scarcity make it a good symbol of the wildness and beauty that remains in the refugia of the Southern Highlands. This species favors deep woodland habitat: forested valleys with streams and mountainsides with rich, moist soils. The cutting and conversion of forests has excluded this species from large portions of its former range. It now occurs in four disjunct ranges, the largest of which is the Southern Appalachians. The Diana is still common in parts of the Great Smoky Mountain National Park.

Directions

The Hemp Top Trailhead at Dally Gap can be most easily reached from Access Points 7 and 8. (See the detailed description of the Access Points at the beginning of this guide.)

Access Point 7: From the paved, three-way intersection of FS 221, FS 65, and County Road 251, continue across the bridge over Tumbling Creek and proceed straight ahead (south) on FS 65—then FS 22—for approximately 8.0 miles to the Dally Gap Trailhead. Forest Service 65 turns to dirt-gravel after 0.5 mile, enters Georgia, then becomes FS 22. Two signed and gated trails begin to the right side of the road at Dally Gap. Jacks River heads downhill past the bulletin board; Hemp Top starts up and to the right.

Access Point 8: From the four-way intersection at Watson Gap, turn right and uphill onto FS 22, then travel approximately 3.5 miles to the obvious (bulletin board, trail signs, pull-off parking to the left and right) trailhead at Dally Gap. Two signed and gated trails begin to the left side of the road at Dally Gap. Jacks River heads downhill past the bulletin board.

Notes

Chestnut Mountain Trail

Foot Trail 63: 1.9 miles

- **Dayhiking In** Easy to Moderate
- **Dayhiking Out** Easy
- **Backpacking In** Moderate
- **Backpacking Out** Easy to Moderate
- **Start** Chestnut Mountain Trailhead, 2,210 feet
- **End** Wolf Ridge Trail, 3,020 feet
- **Trail Junction** Wolf Ridge
- **Topographic Quadrangles** Hemp Top GA-TN, Caney Creek TN
- **Features** Winter views; shortest route to Big Frog Mountain (see description)

ONE OF THREE TRAILS in the combined wilderness with a length of less than 2.0 miles, Chestnut Mountain—a short, Wolf Ridge approach—is the only Cohutta Wilderness trail totally within Tennessee's Cherokee National Forest. Following a perimeter escarpment ridge, Chestnut Mountain is also the only combined wilderness trail that has nonwilderness land to one side for all or most of its length. Walked in combination with the uppermost 1.8 miles of Wolf Ridge Trail, the Chestnut Mountain–Wolf Ridge route is the shortest, though not the easiest, way up to Big Frog Mountain's broad crown.

From its beginning behind the vehicle-blocking gate, the wide walkway rises easily through a predominantly hardwood forest of thin trees to 0.1 mile, where the route reaches the exact crest of the ridge and the first stands of Virginia pine. For the next 1.5 miles the trail follows the familiar pattern of old, ridge-running roads as it heads to the northeast on or near the spine of Chestnut Mountain, one of numerous spur ridges leading to Big Frog. Here the walking is mostly easy or easy to moderate as the track either continues with the crest line up and over low knobs, or slabs to the right onto the upper southeastern slope, the dry side, to avoid the harder grades over the steeper knobs. Many of the level sections remain wide and grassy; some of the steeper segments are gullied to bare rock in the middle.

The woods along the ridgetop is not all pine, nor has it all been recently cut. As you gain elevation, pockets of second-growth hardwoods—mostly dry-site oaks, pignut hickory, sassafras, red maple, and blackgum—become more common, especially on the moister, northwestern side of the ridge. The nearby spur to the right (east) is Fork Ridge. The west fork of Beech Creek begins its run to the Jacks River down in the hardwood cove between the ridges.

With 0.3 mile remaining Chestnut Mountain Trail switchbacks up and to the left, crosses over the ridgetop to the northwest slope for the first time, then climbs an overall moderate grade (progressively easier after the one short, steep pull) to its junction with the Wolf Ridge Trail. Near its end the treadway levels out in a spur-top forest of crooked, low-limbed oaks. Chestnut Mountain ties into Wolf Ridge Trail at a usually signed, worn-bare spot on the narrow crest of the Blue Ridge.

Wolf Ridge Trail makes a sharp turn to the east at its Chestnut Mountain junction. Following Wolf Ridge down and to the left (approximately 30 degrees) leads toward its trailhead at Pace Gap. To finish the hike to the top of Big Frog, angle to the right and gently up (approximately 100 degrees) onto the upper south slope of the Blue Ridge.

Like other upper-slope and ridgecrest trails, Chestnut Mountain affords numerous bare-branch views. To the right of the trail at 80 to 90 degrees is the highest mountain around—Big Frog at 4,224 feet— and a portion of the Blue Ridge rising toward its peak from Double Spring Gap. To the left of the trail are views west and north of long, low ridges that stretch away to the Ridge and Valley physiographic province. The sharp peak at approximately 335 degrees is Chilhowee Mountain, nearly 10 miles away.

There is nothing but ooze water even during wet weather on or close beside this trail. The section of Wolf Ridge Trail rising to the top of Big Frog offers no help either. Three trails—Big Frog, Wolf

Ridge, and Licklog Ridge—join together at a usually signed, high-elevation junction atop Big Frog Mountain. Usually reliable Elderberry Spring, rocked in to form a basin, is just to the right of Licklog Ridge Trail slightly more than 0.1 mile southeast of the mountaintop junction.

Nature Notes

For both species diversity and individual size, the best days of the forest beside this trail are definitely in the future. Especially near the trail's beginning, the forest appears to be small, relatively young third-growth. The most recent topo sheet of the area, however, still shows the white of cleared land near the lower-elevation end of the trail. It may be that some of this ridgetop terrain was cleared for a number of years, and that the thin-boled forest is actually young second growth.

Beyond the first few tenths of a mile, the forest is oak-pine in various stages of recovery. Virginia pine (*Pinus virginiana*), a succession species, is numerically dominant over much of the ridgetop. Many of the lower-elevation stands of this pine were still in a stunted, thicket stage in 1990. Since that time, competition within the stand for water, nutrients, and light has noticeably thinned out these shade-intolerant trees. Near the end of the route, the pines become larger and fewer while the oaks—especially the chestnut and northern red—become larger and more numerous.

The Virginia pine is abundant and easy to identify. It is the only pine in the combined wilderness that always has two needles per bundle, and it also has the shortest needles (1½ to 3 inches) of any pine in the wilderness. The dull yellow-green to gray-green needles are stout, slightly flattened, and often somewhat twisted.

This conifer's cones, bark, and thickly branched growth habit are also distinctive. The diminutive, reddish brown cones are only 1½ to 2¾ inches long. The bark on a mature bole is orangish brown and shaggy, with small, thin, scaly plates that flake off easily when touched. Especially in the open canopy of sunny ridges, Virginia pines have numerous twisting limbs, quite different from those of white and shortleaf pines. Unlike many others in its genus, the Virginia's lower limbs often persist for years, even after dead.

Slow-growing and relatively short-lived, this species is most often a small- to medium-sized tree, usually 30 to 65 feet tall and 16 to 22 inches in diameter at maturity. The tallest Virginia pines in the wilderness are the occasional 80- to 90-footers that fought for and won a place in the streamside canopy after the logging along the Jacks and Conasauga Rivers. The thickest ones—wide-crowned dry-slope or ridgetop specimens—are a little more than 2 feet in diameter.

The Virginia, also known as scrub pine, is most common on dry, low-elevation ridges. The poorer and rockier the soil, the better this pine competes. These pines are most abundant from the lowest elevations to 3,000 feet. Above 3,600 feet they become increasingly scarce. This conifer is often numerically dominant on the low- to middle-elevation ridges in the Big Frog Wilderness.

Virginia pine

Especially where fire is suppressed, the Virginia is a very successful succession species on the drier, recently disturbed sites within the oak-pine forest. After timber cutting, infestation, or storm, incredibly dense stands of saplings quickly claim the forest floor. At first there is little life below the solid green shade cast by the young trees. But the saplings soon thin themselves out and other trees—in this case white pines and dry-site hardwoods—invade and, if there are no further disturbances, gradually replace the scrub pines. The Virginia is intolerant of heavy shade and soon dies after other trees block the sun.

Although often despised by lumbermen and ignored by hikers, this evergreen plays an important ecological role. Its role became especially apparent after millions of acres of the highly erodable Southern Appalachians were subjected to the one-two punch of clear-cutting followed by the frequent fires that raged through the slash. It was then that this lowly tree, as only it could on certain sites, protected the steepest, rockiest, poorest-soiled environments from further degradation. It held the soil, added to the duff, and started the healing process that continues today.

A member of the Primrose family, whorled loosestrife (*Lysimachia quadrifolia*) is common throughout the wilderness in dry, open, oak-pine forest. These unbranched wildflowers range from 1 to 3 feet tall and have at least three or four whorls of 2- to 4-inch-long leaves. Each whorl consists of three to six pointed leaves.

The loosestrife's delicate, star-shaped flowers are borne singly on long, slender stems that arise from the axils of the leaves. Yellow with reddish centers, the five-petaled blooms are only ½ inch across. This herbaceous perennial starts blooming from mid- to late-May at the lower elevations and lasts until early July at the higher elevations.

Both the common and generic names of this plant allude to the accepted potency of loosestrife to pacify draft animals—to loose them from their strife. Colonists often fed their oxen loosestrife to calm them enough to work together. Sometimes they tied bunches of the herb to the yokes of the oxen to accomplish the same purpose. Some think the loosestrife may have actually repelled insects, thus soothing the beasts.

whorled loosestrife

Directions

The Chestnut Mountain Trailhead can be most easily reached from Access Points 3, 4, and 5. (See the detailed description of the Access Points at the beginning of this guide.)

Access Point 3: From the three-way FS 16–FS 17 intersection, continue straight ahead on FS 16 (then FS 221 beyond the big iron bridge over the Jacks River) for approximately 6.5 miles to the sharp right turn uphill onto FS 62 (Big Frog Loop Road). Once on FS 62, proceed approximately 6.2 miles (prominent Beech Bottom Trailhead after approximately 4.5 miles) to the trail sign that marks the right turn up into the Chestnut Mountain Trailhead and parking area. The gated old road directly opposite the bulletin board is the trail.

Access Point 4: From the three-way FS 221–FS 16 intersection at the Jacks River Trailhead, curl left with FS 221 and continue approximately 1.1 miles to the sharp right turn up onto FS 62 (Big Frog Loop Road). Travel FS 62 for approximately 6.2 miles (bulletin board and parking area for Beech Bottom Trail after approximately 4.5 miles) to the trail sign and right turn to the Chestnut Mountain Trailhead and parking area. The gated trail is the old road straight across from the bulletin board.

Access Point 5: From the three-way FS 55–FS 221 intersection, turn left onto FS 221 and follow that road for approximately 1.8 miles to the right turn onto FS 62. Proceed on FS 62 (Big Frog Loop Road) approximately 4 miles to the trail sign and left turn up into the Chestnut Mountain Trailhead and parking area.

With two intersections on FS 221—southwestern and northeastern junctions approximately 3.7 miles apart—the Big Frog Loop Road (FS 62) forms a complete loop in combination with FS 221. The 4.5-mile segment of FS 62, from its southwestern junction to the Beech Bottom Trailhead, is usually well maintained. But beyond the Beech Bottom Trailhead, and especially the uphill section from Beech Bottom to the Chestnut Mountain Trailhead, the road becomes significantly rougher in places all the way to the northeastern junction. Access Points 3 and 4 follow FS 62 from its southwestern junction; Access Point 5 takes you uphill from the northeastern junction. Although it is often rutted, the uphill stretch beyond Beech Bottom Trailhead usually remains passable for all but the lowest-clearance vehicles.

Notes

Big Frog Wilderness

The love of wilderness is more than a hunger for what is always beyond reach, it is also an expression of loyalty to the earth, (the earth which bore us and sustains us), the only home we shall ever know, the only paradise we will ever need—if only we had the eyes to see.

—Edward Abbey

Big Frog Wilderness

West Fork Rough Creek

Trails

Wolf Ridge Trail
Grassy Gap Trail
Big Creek Trail
Yellow Stand Lead Trail
Big Frog Trail

Rough Creek Trail
Fork Ridge Trail
West Fork Trail
Licklog Ridge Trail

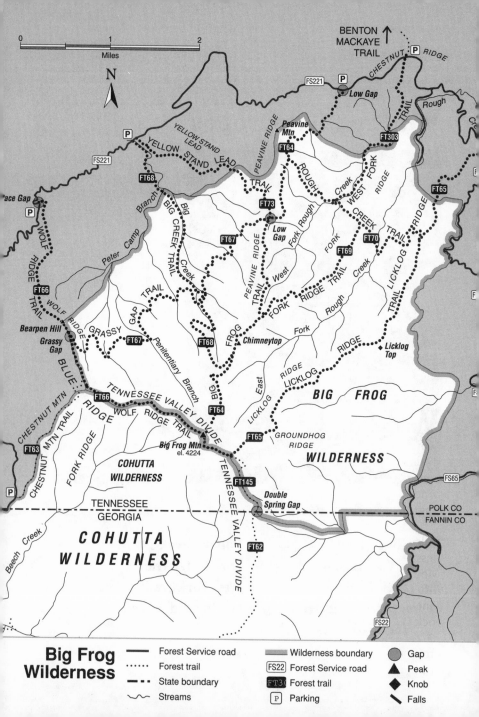

Wolf Ridge Trail

Foot Trail 66: 4.5 miles

- **Dayhiking In** Moderate
- **Dayhiking Out** Easy to Moderate
- **Backpacking In** Moderate to Strenuous
- **Backpacking Out** Moderate
- **Start** Wolf Ridge Trailhead at Pace Gap, 1,700 feet
- **End** Big Frog Trail and Licklog Ridge Trail atop Big Frog Mountain, 4,220 feet
- **Trail Junctions** Grassy Gap, Chestnut Mountain, Big Frog, Licklog Ridge
- **Topographic Quadrangle** Caney Creek TN
- **Features** Winter views; excellent spring wildflower display; narrow, rocky ridgecrest; Big Frog Mountain

WOLF RIDGE, BIG FROG, AND LICKLOG RIDGE Trails all end at an important junction very close to the highest point on Big Frog Mountain. Of these three trails, Wolf Ridge is the shortest and most difficult. In fact, it gains 2,520 feet—the most of any trail in the combined wilderness—in a relatively short distance. Unlike the other two trails, Wolf Ridge does have some moderate-to-strenuous upgrades.

This trail is a ridgetop and upper-slope route. Beyond the first mile it follows the famous Blue Ridge, which doubles as the Tennessee Valley Divide. After Wolf Ridge turns east from its Chestnut Mountain junction, the character of the trail becomes distinctively different from all others in the wilderness. Over most of the combined wilderness, the ridges lack the pleasing ruggedness and color of rock outcrops. But here, near the end of this trail, the ridge often narrows to a topknot of rock. And the trail often slabs below outcrops or snakes side to side around rock as it heads up the scenic crest.

Starting behind the trailhead gate, the route rises easily on Forest Service road to 0.3 mile, where it turns to the right and enters the oak-pine forest on path. Here the treadway quickly angles onto the upper west slope of lowermost Wolf Ridge and continues its steady grade, no harder than easy to moderate, to the south. Virginia pines and chestnut oaks are abundant on the dry, west-facing soils. The trail switchbacks to the left at 0.5 mile, crosses over the ridge, then ascends steadily and gradually on an old woods road. Several old-growth chestnut oaks, poor-form boles skipped by loggers, are the largest trees along this section.

Soon after a second switchback takes it back to the west slope, the track follows the ridgecrest up and over a low knob. An easy 0.2-mile descent from the knob leads to a slight gap (2,260 feet) at mile 1.4. The route follows a pattern from this gap to the next one. Maintaining a steady, easy upgrade, the walking slips onto slope, first on the east side then on the west, where the ridge rises harder. The forest, still second-growth oak-pine, is now more open with larger trees. After skirting the upper west side of Bearpen Hill, the footpath reaches Grassy Gap (2,510 feet) and the usually bear-clawed sign that marks the Grassy Gap Trail junction at mile 2.0. From Pace Gap southward to Bearpen Hill, both sides of the trail are outside of the wilderness. From Bearpen Hill to Chestnut Mountain, the wilderness boundary follows the crest of Wolf Ridge. The land east of the ridgeline is wilderness; that to the west is nonwilderness, Cherokee National Forest.

Wolf Ridge Trail continues straight ahead, southward and upward, from its Grassy Gap connection. Beyond the gap, the hiking becomes harder—easy to moderate, then moderate as it nears Chestnut Mountain. The final 0.1 mile of the climb rises on the sunset side of the Big Frog spur, well below ridgeline, through an increasingly open and deciduous forest. The path pops up to the spine of Chestnut Mountain and its junction with Chestnut Mountain Trail (3,020 feet) at mile 2.7. Chestnut Mountain Trail ends here at the sign; Wolf Ridge Trail curls sharply to the left (east) and gains elevation on the Tennessee Valley Divide all the way to the peak of Big Frog.

After turning east, the treadway closely follows the boundary between the Cohutta and Big Frog Wildernesses. It gradually ascends on the upper south slope through a dry-soiled forest of Virginia pine and chestnut oak. The track soon gains the crest, traverses its rocky spine (up harder, moderate), then slants onto the south side where the keel heads for a jumble of rock and downed trees. The route now climbs a moderate-to-strenuous grade through a rich, rocky area full of wildflowers in the spring. After less than 0.1 mile of steep hiking, the footpath winds back up to the top of a wide, flat-enough-to-farm ridge at mile 3.1.

Here the unusually deep and fertile dark soil supports a diverse forest of moist-site hardwoods—sugar maple, black cherry, basswood, and white ash—often found in coves or on higher north-facing ridges. Prior to Hurricane Opal, the trail ran straight through this stand of relatively undamaged trees. Now the course winds around windthrows and dodges deadfalls. As the walking dips gently to a slight saddle (3,500 feet) at mile 3.5, you can see your destination, Big Frog, through winter's (November through the beginning of May) stick-figure hardwoods.

The trail continues to rise from the gap, working and winding its way up the rocky and often narrow ridgeline. The grade, steady easy to moderate with occasional short surges, passes through a Catawba rhododendron thicket along the way. With 0.2 mile remaining, the upridge run—a slaloming, side-to-side obstacle course around rock outcrops—becomes tougher and more scenic. Yellow birch, this area's version of a highcountry tree, is common here. The final 0.1 mile swings onto slope, then finishes with a kick—a steady, moderate-to-strenuous pitch to the top of Big Frog.

Wolf Ridge, Big Frog, and Licklog Ridge Trails all end at the prominently signed intersection near the high point of the mountain. Big Frog Trail heads northeast from the junction; Licklog Ridge leads to the southeast. A fourth trail, the Benton MacKaye, which shares treadways with portions of both Big Frog and Licklog Ridge, also passes through this major high-elevation connection.

Wolf Ridge Trail has no water of its own. You can find water at Elderberry Spring, slightly more than 0.1 mile down the uppermost end of Licklog Ridge Trail.

Nature Notes

The lone colony of cow parsnip—a large herbaceous plant standing 3 to 4 feet tall with purple-dotted stems and huge, coarse leaves—is hard to miss on the wide ridgetop beyond the Chestnut Mountain junction. Since this is the only place where this poisonous plant occurs beside the trails in the combined wilderness, the botanically curious tend to gather round to examine it. But like poison ivy, cow parsnip is one of those look-but-do-not-touch plants that can cause contact dermatitis.

Once it rises above the Virginia pines, Wolf Ridge Trail offers an excellent wildflower display in the spring. You may see a few first-wave flowers, such as squirrel corn, spring beauty, and bloodroot, in very late March or early April. But for the peak in variety and abundance, wait till late April through May 20. During that time rose-colored Catesby's trillium bloom all the way to the top beyond the Chestnut Mountain Trail junction. Lily-of-the-valley becomes increasingly common as you gain elevation on the final mile of the footpath. At trail's end, the top of Big Frog Mountain is a wildflower garden during most of May. If your timing is right, you should be able to spot columbine, sweet cicely, yellow mandarin, rue anemone, mayapple, foamflower, lousewort, toothwort, bellwort, wood lily, and both the false and the real-deal Solomon's seals.

Bloodroot are so abundant along this trail's high hardwood ridge that for more than a mile they are rarely out of sight during blooming season. For many, this beautiful early bloomer symbolizes the ephemeral quality of spring wildflowers. Closing at night and during cloudy weather, the petals normally drop off in two to five days. A hard rain, however, can plaster the fragile folded petals to the forest floor at any time.

Bloodroot blossoms are the largest and showiest of the early spring wildflowers at higher elevations. Its single, bright white corolla—usually 1¼ to 2¼ inches wide—is impossible to miss against the brown thatch of last year's leaves. Eight to twelve (normally eight) petals encircle the bright yellow stamens in the center.

Unlike the leaves of many other wildflowers, bloodroot leaves are large, distinctive, and easily recognized long after the blooms have faded. Roughly circular in outline, the deeply divided, palmately scalloped leaf has five to nine lobes. When the usually solitary basal leaf first appears, it is folded around the top of the flower stalk. The thick, slightly leathery leaf grows substantially after early spring, reaching 4 to 7 inches across by mid-June.

The bloodroot forms colonies by means of rhizomatous runners. These colonies most often occur in open, predominantly deciduous forests up to at least 4,000 feet. As long as there is plenty of early spring light, you will find the bloodroot on a variety of sites—high slopes and ridges, hardwood coves, and the sunny woods above streams where rhododendron and hemlock are absent.

A member of the Poppy family, bloodroot is the only plant of its genus. As its name implies, the root of this perennial has acrid, orange-red sap. Native Americans utilized its somewhat poisonous juice for war paint, dye, and insect repellent. In addition to using the root sap as red dye, pioneers made cough medicine by putting a drop of the sap on a lump of sugar.

bloodroot

Beginning at mile 3.1, this trail winds eastward along a wide ridgetop that is remarkably flat and fertile, even for the Cohuttas. This fertility, plus the added moisture of elevation (approximately 3,400 feet), supports a ridgecrest forest with tall black cherry, white ash, and sugar maple—species that normally remain in the understory on most ridges within the wilderness. The number of white ash (*Fraxinus americana*) in the canopy is particularly surprising. This species usually thrives in other habitats—moist coves, north-facing slopes, and certain riverine sites. But here on the deep-soiled, ridgetop flat, numerous specimens stand close beside the trail, easily seen and identified from the level ground.

The largest and most common of the ashes, the white ash is a beautiful tree with a tall, straight, clear trunk. When foliage has fallen or is out of sight, however, most hikers mistake this species with its gray bark and straight bole for yellow poplar.

Even when its leaves are close at hand, most people still misidentify white ash, in this case as a hickory. The two do have a similar appearance. The pinnately compound leaves of the white ash are 8 to 12 inches long with five to nine (usually seven) oblong leaflets. These leaflets—finely saw-toothed or almost smooth, dark green above and pale green to whitish below—are 3 to 5 inches long and 1½ to 2½ inches wide. Hickories not only have pinnately compound leaves like the ash, but they also have about the same number of similarly shaped leaflets per leaf. Despite these similarities, though, there are

two easy ways to distinguish them. First, ashes have opposite leaves and branches; hickories have alternate leaves and branches. Second, the leaflet stems of the ashes are long and thin, while the leaflet stems of the hickories are short (sometimes almost nonexistent) and thick.

The grayish brown bark of the white ash is roughened by networks of crisscrossing, diamond-shaped furrows and forking ridges. It is also often corky or somewhat spongy to the hard touch. And you can almost always find several patches of small, white, flaky squares somewhere on the trunk.

white ash

This species grows well only in deep, moist, fertile soils, ranging from the lowest elevations to approximately 5,200 feet in the Southern Blue Ridge. As one of the dominant trees in the cove hardwood forest, this ash often associates with yellow poplar, black cherry, yellow buckeye, basswood, sugar maple (in range), cucumbertree, northern red oak, and hemlock. On good sites, white ash is commonly 70 to 100 feet in height and 2½ to 4 feet in diameter. Its record dimensions are roughly 140 feet in height and 6 feet in diameter. Maximum life span is 300 to 350 years.

Ash wood brings back muscle memories of yesteryear's outdoor activities and athletics. Before the switch to aluminum bats, all baseball bats, including the famous Louisville Sluggers, were made of ash.

Today, the major leagues still use wooden bats, and the sound of ash wood flush on a high fastball still crackles across the airwaves. Canoe paddles, oars, hockey sticks, and tennis rackets were all traditionally made of ash.

Directions

The Wolf Ridge Trailhead can be most easily reached from Access Points 3, 5, and 6. (See the detailed description of the Access Points at the beginning of this guide.)

Access Point 3: From the three-way FS 16–FS 17 intersection, continue straight ahead on FS 16 for approximately 5.5 miles to its junction with FS 221, located on the Georgia-Tennessee border immediately across the big iron bridge over the Jacks River. Once across the river, stay straight ahead on FS 221 for approximately 7.3 miles to the right turn onto FS 221 E. A prominent trail sign usually signals the entrance of FS 221E, which leads just uphill to the trail-head parking area and bulletin board. If you miss the trail sign on FS 221, or if the sign is missing, you will come to FS 374 to the left side of the road a little more than 0.1 mile beyond the entrance to FS 221E.

Access Point 5: From the three-way FS 55–FS 221 intersection, turn left onto FS 221 and proceed approximately 4.3 miles to the right turn onto FS 221E, usually marked with a Wolf Ridge Trail sign.

Access Point 6: From the three-way FS 45–FS 221 intersection, turn right onto FS 221 and follow that road for approximately 7.3 miles to the left turn onto FS 221E, usually marked with a Wolf Ridge Trail sign. The entrance to FS 374, which is on the right side of FS 221, is a little more than 0.1 mile before the left turn onto FS 221E.

Notes

Grassy Gap Trail

Foot Trail 67: 5.0 miles

- ■ **Dayhiking** Easy to Moderate walked in either direction
- ■ **Backpacking** Moderate walked in either direction
- ■ **Interior Trail** Southwestern terminus on Wolf Ridge Trail at Grassy Gap, 2,510 feet; northeastern terminus at the junction of Yellow Stand Lead Trail and Big Frog Trail at Low Gap, 2,460 feet
- ■ **Trail Junctions** Wolf Ridge, Big Creek, Yellow Stand Lead, Big Frog
- ■ **Topographic Quadrangle** Caney Creek TN
- ■ **Features** Small streams; hardwood hollows; good spring wildflower display; winter views

GRASSY **GAP IS THE ONLY TRAIL** in the combined wilderness that winds its total distance on the midslope. Straight-line walking, as on ridgecrest or along riverbank, is all but impossible in this rugged terrain. The only reasonable way to traverse the midslope is to follow a squiggling, snaking, S-loop pattern: half-looping around the hollows as high as practical in one direction, and half-looping around and over the spurs as low as practical in the opposite direction.

Civilian Conservation Corps workers planned, surveyed, and constructed this midslope trail in the early 1930s. Well built and made to last, Grassy Gap exemplifies the CCC legacy of money, manpower, hard work, and pride. The CCC boys laid this rugged-country route out to maximize scenery and minimize leg strain. Except near either end, the path remains between the 2,200- and 2,400-foot contour lines. And even though it frequently rises and falls, most of this trail is easy walking. There are no sustained grades more difficult than easy to moderate.

Grassy Gap meanders through a series of hardwood hollows, some wet and some dry, that generally face from 290 degrees to 25 degrees. Because these hollows are more or less north facing, they are often surprisingly moist and rich for their relatively low elevation.

One of the least traveled trails in the combined wilderness, Grassy Gap could use some more feet to help keep its treadway open. This path is at its best during spring before leaf-out. Then you can enjoy the wildflowers, the views of ridges near and far, and the largely unobstructed vision of the small streams spilling and sliding down the rocky notches of the hollows.

This trail is described from southwest to northeast, from Grassy Gap on Wolf Ridge to Low Gap on Peavine Ridge. Starting at its namesake gap, the footpath drops onto slope, then quickly swings parallel to the notch of the first steep-sided hollow. As is usual at low-to-middle elevations, tall, straight stands of yellow poplar dominate the second-growth cove hardwood forest. The route descends to and crosses its first hollow notch (wet in spring) at 0.3 mile. The stream that arises straight down the hollow is a headwater rivulet of Peter Camp Branch.

After rounding its first hollow, the track crosses over a broad spur before swinging parallel to the next one. Another headwater prong of Peter Camp Branch pours over rock way below. At 0.8 mile the treadway crosses the wide, rocky bottom of a hollow—full of early spring wildflowers before the canopy of yellow poplar, basswood, and yellow buckeye closes overhead. After rising over an inconspicuous spur, the course crosses a northwest-facing hollow, then ascends gently over the next spur, this one well defined and pine topped.

At mile 1.4 the wilderness path crosses a creekbed—a sliding veneer of water during spring that falls sharply down a wide hollow with multiple notches. The open, rocky terrain of the hollow is scenic and botanically rich. Here the second-growth forest—hemlock and cove hardwoods including sugar maple and white ash—has come back straight and tall canopied. This rivulet and the permanent stream pouring down the rocky notch of the next hollow, a little more than 0.1 mile further, are both forks of Penitentiary Branch, a Peter Camp tributary.

Since this trail follows the same pattern—winding over spurs in one direction and half-looping around hollows in the other—over and over again, there is no need to describe each spur, each hollow.

Generalities will suffice. Most often the walking is level or easy down to the center of the hollow, then level or easy up to the next spur. Hiked as described, the path first parallels a hollow on relatively moist east- to northeast-facing slope, crosses the moister northwest- to north-facing notch, then quickly rises up and away from the hollow on dry, west- to southwest-facing slope. The dry slope is wooded in oak-pine forest, where Virginia pine, chestnut oak, mountain laurel, galax, and deciduous heath, including flame azalea, are abundant. In spring, you can find crested dwarf iris blooming on the moist, hardwood side of the hollow, and its dry-site counterpart, dwarf iris, blooming in an oak-pine forest only 200 yards away.

After winding over the ridgeline of Bark Legging Lead and crossing a permanent, bouldery fork of Big Creek at mile 3.1, Grassy Gap intersects Big Creek Trail at a usually signed and always rock-cairned junction at mile 3.3. Over the years wise guys have turned this sign around so that its arrows point in the wrong direction. (Missing, vandalized, and turned-around signs are additional reasons for carrying map and compass when walking interior trails.) Grassy Gap crosses Big Creek Trail, quickly dips down and steps over another rocky Big Creek fork (often dry after leaf-out), then doubles back downstream toward the next spur.

Beyond the Grassy Gap–Big Creek connection, the course continues to S-curve—around hollows and over intervening spurs—to the northeast. The treadway crosses a 10-foot-wide rocky branch, a Big Creek tributary, at mile 4.2. Grassy Gap ends at a usually signed, four-way junction in Low Gap on Peavine Ridge. Yellow Stand Lead Trail ends to the left, due north. Big Frog Trail enters the gap from the east, opposite Grassy Gap's end, then rises with the ridge toward its mountain to the right (south).

Grassy Gap affords numerous wintertime (middle of November through middle of April) views of the surrounding ridges and mountains. Walked as described, the trail offers views to the east of pine-crested Bark Legging Lead for the first few miles. Vistas to the south (150 degrees) are of the Blue Ridge near Big Frog's high point. To the southeast Peavine Ridge climbs toward Big Frog. To the north (330 degrees), you might see Chilhowee Mountain—a sharp peak on a long ridge well out of the wilderness. Beyond the Grassy Gap–Big Creek connection, the prospect to the left (west) encompasses nearby Bark Legging Lead and Wolf Ridge further away. A gaze eastward brings Peavine Ridge, the next wall over, into focus.

Nature Notes

Despite its relatively low elevation, Grassy Gap has a good spring wildflower display. Scores of flame azalea bloom from late April through most of May, and the abundant sweetshrub reaches its flowering peak from mid-April through early May. Bloodroot begins the show on the forest floor in late March. Crested dwarf iris, dwarf iris, rue anemone, windflower, giant chickweed, foamflower, squawroot, yellow mandarin, bellwort, and several violet species take turns blooming from April 10 to April 25.

rue anemone

The most plentiful of the early spring wildflowers in Grassy Gap's many hollows is the rue anemone. Clumps of this member of the Buttercup family are sprinkled throughout the richest hollows. This perennial is one of early spring's smallest (4 to 8 inches high) ephemeral wildflowers. Numerous across a colony, the rue anemone's small white flowers, consisting of five to ten petals (actually sepals), are only ½ to 1 inch wide.

This plant's name came from its resemblance to the wood anemone or windflower. Both species, which often grow in the same habitat, have delicate blossoms that vibrate in the slightest breeze, while sturdier neighboring plants remain perfectly still. Although the corollas of the rue anemone look like those of the windflower, the foliage is quite different. The rue anemone's small leaflets have smooth margins and rounded, three-lobed tips; the wood anemone's leaflets are longer, narrower, notched along the margins, and pointed at the tip.

The rue anemone, which is much more abundant than the wood anemone, is found on rich slopes at low and middle elevations. This wildflower normally reaches its flowering peak just before mid-April.

The squawroot is a member of the Broomrape family, a group of parasitic flowering plants that lack chlorophyll. This species is an obligate parasite on the roots of trees and shrubs, primarily oaks. Because this herb is a parasite, it has no need for green chlorophyll.

squawroot

And because it has no chlorophyll, it has no need for leaves. So over time the leaves have become vestigial afterthoughts—a scaly covering of overlapping bracts.

This fleshy and unbranched perennial has 3- to 8-inch-tall stalks. The small, closely bunched clusters, yellow or brownish yellow when they first break ground, resemble small ears of corn. After quickly drying out and turning brown, they look like skinny pinecones.

The squawroot's inconspicuous, pale yellow flowers are not readily recognized as such unless your eyes are near plant level. These thin flowers, only ½ inch long and tightly two lipped, bloom between the bracts in April. From standing eye level, the blossoms look like evenly spaced spikes protruding from the stem.

Chiefly a mountain species, this parasitic plant is occasional to common in predominately deciduous forests where oaks are plentiful. The yellow clusters first emerge at the lower elevations within the combined wilderness from late March through early April. As soon as the clumps poke up, bears avidly seek and eat the fleshy stalks. You can often see where a bear has walked the trail, grubbing up squawroots along the way.

Directions

Grassy Gap is an interior trail that has its southwestern end on Wolf Ridge Trail at Grassy Gap and its northeastern end on Big Frog and Yellow Stand Lead Trails at Low Gap.

To reach Grassy Gap's southwestern end, walk 2.0 miles on Wolf Ridge Trail to the usually signed junction in the small opening at Grassy Gap. Wolf Ridge continues straight ahead on the ridgecrest to the south; Grassy Gap drops down and to the left (east) off the ridgetop. (See Wolf Ridge, the preceding trail, for further information.)

You have two options to reach Grassy Gap's northeastern end at Low Gap: walk 2.3 miles on Yellow Stand Lead to its end at Low Gap, or walk 2.4 miles on Big Frog to the gap. You will encounter a usually signed, four-way trail junction in Low Gap. Frequently walked Big Frog passes through the gap; Yellow Stand Lead and Grassy Gap end there. If the sign has been smashed by bear or human, this junction is potentially confusing. Big Frog enters the gap from the east, bends to the left, then heads toward its namesake mountain at 210 degrees. The end of Yellow Stand Lead is due north. The faint track of Grassy Gap, between Yellow Stand Lead and Big Frog's upward-bound segment (210 degrees) heads away from the gap to the west. (See Yellow Stand Lead Trail, page 193, and Big Frog Trail, page 199, for further information.)

Notes

Big Creek Trail

Foot Trail 68: 4.2 miles

- ■ **Dayhiking In** Moderate
- ■ **Dayhiking Out** Easy
- ■ **Backpacking In** Moderate to Strenuous
- ■ **Backpacking Out** Easy to Moderate
- ■ **Start** Big Creek Trailhead, 1,375 feet
- ■ **End** Big Frog Trail on Peavine Ridge, 3,660 feet
- ■ **Trail Junctions** Yellow Stand Lead (at trailhead), Grassy Gap, Big Frog
- ■ **Topographic Quadrangle** Caney Creek TN
- ■ **Features** Big Creek; old-growth beech; excellent spring wildflower display; winter views; rich, north-facing slope

IF YOU LIKE MOUNTAIN STREAMS, spring wildflowers, and diverse forests, you will probably enjoy this scenic trail. As it winds up to Peavine Ridge, Big Creek frequently changes elevation, exposure, and habitat—riparian, hardwood cove, and hardwood slope; dry ridge-top, steep-sided hardwood hollow; and lush, high, north-facing slope. Hiking this trail is particularly pleasurable in early spring, when full streams, wildflower patches, and winter views come in quick succession.

Both for sheer numbers of blooms and for the variety of species, this is the best spring wildflower trail in the combined wilderness. Blooming usually begins from April 1 to April 15 at the trailhead. The second wave of spring wildflowers—white wake robin, bellwort, yellow mandarin—usually colors the rocky hardwood slopes above Big Creek during the last half of April into early May. The uppermost north-facing slope has blossoms through mid-May.

Because the Big Creek and Yellow Stand Lead Trailheads are only a strong-armed stone's throw apart, Big Creek can be walked as the first or last leg of numerous, convoluted-as-you-want, no-backtrack loops. The three most straightforward routes are the 6.4-mile Big Creek–Grassy Gap (to the northeast)–Yellow Stand Lead loop, the 8.4-mile Big Creek–Big Frog–Yellow Stand Lead loop, and the 13.6-mile Big Creek–Grassy Gap (to the southwest)–Wolf Ridge–Big Frog–Yellow Stand Lead route.

For a trail that has an easy first half and ends well short of Big Frog's 4,224-foot crown, Big Creek gains a surprising amount of elevation—2,285 feet. Its trailhead has the second lowest elevation in the combined wilderness (Jacks River Trail's northwestern end in Alaculsy Valley is the lowest). The final 1.8 miles above the Grassy Gap junction gain approximately 1,420 feet on numerous easy-to-moderate or moderate grades. This section of trail could use more maintenance and more hikers' feet to help keep the treadway clear.

The trail begins on the wide walkway of an old road that closely parallels its namesake creek. Twenty-five to 35 feet across when there is plenty of water, Big Creek is wide enough for the noonday sun to sparkle on its shoaling runs. The creekside vegetation—hemlock, white pine, rhododendron, and moist-site hardwoods—is typical of low-elevation Southern Appalachian streams. After a few tenths mile of easy walking close beside the brook, the route gradually swings up and away on cut-in path, curls around a ravine, then angles back to and above Big Creek. At one point the track passes along a narrow bench above a steep pitch to the water almost directly below. The trail, on old roadbed again, enters the wilderness just before crossing shallow Peter Camp Branch at 0.9 mile.

Across the branch, the treadway passes beside a dense grove of saplings, mostly sweetgums and yellow poplars, that has grown very rapidly since the former wildlife opening became wilderness. The former road quickly comes to the first and largest (if it is still standing) of the dozen or more old-growth beeches near this short section of the trail. Still heading south, the path works its way up the Big Creek watershed, always within earshot and occasionally within close sight of the stream. Starting at mile 1.6, the route rises on a rich, rocky slope where patches of wildflowers crowd against one another in the spring. Here the second-growth forest—sugar maple, basswood, black cherry, yellow buckeye, white ash, and yellow poplar—is tall, straight, and largely deciduous.

The trail continues its easy ascent up the rich hardwood slope. At mile 2.1 the footpath nears the now small stream for one last look— a boulder-jumble cascade when the water is up—at what remains of the creek below its two headwater forks. A tenth of a mile further, the track crosses the larger of the forks, parallels that branch for a little over 100 yards, then switchbacks up and to the left at a cairn. After rising through open forest toward the other fork, it reaches its sometimes signed intersection with Grassy Gap Trail at mile 2.4 (2,260 feet). If the sign is missing, look for the rock pile that supports the post very near to the barely flowing fork. Grassy Gap passes through the junction; Big Creek makes a rounded switchback up and to the right (260 degrees).

Above the connection, the grade heads upslope on the lower-most end of the spur that drops to the northwest from Chimneytop. The route switchbacks up and to the left at mile 2.5 (add a stone to the cairns at sharp turns); one tenth of a mile further it switchbacks again, to the right onto the drier, oak-pine, western slope of the spur. Here the treadway angles uphill toward the Big Creek fork it crossed below (mile 2.2). The forest increasingly becomes cove hardwood as you near the notch. Following a short descent, the course crosses the branch on rock rubble at mile 3.0. High, sheltered, and north-facing, this cove is especially lush and scenic in early May after rain. Tall, arrow-straight white ash rival the yellow poplars. Clear drops trickle off the mossy rock outcrop to the left; bright water spills through boulders to the right. Herbaceous plants color the forest floor various shades of spring green.

Beyond this last chance for water, the trail turns to the northwest and makes a 0.3-mile climb (easy to moderate and moderate) to the ridgecrest of Bark Legging Lead. Along the way, there is an excellent winter view of the Big Creek valley and a long line of low ridges to the northwest. Here the trail curls back and resumes its usual direction of travel, generally southward, as it rises easily up the oak-pine ridgeline. After 0.1 mile on top of the lead, the track slants onto the sunrise slope and continues its steady upgrade parallel to, but progressively further below, the crest. The route burrows through a rhododendron thicket at mile 3.7, then swings toward another north-facing hollow, this one moister and more lush than the last.

Most of the path's final 0.5 mile half-loops around this large, steep-sided hollow. The open forest in this picturesque cove is mostly northern hardwood—yellow birch, sugar maple, and yellow buckeye, among others. Beneath the well-spaced broadleafs, a solid forest garden, including extensive colonies of ramp, carpets the slope. After rounding the notch at mile 3.9, the walkway curls to the northeast and makes an easy-to-moderate, diagonal ascent to the top of the ridge. Big Creek ends at its junction with Big Frog Trail on Peavine Ridge's narrow crest just south of Chimneytop.

Nature Notes

Over fifty species of wildflowers bloom in intermingled profusion along three widely separated sections of this trail before the summer solstice. In addition to the easily found and nearly ubiquitous wildflowers, Big Creek offers a parade of herbaceous perennials that are absent or much less common along most of the other trails in the combined wilderness. Among them are Vasey's trillium, bellwort, and nodding mandarin; squirrel corn and Dutchman's breeches; long-spurred violet, showy orchis, sweet cicely, hepatica, spring beauty, and fringed polygala (also known as gaywings).

One-tenth mile beyond the crossing of Peter Camp Branch, the trail passes the largest of the dozen or so old-growth beeches scattered along the next half mile of the route. The big beech just to the left of the trail—initialed, bent slightly, and totally hollowed out in the back—is 11 feet 5 inches in circumference. These old-growth trees, remnants of the virgin forest before logging, escaped with their gray hides because they were deemed useless. The settlers didn't want them for firewood, and the loggers didn't want them for lumber. Lucky for those few trees and lucky for us. Large beeches, 9 to 12 feet in circumference, 175 to 300 years old, scarce over most of Southern Appalachia, add beauty and diversity to this wilderness.

Classified as a northern hardwood, the American beech (*Fagus grandifolia*) is characterized by its smooth, smoke gray bark, which remains unwrinkled and unfurrowed even in old age, and by its saw-toothed, sharp-pointed dark green leaves. A few other trees, primarily Fraser magnolia and the rare yellowwood, may be mistaken for beech in winter. But if you see the gray bark and slender, reddish brown buds, sharp pointed and up to 1 inch long, you will not mistake the beech for another tree. You can also distinguish a beech in winter by looking for the light tan, withered leaves on its branches. It is the only deciduous tree in the wilderness that regularly retains most of its leaves through the winter and into spring.

Mature beeches on good sites average 60 to 80 feet in height and 2 to 4 feet in diameter at breast height (DBH), 4½ feet from the ground. Its maximum size is 150 feet in height and 6 feet in diameter.

American beech

Even under the best of conditions, American beeches grow slowly. But like the hemlock, they grow slowly for a long time: they may attain an age of 400 to 450 years.

The beech offered a welcome look of stability and familiarity to the early colonists because our species does not differ significantly from the beech trees of Europe. The European beech is closely linked with the history of written language. Historians write that the earliest Sanskrit characters were carved on strips of beech bark. This practice spread to Europe, where the earliest scribblings of the Germanic people were inscribed upon beechen tablets. In fact, our modern word "book" was derived from the ancient Anglo-Saxon word for beech. Gutenburg printed the first Bible from movable type carved from beech wood.

Two diminutive irises with nearly identical blooms, the crested dwarf iris and the dwarf iris, are commonly found in the combined Cohutta–Big Frog Wilderness. These small but colorful wildflowers, however, are easily distinguished from one another by habitat, by leaf shape, and by the sepals which are either crested or uncrested.

The crested dwarf iris (*Iris cristata*) is common to abundant in very moist sites from lower to upper elevations. The dwarf iris (*Iris verna*) is occasional to common in the dry oak-pine forest. (See Yellow Stand Lead, the following trail, for a description of the dwarf iris.)

A few tenths of a mile after it crosses Peter Camp Branch, this trail enters a moist, level stretch where crested dwarf iris, Tennessee's state flower, are exceedingly abundant. Here dense colonies of this native perennial, which clones itself by means of creeping rootstocks, often flank the path. Even when not in bloom, this plant is easily recognized by its typical iris leaves—sword shaped, sheathed at the base, and fanning out from the bottom. The leaves of this species are shorter, usually only 4 to 7 inches long at blooming time, and much wider (½ to 1⅛ inch across) than the grasslike leaves of the dwarf iris.

Iris cristata usually begins blooming along the lower-elevation end of Big Creek Trail sometime between April 5 and April 15. Spring moves up the mountain for nearly a month. This iris opens along the higher elevations of Big Frog Trail in mid-May.

Blossoming atop a stem rarely over 5 inches high, the 1½- to 2½-inch-wide flower has three sepals and three petals. Yellow-orange crests run along the centers of the downward-curving sepals. These crests, slightly raised, tufted strips that are soft and velvety to the touch, are absent **crested dwarf iris** from the dwarf iris. The color of the *Iris cristata* corolla ranges from light blue to darker violet-blue.

Directions

The Big Creek Trailhead can be most easily reached from Access Points 3, 5, and 6. (See the detailed description of the Access Points at the beginning of this guide.)

Access Point 3: From the three-way FS 16–FS 17 intersection, continue straight ahead on FS 16 for approximately 5.5 miles to its junction with FS 221, located on the Georgia-Tennessee border immediately across the big iron bridge over the Jacks River. Once across the Jacks, travel straight ahead on FS 221 for approximately 9.3 miles to the Big Creek Trailhead on the right just before the bridge over Big Creek. This trailhead is hard to miss: a prominent hiker sign signals the turn into a large parking/primitive camping area complete with bulletin board at the far left corner.

Access Point 5: From the three-way FS 55–FS 221 intersection, turn left onto FS 221 and proceed approximately 6.3 miles to the trail sign and parking/primitive camping area to the right immediately before the bridge over Big Creek.

Access Point 6: From the three-way FS 45–FS 221 intersection, turn right onto FS 221 and travel that road for approximately 5.3 miles to the signed trailhead, which is to the left immediately after the bridge over Big Creek.

Notes

Yellow Stand Lead Trail

Foot Trail 73: 2.3 miles

- ■ **Dayhiking In** Easy to Moderate
- ■ **Dayhiking Out** Easy
- ■ **Backpacking In** Moderate
- ■ **Backpacking Out** Easy to Moderate
- ■ **Start** Yellow Stand Lead Trailhead, 1,380 feet
- ■ **End** Big Frog Trail and Grassy Gap Trail at Low Gap, 2,460 feet
- ■ **Trail Junctions** Big Creek (at trailhead—see directions), Big Frog, Grassy Gap
- ■ **Topographic Quadrangle** Caney Creek TN
- ■ **Features** Winter views; hardwood hollows

THE GEOGRAPHICAL TERM "lead," which occasionally appears on topographic maps throughout the Southern Appalachians, is just another word for a prominent spur ridge that leads to a higher mountain or ridge, in this case Peavine Ridge.

Before 1990, hikers traveled an open Forest Service road 0.8 mile in from FS 221 to reach the Yellow Stand Lead Trailhead. During the early 1990s, the Ocoee Ranger District gated the road and moved the trailhead out to FS 221, lengthening the trail by 0.8 mile of usually closed road. The majority of this lightly used trail, 1.4 miles, is outside of the Big Frog Wilderness.

Because the Yellow Stand Lead and Big Creek Trailheads are less than 100 yards apart, Yellow Stand Lead can be walked as the first or last leg of numerous, convoluted-as-you-choose, no-backtrack loops. (See Big Creek, the preceding trail, for the mileages of the three most straightforward routes.)

Starting behind the gate, the trail heads southeastward on the easy grades of a logging road for the first third of its distance. Near the beginning the downslope falls away steeply to Big Creek. You can see the riffling water below through a maturing riparian forest of hemlock, tall white pine, and moist-site hardwoods. The upslope, in fairly stark contrast, is regenerating from a relatively recent cut. The road quickly pulls away from the creek and soon passes close beside a small, sliding Big Creek tributary—Graham Branch.

At 0.8 mile near the old bulletin board which marked the former trailhead, the route turns to the left from the road onto the wide walkway of an old woods road. Here the track continues to the southeast through an oak-pine forest, sections of which are thin third-growth dominated by Virginia pine and stump-sprout hardwoods. Two-tenths mile beyond the first left turn, the treadway rises to the top of a low spur, then turns 90 degrees to the left. A less prominent path, partially maintained by hikers missing the turn, continues straight ahead and down.

After a short stretch of easy walking, the trail crests another low spur in a slight saddle, turns right, then ascends the spur up the first grade worth mentioning. The route heads upridge through a more open forest of larger trees dominated by chestnut oak and tall Virginia pine. Hardwood hollows drop away to the left. The 0.2-mile-long grade (easy to moderate or moderate) curls onto Yellow Stand Lead and continues climbing for a short distance before slabbing to the right onto upper slope and entering the wilderness at mile 1.4.

The large, gray, wooden Big Frog Wilderness markers are often appropriated as signposts by another species. Bear writing appears on nearly all of the large signs in the Big Frog Wilderness. While they lack power tools, bears use their teeth and claws with equal effectiveness, and their territorial claims are no doubt well understood by other bears. Some messages are more emphatic than others. The top halves of several signs have been ripped to expensive kindling. The claw-marked signs have meaning for humans too. Trace the long, deep gouges in the wood with your fingers and feel the power of the animal. The evidence these carvers leave behind adds spirit and a tangible physical presence to the wilderness. Big Frog nothing—this is big bear country.

Once in the wilderness, the footpath follows the same pattern the rest of the way to its end at the level loafing spot in Low Gap.

Here, on the upper southwestern and western slopes of the lead, the trail half-loops around the head of a hollow, half-circles over a dry spur, then rounds the notch of the next hollow. On the ridgetops and upper slopes the path passes under a low-canopied oak-pine forest; on the steep-sided hollows it travels beneath taller, straighter cove hardwoods. With 0.3 mile remaining, the treadway crosses a rocky hollow with a year-round rivulet, the beginning of Low Gap Branch. This is last-call water if you are planning to hike further south on Big Frog Trail.

Low Gap is an important trail junction. Two trails, Yellow Stand Lead and Grassy Gap, end here. A third trail, Big Frog, passes through the gap on the way up to its namesake mountain. If the trail signs are missing, the four paths leading away from the gap can be confusing. Grassy Gap's northeastern end is at 240 degrees. Big Frog enters the gap at 90 degrees, then rises toward its high-elevation end on the other side of the gap at 210 degrees.

Winter views to the right of the trail are primarily of nearby Peavine Ridge and Bark Legging Lead. The sharp knob almost due south is Chimneytop, a named high point on Peavine Ridge. Rising from 250 to 160 degrees is Bark Legging Lead. The best look off the left side of the lead focuses on twin mountaintops—one at 320 degrees and the other at 340 degrees—at opposite ends of a long ridge. The taller of the two peaks of Chilhowee Mountain, the one further north and nearly 10 line-of-sight miles away, is 3,000-foot Oswald Dome.

Nature Notes

The route doesn't leave the sometimes scraggly mosaic of recently managed, nonwilderness land until mile 1.2. The remainder of the trail travels through second-growth forest—oak-pine on the ridgecrests and upper slopes, cove hardwood in the hollows. The oaks—chestnut and reds (northern red, black, scarlet)—and tall Virginia pine dominate the oak-pine canopy. White pine saplings, rocketing up through the understory, are quickly changing the face of the forest.

As they almost always do, tall, straight yellow poplars dominate the second-growth cove hardwood forests in these low- and middle-elevation hollows. Several of the uppermost hollows have fair spring wildflower displays. Early bloomers include rue anemone, crested dwarf iris, and halberd-leaved violet.

As soon as the male red-eyed vireo (*Vireo olivaceus*) settles into his breeding territory, during the first half of April in the combined wilderness, he begins to sing. And he sings and sings and sings. He sings his fool head off. He makes the Energizer bunny look like a couch potato. Classified as a neotropical migrant, this small perching bird sings incessantly from dawn until dusk, even during the hot midday when other birds are silent. The red-eyed has been recorded averaging thirty songs per minute all day long. When really in the mood, it can average up to seventy songs per minute for a half hour at a time. This obsessive-compulsive songbird even sings, though probably not as melodiously, while wrestling with a large insect or choking down a big caterpillar. Its nonstop singing has earned the red-eyed the nickname of "preacher bird."

If you still the chatter of your brain and the fall of your feet, you will often discover that what normally passes as background forest noise is in part red-eyed vireo. Its song is a series of ascending and descending two- to three-syllable phrases—short, deliberate, and musical—warbled endlessly between catch-breath pauses. As they have done for most songbirds, birdwatchers have decoded the vireo's singsong phrases as *see me...here I am...up here...that's right...still higher...you fool*—or something like that.

The red-eyed vireo breeds throughout most of the eastern U.S., the northern Great Plains states, and all the way across southern Canada and northward into the Northwest Territories. It winters in the Amazon Basin of South America. This passerine is a common summer resident throughout the predominantly deciduous Southern Appalachians below 4,600 feet.

The red-eyed was once considered one of the three most abundant birds in the deciduous forests of eastern North America. Although it remains plentiful, this species has declined over the last thirty years. Forest fragmentation and cowbird brood parasitism in North America, as well as loss of winter habitat in the Amazon Basin, have reduced its numbers.

After the trees leaf out, visual identification of this bird of the high canopy is particularly difficult. Even before the forest greens, you need patience and probably binoculars to get a good look at this unobtrusive songster. Six inches long with a prominent insectivore bill, the red-eyed has a blue-gray crown and a white eyebrow bordered above and below with black streaks. Its back is brownish olive-green; the tail and the wings (no wingbars) are a somewhat darker dull green. The chin is white, the belly is dull beige, and the sides below the wings have a wash of light, pastel yellow. And as its common name suggests, its eyes are noticeably red at close range. The sexes are identical in appearance.

Two native irises with nearly identical corollas, the dwarf iris and the crested dwarf iris, bloom in the wilderness every spring. These small, rhizomatous perennials, however, are easily distinguished by leaf shape and habitat. The dwarf iris (*Iris verna*) is occasional to common in the dry oak-pine forest. The crested dwarf iris (*Iris cristata*) is common to abundant in the moist habitats of coves, north slopes, and stream margins. The dwarf iris has noticeably longer, narrower leaves, uncrested sepals, and most often occurs in clusters of half a dozen to twenty plants. The crested dwarf iris, however, has shorter, wider leaves, crested sepals, and often grows in dense, extensive colonies. (See page 190 for description).

dwarf iris

Like other early spring wildflowers in the dry forests along this trail, the dwarf iris begins blooming well before the canopy closes. This fragrant iris usually starts to flower here from April 5 to April 15 and finishes, except for a few stragglers, by May 1. After the blossoms disappear, these herbaceous plants can be identified by their essentially straight, swordlike leaves—more or less 12 inches high and thinner than ½ inch wide. When these skinny leaves and iris flowers are discovered in dry habitat, you know you're looking at a dwarf and not a crested dwarf iris.

The colorful blossoms, which have three sepals and three petals, appear singly atop stems usually only 3 to 4½ inches high. The flame-orange honey guides—landing strips for pollinating insects—flicker out of the center of the sepals. The orange streaks of the dwarf iris lack the fuzzy, raised crests that characterize the crested dwarf iris. At 2 to 2¾ inches wide, dwarf iris blossoms are richer in color and slightly larger than the crested species. Corolla colors range from washed out violet and pale yellow-orange to a vibrant blue that becomes deep purple near the flame-colored streaks down the center.

Iris was the Greek goddess of the rainbow, the deity who brought peace after stormy weather caused by the violent confrontations between the gods. The Greeks named this family of wildflowers after the goddess of the rainbow because of their multicolored flowers, which often included stormy-sky dark blue and lightning-flash yellow-orange. The word "iris," translated as "eye of heaven," refers both to the center of the eye and to the rainbow.

Directions

The Yellow Stand Lead Trailhead—a trail sign next to a gated Forest Service road—has neither bulletin board nor parking area. But it really doesn't need them; the large, well-marked, Big Creek Trailhead parking area is nearby. Starting from the entrance to the Big Creek Trailhead, cross the bridge over Big Creek, then continue less than 100 yards to the Yellow Stand Lead Trail sign and the orange gate blocking the Forest Service road to the right. The trail starts behind the gate.

If you decide to park at the Yellow Stand Lead Trailhead, the Forest Service requests that you not block access through the gate. (See Big Creek, the preceding trail, for directions to its trailhead.)

Notes

Big Frog Trail

Foot Trail 64: 5.5 miles

- ■ **Dayhiking In** Easy to Moderate
- ■ **Dayhiking Out** Easy
- ■ **Backpacking In** Moderate
- ■ **Backpacking Out** Easy to Moderate
- ■ **Start** Big Frog Trailhead at Low Gap, 2,160 feet
- ■ **End** Wolf Ridge Trail and Licklog Ridge Trail atop Big Frog Mountain, 4,220 feet
- ■ **Trail Junctions** Rough Creek, Yellow Stand Lead, Grassy Gap, Fork Ridge, Big Creek, Licklog Ridge, Wolf Ridge
- ■ **Topographic Quadrangle** Caney Creek TN
- ■ **Features** Winter views; excellent spring wildflower display; Big Frog Mountain; hardwood hollows with mature yellow poplars

THIS TRAIL IS THE CENTER OF CONVERGENCE for the Big Frog Wilderness trail system. Seven of the other eight trails lead—sooner or later, lower or higher—to the Big Frog Trail. Wolf Ridge, Licklog Ridge, and Big Frog Trails all end at an important, high-elevation junction on Big Frog Mountain's crown. The second longest of the three trails, Big Frog is the easiest to hike. It gains its 2,060 feet in a remarkably steady manner—usually easy, occasionally easy to moderate, and nowhere harder than moderate.

Big Frog leads through a wide range of elevations, exposures, and habitat-dependent forest types. It winds around cove hardwood hollows where wildflowers thrive beneath the tall yellow poplars. It traverses dry, low-elevation oak-pine slopes and ridges; moister, middle-elevation mixed hardwood slopes; moist, upper-elevation north-facing slopes with buckeye and basswood; and open oak ridges. The trail ends in a northern hardwood forest cool enough for yellow birch. Yet even though it offers such diversity and the highest mountain in the combined wilderness, Big Frog draws only light-to-moderate usage, especially compared to many other trails in the Cohutta Wilderness.

Big Frog begins with easy walking on a woods road heading southwest on the southeastern slopes of Peavine Ridge. The gently ascending track passes through a second-growth forest with an oak-pine canopy above an understory of mountain laurel and deciduous heath (blueberries and huckleberries). At 0.7 mile the route reaches the Big Frog Wilderness, posted with a large, wooden, bear-clawed sign. Once in the wilderness, the trail continues level or easy up as it half-circles a few largely hardwood hollows.

Big Frog arrives at its usually signed junction (2,460 feet) with Rough Creek Trail at mile 1.5. (Rough Creek leads to the left, east.) The next 0.9 mile is as easy as it gets in a mountain wilderness. Here the treadway closely follows the contour as it winds around hollows and crosses over broad, flat-topped spurs. A little less than 0.1 mile beyond the connection, the footpath rounds a hollow with a flowing spring (probably dry in drought). The trail often seems to divide the forest, oaks dominating below, pines above. A few poor-form chest-nut oaks were spared by the loggers. Sassafras and white pine saplings often flank the trail. Barring fire or disease, the white pines will quickly supplant the successional Virginia pines.

The route first gains the top of Peavine Ridge at a usually signed, four-way junction in Low Gap (mile 2.4, 2,460 feet). Yellow Stand Lead ends at the gap; Grassy Gap's northeastern terminus is on the west side of the gap, and Big Frog bends to the left and con-tinues to the southwest (210 degrees). Once across the saddle, the track makes an easy-to-moderate upridge run—the first grade worth mentioning—for less than 0.1 mile before slipping onto the sunrise slope. It then continues on a steady, easy upgrade through an oak-dominated forest on cut-in path. Where the footpath swings parallel to a northeast-facing hollow, you will see two large yellow poplars to the left, the second 70 yards beyond the first (if they are still standing). The first second-growth tree has a girth of 11 feet 4 inches, and the second measures 12 feet 8 inches.

From Low Gap to Fork Ridge, the trail heads south, rounding hollows and crossing spurs, on the upper east flank of Peavine Ridge. Most of the sidehill forest remains oak-pine, but the hollows—now higher, cooler, and moister—are increasingly rich with tall cove hardwoods, ferns, and herbaceous wildflowers. At mile 3.1 the hiking half-circles a hollow with a dense ground cover of New York fern. Following a short, easy-to-moderate ascent, it passes another large, lush hollow where basswood, sweet birch, and black cherry rise above mayapples, Vasey's trillium and foamflower, all abloom in mid-May.

The path curls up to the crest of uppermost Fork Ridge and its junction (3,380 feet) with Fork Ridge Trail at mile 3.7. The Benton MacKaye Trail shares the Big Frog treadway from the top of Big Frog Mountain down to this connection. Here Benton MacKaye switches tracks and follows Fork Ridge Trail.

Big Frog curls to the right (southwest) and upridge from the junction, then quickly swings onto the southeastern slope and rises gradually around an unnamed knob. Depending upon your direction of travel and perspective, Peavine Ridge and Fork Ridge either join together or split apart at this knob. The course regains the ridgetop at a shallow saddle and heads up the spine toward Chimneytop, a named peak on the crest line. Just as the trail heads up and the walking gets harder (easy to moderate), it slabs to the right onto lush north and northwest slope. Here elevation and exposure have combined to create a habitat cool and moist enough for sugar maple and yellow buckeye. Colonies of wake robins bloom white during the first half of May.

Following more easy hiking on the contour around Chimneytop, the treadway gains the keel of the ridge and the Big Creek Trail connection (3,660 feet) in quick succession at mile 4.3. Big Frog continues straight ahead on narrow crest through a low-limbed, windgnarled deciduous forest dominated by oaks. Winter views—Licklog Ridge to the left (east) and your destination, Big Frog Mountain, straight ahead—are still possible into mid-May. Lily-of-the-valley and Catesby's trillium are plentiful and reach peak bloom somewhere along the upper trail from May 5 through May 20.

After 0.1 mile of level walking past the Big Creek junction, the track shifts gears to a short, moderate upgrade before angling to the right onto a rich wildflower slope. Here it gains elevation more gradually toward the top of Bark Legging Lead, a major Big Frog Mountain spur. The trail tunnels through rhododendron, rises harder (easy to moderate), then switchbacks to the left side of the ridgetop where Bark Legging Lead and Peavine Ridge come together. At mile 4.9 the route levels on a broad ridgecrest with a largely northern hardwood forest that includes increasing numbers of yellow birch.

lily-of-the-valley

The remainder of the path is easy walking, level to easy up, on or very near the narrowing crest.

Big Frog ends at an important, three-way junction very close to its namesake mountain's high point (4,224 feet). Wolf Ridge and Licklog Ridge Trails also end at the usually signed intersection. The Benton MacKaye Trail, sharing the Licklog Ridge and Big Frog treadways, passes through the connection.

Usually reliable Elderberry Spring is slightly more than 0.1 mile to the left (southeast) and down on Licklog Ridge Trail.

Nature Notes

Lily-of-the-valley flourishes on two islands of high-elevation habitat within the contiguous wildernesses. This herbaceous perennial is common atop Cowpen Mountain and its upper ridges, and it is abundant atop Big Frog and its upper ridges. From this trail's Big Creek junction to its upper-elevation end, thousands of lily-of-the-valleys grace the trailside and bloom among hundreds of Catesby's trilliums in May. On warm breezy days in mid-May their fragrance floats across this section of trail.

The native lily-of-the-valley is restricted to widely scattered areas of rich forest in the Southern Appalachians. The native is not highly colonial, does not form dense stands, and is usually listed as rare to locally common. The popular lily-of-the-valley grown in gardens was introduced from Europe. This exotic species is a close relative of the native, frequently escapes into the wild, and is densely colonial. While the native species certainly could occur on these two mountains, most of the patches on Big Frog appear to be highly colonial. Therefore, if the botanical descriptions are accurate, the lily-of-the-valley in this area must be the European variety.

The escapees on Big Frog are generally 4 to 10 inches high and have two (rarely three) sheathing leaves from 4 to 8 inches long. The small, dainty blossoms—white, bell-shaped, and very fragrant—hang singly in a row beneath the arching flowering stalk.

Catesby's trillium

The Catesby's is by far the most numerous of the five or possibly six trilliums within the wilderness. Unlike the other trilliums, this species tolerates the drier, more acidic environment of the oak-pine forest. And although this native perennial is common to abundant on many low and middle elevation sites, it is most plentiful across Big Frog's broad crown. There it blooms, often mingled with lily-of-the-valley colonies, by the thousands in May.

Catesby's, also known as rose trillium, is easily distinguished from the other species. Much smaller than either the wake robin (second in abundance) or Vasey's (a distant third), this member of the Lily family is usually between 4 to 12 inches in height. Its characteristic three leaves are relatively short, only 2 to 4 inches long, and often wavy edged.

The strongly recurved flowers, which almost always hang at or below leaf level, range from white tinged with pink, to pink, to dark pinkish red. The corollas become deeper pink or darker pink-red as they age. The darkest color predominates up on Big Frog and its radiating ridges. Like the leaves, the petals of the 1- to 1¼-inch-wide blossoms are wavy margined. Curling, bright yellow anthers in the center of the nodding bloom complete the easy identification.

Catesby's were blooming at the Big Creek Trailhead on April 10 and on the top of Big Frog on May 10 during a recent late spring. The study of natural phenomena that recur periodically, migration and flowering dates for instance, and their relation to climate and change in season is called phenology. Due to their major elevation change, more than any other region in the eastern United States, the Southern Appalachians are a good place to study phenological changes—to see color move slowly up the mountains.

The best place within the wilderness to hear the Southern Appalachian's most ethereal birdsong is on top of Big Frog during spring. If you are at the upper end of this trail early in the morning or late in the afternoon, you will probably hear the veery's downward-spiraling slide-whistle song—a ventriloquial *vee-ur vee-ur veer veer* that rolls down the scale. You'll know the sound when you hear it, especially if you hear it for the first time in a dense fog, when it flows through the gray as though coming from a hole in the ground, somewhere 20 or 100 yards away, seemingly from several different directions. The veery's call note—*peer*—is heard often throughout the day. Like most birds, this member of the thrush family sings less and less as summer progresses.

The veery is a northern breeding bird whose range fingers down into the hot South only along the high ridges of the Southern Appalachians. The southernmost limit of its range in the eastern United States barely reaches into the highest mountains of northernmost Georgia. Here this essentially northern bird seeks the coolest, moistest, deciduous forests for its breeding ground. Because of this requirement, the veery's southernmost range is spotty and discontinuous. Within the wilderness it nests on small, isolated islands of mountaintop habitat, usually above 3,800 feet. Sometimes there is only room enough for one pair.

Common but shy within its limited habitat, this neotropical migrant arrives atop Big Frog at the end of April. By mid-October it is already heading southwest to its winter home in Central America and northern South America. Without making a concerted effort to see one, your chances of identifying a veery are somewhat slim. This 7-inch-long thrush—cinnamon brown above, white below—usually remains in dense cover on or near the ground. The faint spotting on its upper breast makes it the least speckled of the brown thrushes. If you notice a slightly larger (7¾ inch) reddish brown backed thrush with a prominently polka-dotted breast after spring migration is over, after June 1, you have identified a wood thrush, a species that is most common at low and middle elevations within the wilderness.

Directions

The Big Frog Trailhead is very close to Access Point 6. (See the detailed description of the Access Points at the beginning of this guide.)

Access Point 6: From the three-way FS 45–FS 221 intersection, turn right onto FS 221 and travel 0.5 mile to the Big Frog Trailhead sign and graveled parking area on the left side of the road.

Notes

Rough Creek Trail

Foot Trail 70: 2.9 miles

- ■ **Dayhiking** Easy to Moderate walked in either direction
- ■ **Backpacking** Moderate walked in either direction
- ■ **Interior Trail** Northwestern terminus on Big Frog Trail, 2,460 feet; southeastern terminus on Licklog Ridge Trail, 2,480 feet
- ■ **Trail Junctions** Big Frog, West Fork, Fork Ridge, Licklog Ridge
- ■ **Topographic Quadrangles** Caney Creek TN, Ducktown TN
- ■ **Features** Small pond; streams; winter views

THE BIG FROG WILDERNESS, which receives much less use than the Cohutta, has three lightly used interior trails—Rough Creek, Fork Ridge, and Grassy Gap. Hikers sometimes walk sections of Grassy Gap as part of no-backtrack loops involving moderately used Big Creek Trail. Fork Ridge now attracts more hikers because it shares its entire treadway with the Benton MacKaye Trail. For these two reasons Rough Creek, even though it shares 0.6 mile of its treadway with the Benton MacKaye, is probably the least traveled trail in the combined wilderness. This route could use better Forest Service maintenance, as well as more hikers and volunteers to help keep it open.

Rough Creek's 20-foot end-to-end elevation differential does not give any indication of what happens between the two ends. Either way you walk this trail, northwest to southeast or vice versa, you will descend to and cross a Rough Creek fork, ascend to and pass over Fork Ridge, descend to and cross the other Rough Creek fork, then rise to an end. While this trail is seldom level for long, its toughest long grades are no more difficult than easy to moderate.

Rough Creek is described from northwest to southeast, from Big Frog Trail to Licklog Ridge Trail. Walked in this direction, the path quickly skirts the upper edge of a former wildlife opening. Downhill and to the right, through what soon will be saplings, you will find a small, man-made pond, full of salamanders and tadpoles in the spring. The route continues on a former logging road through a forest of thin, third-growth trees, mostly red maple, sourwood, and thicket-growth Virginia pine.

At 0.3 mile the walkway veers down and to the right onto another woods road, then descends through a still-young oak-pine forest of larger trees. The steady downgrade soon enters a once-cut woods of hemlock, hardwoods, and pines. After rounding a hollow and making a quick, double switchback dip, the trail comes to a former system road and its usually signed junction (1,880 feet) with West Fork Trail at 0.9 mile. The Big Frog Wilderness Addition of 1986 turned the road into trail.

Rough Creek Trail turns right (240 degrees) at the connection and follows the former road for 40 yards before turning left and downhill (turn may be marked with a cairn) to its crossing of West Fork Rough Creek. The West Fork—15 or 20 feet wide and shallow—can often be crossed dry shod after leaf-out. Once across the creek, the footpath heads uphill beside a feeder branch and quickly crosses the small stream. The riparian forest here consists of hemlock and hardwoods such as yellow poplar, sweet birch, and basswood.

The track climbs up the cove on a steady easy-to-moderate grade, crosses the trickling notch, then continues ascending through a drier oak-pine forest. After following a spur to the crest of Fork Ridge, the route reaches its junction with Fork Ridge Trail (2,290 feet) at 1.5 miles. Fork Ridge Trail heads up the spine (southwest) of its namesake ridge; Rough Creek crosses over the ridgecrest at nearly a right angle and immediately heads down to the southeast. The segment of Rough Creek Trail from its West Fork junction to its Fork Ridge junction shares its treadway with the well-maintained Benton MacKaye Trail. To the southeast beyond its Fork Ridge connection, Rough Creek is likely to be in worse condition than its previous 0.6 mile.

The treadway steadily descends from this midtrail high point on oak-pine slope and hardwood hollow to another former system road at mile 2.0. Here at a cairn the route turns right (240 degrees) onto the road and follows it upstream near East Fork Rough Creek. Sweet birch, basswood, yellow poplar, northern red oak, and hemlock are common in the streamside forest downslope. After following the roadbed for 0.1 mile, you come to a rivulet that flows through a culvert. A few feet beyond the rivulet (at another cairn if the rocks have not been moved), the trail turns left and down to cross two channels of the East Fork (1,820 feet). Narrow and shallow, both are an easy rock-hop in summer.

The remainder of the walking is uphill, an easy-to-moderate grade overall. The track heads away from the creek on an old, rocky woods road through a moist forest of hemlock, rhododendron, yellow buckeye, beech, and sugar maple. It quickly turns to the northeast and angles up a drier oak-pine slope with deciduous heath thick in the understory. At mile 2.5 the route rounds the barely wet notch of a hardwood hollow. Look up and to the right for partial summer and good winter views of your destination—Licklog Ridge.

The final few tenths of a mile curl and wind through an increasingly deciduous forest. After passing over the last spur, the path slants up to the south to its usually signed junction with Licklog Ridge Trail at the upper edge of a slight saddle.

Nature Notes

If you walk this or any other trail in the wilderness from mid-April through June, you will probably hear the ovenbird repeatedly as you hike through one nesting territory after another. You will hear this warbler because it is abundant and loud. Most bird guides describe its song as *teacher-teacher-teacher...*, repeated up to ten times louder and faster. Ovenbirds do say *teacher* in the northern part of their large range. Here in Dixie, however, they sing with a regional variation. Southern Appalachian ovenbirds leave off the "er," make the noun an imperative verb, and chant *teach-teach-teach...*, usually in an emphatic, ringing, slightly louder staccato. Early on cold mornings their songs often sound weak. But after the sun shines on the forest floor, they warm to the task and belt out their "teach" songs loud and clear.

This sparrow-sized (6 inch) wood warbler breeds no farther south than the upper Piedmont of Georgia and Alabama. During late May and much of June, probably when there are young to feed and protect, this normally secretive bird pops up and fusses at intruders. Sometimes it makes a complete circuit of short flights around you, steadily scolding with call-note *chips.*

Also known as the teacher-bird, the ovenbird lacks the tropical coloring and flashy flight patterns characteristic of most wood warblers. It is olive-brown above and white with prominent streaks of dark spots below. From the neck down it resembles a small thrush. For a positive visual identification, you must see the diagnostic band-stripe-ring color pattern on its head. The band is a mohawk brushstroke of bright orange-brown from the base of its bill back across the top of its crown. The stripe is a thin black eyebrow, bordering the band and accentuating the white of the eye ring below.

This perching bird is named for the domed, ovenlike nest it builds on the ground. The ovenbird fits leaves on top of its grass-lined nest to further camouflage its stoop-in entrance.

Unlike some wood warblers, this species does not have stringent habitat requirements. You will hear them chant at all elevations within the wilderness in all but the driest or the wettest forests. Listen for them in the spring and summer on low- and middle-elevation oak-pine ridges and upper slopes. Most have headed south by the end of September; all but a few genetically encoded stragglers are gone by the end of October.

If you hike during spring migration before leaf-out, from April 10 down low to mid-May in the highcountry, you have a good chance of spotting one of Southern Appalachia's most strikingly colored songbirds. As soon as the bright red body and jet black wings and tail catch your eyes, you cannot mistake the male scarlet tanager for any other bird. In fact, the color pattern of the male scarlet tanager's breeding plumage is unique among North American avifauna. The intense colors of this 7-inch-long bird make such an impression that years later many hikers remember the trail where they saw one.

This neotropical migrant is occasional to common in deciduous and oak-pine forests. Early spring migrants can be seen at all elevations; resident breeding birds, however, will usually be found above the 1400- to 1600-foot level. During the fall migration you will not see the male's resplendent red and black. In late summer the male tanager molts and switches to its drab olive green winter plumage, which is similar to the female's year-round coloration. After leaving by mid-October, this small perching bird wings its way thousands of miles to its wintering grounds in northwestern South America.

Directions

Rough Creek is an interior trail that has its northwestern end on Big Frog Trail and its southeastern end on Licklog Ridge Trail.

To reach Rough Creek's northwestern end, walk 1.5 miles on Big Frog Trail starting from its FS 221 trailhead. At the usually signed Rough Creek–Big Frog junction, turn left (east) and downhill onto Rough Creek's northwestern end. (See Big Frog, the preceding trail, for further information.)

To find Rough Creek's southeastern end, walk 1.5 miles on Licklog Ridge Trail starting from its FS 221 trailhead. The Rough Creek–Licklog Ridge junction, usually signed, is located in a saddle (slight gap) on Licklog Ridge. Turn to the right (northwest) and down off the ridgecrest onto Rough Creek Trail. (See Licklog Ridge Trail, page 221, for further information.)

Notes

Fork Ridge Trail

- ■ **Dayhiking (low to high)** Easy to Moderate
- ■ **Dayhiking (high to low)** Easy
- ■ **Backpacking (low to high)** Moderate
- ■ **Backpacking (high to low)** Easy to Moderate
- ■ **Interior Trail** Northeastern (low elevation) terminus on Rough Creek Trail, 2,290 feet; southwestern (high elevation) terminus on Big Frog Trail, 3,380 feet
- ■ **Trail Junctions** Rough Creek, Big Frog
- ■ **Topographic Quadrangles** Caney Creek TN, Ducktown TN
- ■ **Features** Winter views; old-growth blackgums; flame azalea display

THIS RIDGECREST AND UPPER-SLOPE TRAIL is the shortest footpath in the Big Frog Wilderness, and it is the second shortest in the combined wilderness. Although this easily walked interior trail gains (or loses) nearly 1,100 feet, it does so in a remarkably steady manner. There are no sustained grades of even moderate difficulty.

Fork Ridge shares its entire treadway with the Benton MacKaye Trail, which is routinely maintained by the volunteers of the Benton MacKaye Trail Association. Its condition is much improved over years past; compared to some of Big Frog's other trails, which are not regularly brushed out, Fork Ridge is now a pleasure to walk.

Fork Ridge forms the southeastern side of a wedge-shaped triangle of three interconnecting trails. Because so many trails either tie directly into this triangle or tie into those that do, you have many options for hiking Fork Ridge as a link in a multitrail loop. Fork Ridge is described from low to high, from Rough Creek southwestward to Big Frog. The trail rises easily on the crest of Fork Ridge, then quickly slides onto the drier, southeastern slope where the ridge begins to gain elevation faster. By 0.3 mile the treadway is well below the keel on a cut-in path. With the exception of a few hollows near the upper end, the entire route runs through a middle-elevation, second-growth oak-pine forest. The pines are white and Virginia; the oaks are primarily chestnut, northern red, and scarlet.

The track continues straight ahead and easy up, closely paralleling the crest line above. Sassafras, sourwood, and red maple are common in the understory. Several Virginia pines are close to 2 feet in diameter, bragging size for that species. Colonies of the evergreen wildflower galax frequently flank the treadway.

The forest footpath gradually works its way back to the ridgetop at a shallow gap at 0.9 mile. It then quickly slants onto the moister, northwestern edge of the crest. Here, where Fork Ridge rises fast again, the route slips back onto upper slope and continues its steady easy ascent. Added moisture from increased elevation and northern exposure has produced a predominately broadleaf forest of taller and thicker trees. This stretch of trail passes near half a dozen old-growth blackgums; the largest of these block-barked trees is almost 3 feet in diameter.

With 0.3 mile remaining, the route rounds the first of two north-facing hollows. The first hollow, the richer of the two, is dominated by sweet birch, basswood, tall red maple, yellow poplar, and distinctively whorled Fraser magnolias. In spring cinnamon ferns unfurl into fountains of light green fronds with orangish-brown topped fertile stalks in the middle. Beyond the second hollow, this wilderness walkway makes its best attempt at a climb (low-range easy to moderate) up to its usually signed, Big Frog junction on the crest of the ridge. Big Frog Trail switchbacks onto Fork Ridge at the connection. Follow the ridge and Big Frog Trail to the southwest (220 degrees) if you want to continue the hike toward Big Frog Mountain.

Partial summer and winter views are mostly to the east and southeast. The next lead over to the left is Licklog Ridge; the well-defined peak on Licklog Ridge to the southeast is Licklog Top.

There is no source of water along this trail.

Nature Notes

The low- to middle-elevation oak-pine forest is too shady, too dry, too acidic, and too shrubby for the ephemeral wildflowers of early spring. But the thick understory of heath shrubs—huckleberries, blueberries, mountain laurel and flame azalea—holds its own pageant in late spring. Clumps of flame azalea appear at regular intervals along the entire trail. Although the clusters are not extensive, their showy flowers are the dark orange-red that predominates on Big Frog and its spurs. Flame azalea ordinarily peaks on some section of this trail during the last half of May.

blackgum

Although many hikers may not be familiar with the blackgum (*Nyssa sylvatica*), this medium-sized tree is common in the low- and middle-elevation forests of the Southern Blue Ridge. The blackgum, a member of the same genus as water tupelo, is found in a variety of habitats, from riverine to dry ridgetop. It competes best, however, as an upland tree in the oak-pine forest—the kind of forest that covers Fork Ridge. Loggers generally considered this quick-to-hollow species worthless. Today in the combined wilderness, many of the trails that traverse dry slopes and ridges pass by at least a couple of old-growth gums. For such a short trail, Fork Ridge has a surprisingly large number of these distinctive trees.

The thick, brownish black bark of an old blackgum is unmistakable. Deep furrows crisscross its surface, splitting it into a pattern of small rectangular or squarish blocks.

Often crowded near the ends of short twigs, the roughly oval, alternate leaves—2 to 5 inches long and 1 to 3 inches wide—have smooth margins and short, blunt tips. Blackgum's foliage, the first to turn (usually starting in August) in the Southern Appalachian forest, is a brilliant, glossy red in the fall. The clusters of blue-black fruits, berrylike drupes, are gobbled down by bears, squirrels, and birds.

Also known as black tupelo, the blackgum often attains a height of 55 to 80 feet and a thickness of 2 to 3 feet. On better sites it can measure 100 or more feet tall and 3 to 4 feet thick. Found by a couple of hikers near Conasauga River Trail's giant hemlock, the Georgia state record, much larger than Tennessee's record, is 124 feet in height and 10 feet 4 inches in circumference.

Throughout the Southern Highlands you will run across the

place name Beegum Gap. The origin of the name comes from a clever pioneer practice. Because decay attacks the heartwood of these trees first, settlers used hollow sections of felled blackgums for beehives.

One of the most abundant wildflowers in the oak-pine forest, galax blooms on this trail's dry slope and ridgetop from the middle of May to the middle of June. Chiefly a Southern Appalachian species, the galax is often one of the first evergreen plants mountain hikers learn. The leathery, shiny green leaves (often turning coppery-bronze in winter), round with heart-shaped bases, and the single flowering stems, wands of tiny white blossoms up to 2 feet high, make this plant easy to recognize. The white flowering spikes range from roughly 4 to 9 inches in height. The flowers bloom in succession from bottom to top as the season progresses.

galax

These perennials, which spread by underground rhizomes, form colonies, many of them quite large. You can often detect these colonies by their scent—a peculiar, sweet, skunky fragrance—well before you see them.

Directions

Fork Ridge, an interior trail, has its southwestern (upper-elevation) end on Big Frog Trail and its northeastern (lower-elevation) end on

Rough Creek Trail. Fork Ridge is one of only two trails in the combined wilderness (the other is Sugar Cove in the Cohutta) that requires walking segments of two other trails to reach one of its ends. To reach the southwestern end of Fork Ridge, walk 3.7 miles on Big Frog from its trailhead to where it curls onto the main ridgecrest leading to Big Frog Mountain. Fork Ridge is downhill and to the left (45 degrees) as you approach the signed junction from below on Big Frog Trail. The Benton MacKaye Trail switches from Big Frog to Fork Ridge Trail as it continues downhill (northeast) from this junction. (See Big Frog Trail, page 199, for further information.)

Fork Ridge's northeastern end is located along an interior trail—Rough Creek. Three different routes—each using segments of two trails, each about the same length—can be walked to the Rough Creek–Fork Ridge junction. The Big Frog–Rough Creek route is 3.0 miles; the Licklog Ridge–Rough Creek route is 2.9 miles, and the West Fork–Rough Creek route is 2.8 miles. (See Rough Creek, the preceding trail; West Fork, the following trail, and Licklog Ridge, page 221, for further information.)

If its sign is missing, the Rough Creek–Fork Ridge junction may be confusing. This junction is located on the exact crest of Fork Ridge. Either way it approaches this junction, Rough Creek Trail rises up to the ridgecrest, crosses over it quickly, then descends the other side. Fork Ridge Trail's beginning treadway heads uphill (230 degrees)on the exact crest of Fork Ridge—a left turn coming from Licklog Ridge and a right turn coming from Big Frog or West Fork.

Notes

West Fork Trail

Foot Trail 303: 2.2 miles

- ■ **Dayhiking** Easy in either direction
- ■ **Backpacking In** Easy
- ■ **Backpacking Out** Easy to Moderate
- ■ **Start** West Fork Trailhead, 1,900 feet
- ■ **End** Rough Creek Trail, 1,880 feet
- ■ **Trail Junction** Rough Creek
- ■ **Topographic Quadrangles** Ducktown TN, Caney Creek TN
- ■ **Features** Few old-growth hemlocks; West Fork Rough Creek; riparian forest

WEST FORK'S GRADES ARE MILD ENOUGH to make the two normally shallow stream crossings the hardest part of the hike. Although it offers the easiest walking in the combined wilderness, the trail is not quite as flat as its 20-foot, end-to-end elevation change might suggest. West Fork actually loses approximately 240 feet to mile 1.0, then gains elevation very gradually to its end. This well-maintained trail shares its entire treadway with the Benton MacKaye Trail, whose volunteers usually keep their trail brushed out.

Starting on the southern slope of Chestnut Ridge, West Fork Trail gently descends to the south on the wide walkway of a logging road. Much of the beginning forest—thin hardwoods, even thinner pines—is regenerating from a cut made in the late 1980s or early 1990s. The dense stand of Virginia pines remains in its stunted, thicket stage that follows disturbance in the dry range of the oak-pine forest. The winter view to the left across the valley is of Licklog Ridge. The peak due south on the ridge is Licklog Top.

At 0.5 mile the route runs onto the top of a descending spur, then forks to the right and down onto cut-in path. The narrow path drops onto the eastern slope of a steep-sided, south-facing hollow. This section of trail is lush with rhododendron and hemlock, dark green and glossy on sunny days before spring's bud break. Several of the nearby hemlocks are old-growth—over 10 feet in circumference. Tall, maturing northern red oaks dominate the hardwoods in the second-growth forest. The treadway descends on an overall easy grade above a small, but steadily growing branch.

The track turns right (west) at mile 1.0 onto a former system road that was closed when this area was added to the Big Frog Wilderness in 1986. The road will narrow steadily to trail; already doghobble thickets and hemlock saplings are filling in the gap. With two minor exceptions, the remainder of the walking follows the very easy grades of the former road as it parallels West Fork Rough Creek upstream. The course affords occasional views of the shallow stream between trunks of the tall, straight, second-growth forest. Basswood, sweet birch, northern red oak, red maple, sweetgum, yellow poplar, white pine, and hemlock are all common on the downslope to the creek.

The trail crosses the West Fork twice, once at mile 1.6 and again at mile 1.7, where the old earth and culvert bridges have flooded out. Now only the two giant culverts remain. The creek is small this high up. Unless there has been recent heavy rain, the crossings should provide no problems beyond wet feet. After the second crossing, the footpath continues to parallel the stream to the southwest toward its usually signed and cairned junction with Rough Creek Trail. Because blazes are not allowed in the combined wilderness, the Benton MacKaye volunteers often mark junctions and sharp turns with rock cairns. If you continue straight ahead from the junction, you will quickly cross the stream as Rough Creek Trail heads toward its southeastern end on Licklog Ridge.

Only the final 0.6 or 0.7 mile of West Fork Trail are completely within the Big Frog Wilderness.

Nature Notes

The thick, heavily shaded duff in this trail's steep-sided ravine provides excellent habitat for Indian pipe (*Monotropa uniflora*). Here where hemlocks are common and there is little understory, colony after colony of these unusual, waxy white plants bloom in late May and

June. The low, fleshy perennials, often mistaken for fungi, usually occur in small, scattered clusters. But on the west-facing slope above the rivulet, their 3- to 8-inch-high stems number in the hundreds—many more than I have ever seen along a similarly short stretch of trail.

The Indian pipe, a non-green, non-photosynthesizing flowering plant, was once believed to be totally saprophytic: dependent upon a symbiotic relationship with wood-rotting mycorrhizal fungi to transfer nutrients from decaying plant matter to its own roots. Recent research, however, has proven that the Indian pipe is not

Indian pipe

always a vulture waiting for other plants to die. It can also thrive as an epiparasite, obtaining nourishment indirectly from the roots of living green plants with the help of mycorrhizal fungi.

Indian pipe's range covers most of the United States and Canada, and even dips southward into Mexico. The plant also occurs in Japan and the Himalayas. Within this vast range, the Indian pipe is most successful in rich, acidic soils beneath the deep shade of conifers. It makes perfect sense that a small plant no longer requiring sunlight for photosynthesis would compete best in the shadiest spots. And because it has no need for photosynthesis, the Indian pipe's leaves have become vestigial afterthoughts, reduced to a few small, scalelike growths clinging alternately up the stem.

The structure of its single, nodding flower led botanists to include this species in the large and diverse Heath family. After pollination, the ¾-inch-long blossom bends upward and begins to darken. As summer progresses, the plants shrivel, become increasingly brittle, and finally fade to black.

Because of its initial white color, its coolness to the touch, and its quick change to black when picked, the Indian pipe has inspired ghoulish names such as corpse plant, ice plant, ghost flower, and ghost pipe. Before its flower straightens to vertical and turns dark, this plant looks like a white clay peace pipe standing on its stem.

Cherokee mythology claims that Indian pipe colonies mark the places where kin quarreled. Their tradition demanded ceremonial pipe smoking only after an agreement was reached. According to legend, clan elders once broke this sacred tradition. The powerful spirits, angered by their disobedience, struck the elders dead, leaving only the ghostly pipes on the forest floor. Today, Indian pipe serves as a reminder to reach a peaceful accord after an argument.

West Fork's final 1.2 miles follows a former system road up its namesake branch of Rough Creek. Here the forest, especially the hemlock, is quickly reclaiming the road, narrowing it to path. Contributing to the takeover is a low, evergreen shrub known as doghobble. This common heath often forms dense thickets in moist, shaded, acidic soils next to or near streams. The doghobble's pointed leaves alternate along its arching, slightly zigzag branches. New growth is usually a reddish color in the spring. In winter, the uppermost leaves turn reddish purple. Hanging clusters of small, white, urn-shaped flowers bloom beneath the branches from late April though early June.

doghobble

This shrub received its colorful name from mountaineer bear hunters. The heavy, powerful bears could force their way through the tangled undergrowth—the dogs couldn't.

Directions

The West Fork Trailhead is very close to Access Point 6. (See the detailed description of the Access Points at the beginning of this guide.)

Access Point 6: From the three-way FS 45–FS 221 intersection, turn left onto FS 221 and travel 0.4 mile to the signed West Fork Trailhead on the right side of the road. A gated Forest Service road, blazed with a white Benton MacKaye diamond, angles downhill opposite West Fork Trail. The Forest Service asks that you not block access through the gate.

Notes

Licklog Ridge Trail

Foot Trail 65: 5.8 miles

- **Dayhiking In** Easy to Moderate
- **Dayhiking Out** Easy
- **Backpacking In** Moderate
- **Backpacking Out** Easy to Moderate
- **Start** Licklog Ridge Trailhead, 1,740 feet
- **End** Wolf Ridge Trail and Big Frog Trail atop
  Big Frog Mountain, 4,220 feet
- **Trail Junctions** Rough Creek, Hemp Top,
  Big Frog, Wolf Ridge
- **Topographic Quadrangles** Ducktown TN,
  Caney Creek TN, Hemp Top GA-TN
- **Features** Winter views; excellent spring shrub display;
  overlook; Big Frog Mountain

THROUGHOUT THE SOUTHERN APPALACHIANS, Licklog—as in Licklog Gap, Licklog Creek, and Licklog Ridge—is an occasional place name, stemming from the old days when farmers ran free-range cattle in the mountains. Back then herdsmen chopped holes in logs and fit salt blocks in the slots. Long after the blocks were gone, the cattle kept right on licking the salty logs.

Licklog Ridge, Wolf Ridge, and Big Frog Trails all end at an important, high-elevation junction atop Big Frog Mountain. Licklog Ridge ranks first of the three in length and second in difficulty. It is the longest trail in the Big Frog Wilderness, and its 2,480-foot elevation gain ranks second in the combined wilderness. Despite this substantial elevation gain, Licklog Ridge is not a strenuous trail. Most grades are easy, and there are no sustained ascents harder than easy to moderate.

After this trail enters the wilderness at 1.0 mile, it remains on ridgetop and upper slope the rest of the way to Big Frog. The forest atop Licklog Ridge took a severe pounding from Hurricane Opal in the summer of 1995. By the winter of 1999, volunteers had cleared and brushed out most of the trail. But the storm left light gaps up on the ridge. Light gaps on ridges fill in with briers, at least until heavier shade comes back, so for a while Licklog Ridge will be a long pants and hiking stick trail.

The beginning of the route passes beside quickly regenerating hardwoods recovering from a cut made in the late 1980s. The trail starts easy up right away and rounds a slight spur before turning left onto a logging road. After roughly fifty paces on the road, the track angles to the right onto cut-in path. At 0.2 mile it crosses a power cut, then continues the steady, easy upgrade around an unprotected nonwilderness hollow with tall yellow poplars and oaks. Just beyond this first hollow, the walking curls over a spur and swings onto the northwest, oak-pine sidehill of Licklog Ridge at 0.5 mile.

From here it rounds another steep-sided, hardwood hollow before slanting toward the ridge on dry west slope, with deciduous heath and mountain laurel in the understory and chestnut oak overhead. You are welcomed into the Big Frog Wilderness by a large, bear-ripped sign, at mile 1.0. The treadway angles its way up through a largely broadleaf forest, with an occasional old-growth oak, to the crest of Licklog Ridge at mile 1.2. Here the hiking follows the ridgeline through a mixed broadleaf-conifer forest. It descends to a shallow gap, heads up to the next bump, then dips to and starts to rise from the next gap before reaching the usually signed Rough Creek junction (2,480 feet) at mile 1.5.

Maintaining its south-southwest course, the footpath's next 0.9 mile—all easy up, easy down, or level—remains on or near the ridgetop in a second-growth forest consisting of white and Virginia pines mixed with oaks—white, chestnut, northern red, scarlet—and other hardwoods such as sourwood, sassafras, blackgum, and Fraser magnolia. As usual, the upper west slope is noticeably drier and supports more mountain laurel, Virginia pine, and deciduous heath than the nearby upper east slope.

At mile 2.4 the route takes the easy way around Licklog Top, a prominent peak on the ridge. Instead of climbing up and over the sharp knob, it skirts the northwestern flank well below the high point. A remarkably steady, easy ascent winds around the heads of several hardwood hollows before rounding a spur and regaining the crest in a shallow saddle at mile 2.9. Several maturing yellow poplars, big for young second-growth, stand in one of the north-facing hollows.

Heading southwest beyond Licklog Top, the wilderness walkway gently undulates on or close to the crest of the ridge for the next 0.6 mile. Most of that distance is an easy uphill grade. The forest along this section is largely deciduous; the majority of the boles are oaks as usual. Fraser magnolia saplings are common and distinctive beside the path; occasional old-growth blackgums, left by the loggers, are easily identified by their blocky bark.

The track slabs onto the southeastern pitch at mile 3.5 and makes an end run around the peak (3,660 feet) of an unnamed knob. The southeastern-facing slope is drier oak-pine, numerically dominated by Virginia pine and chestnut oak. Mountain laurel is common in the understory. At mile 3.8 the trail rounds a hollow with yellow poplar, basswood, and red maple, then gradually works its way up through more oak-pine forest, rocky in places, to ridgetop again at mile 4.4.

Here the pathway, a short, easy-to-moderate climb followed by easy grades, travels along the narrow crest through flowering shrubs—Catawba rhododendron and mountain laurel—under stunted, wind-blasted oaks and gnarled Virginia pine. One tenth mile after the route regains the ridge, look for a year-round view a few feet to the right of the trail. This view, one of only three unobstructed vistas in the combined wilderness, opens to the west. Far below, the U-shaped trough of the East Fork Rough Creek valley deepens to the northeast. Straight out, Peavine Ridge walls in the watershed to the west and rises toward Big Frog to the southwest. White pines poke up, pagodalike, through the canopy of hardwoods on Peavine's eastern slope.

Less than 0.1 mile beyond the look-off, the treadway slants onto the southeastern flank and rises to the southeast toward Groundhog Ridge, a Licklog Ridge spur. Here the hiking heads up a little harder, easy to moderate for a short distance, on a rocky, hardwood mountainside. The path ascends to and curls over the crest of Groundhog

Ridge at mile 4.8. Once over the spur, it heads to the southwest again, and until the middle of May you can see your destination, Big Frog, due west.

The track advances on the southeastern sidehill of the uppermost knob on Licklog Ridge. Here the elevation, closing in on 4,000 feet, has subtracted enough heat and added enough moisture to support a mix of cove and northern hardwoods: yellow buckeye, basswood, black cherry, sugar maple, sweet and yellow birch, northern red and white oak. Beyond the flame azalea colonies, the forest floor is covered with ferns, grasses, and herbaceous wildflowers, including Catesby's trillium and lily-of-the-valley. A tenth of a mile after it regains the keel of the ridge, the route dips to its junction with Hemp Top Trail in a slight gap (4,030 feet) at mile 5.3. This connection is the only point where the trail systems of the contiguous wildernesses meet. It is also where the Benton MacKaye Trail turns left (northwest) from Hemp Top onto Licklog Ridge Trail. Because this final segment shares its treadway with the Benton MacKaye, it is usually well maintained by BMTA volunteers.

Most of the final 0.5 mile ascends gently to the northwest on the north-facing slope of the Blue Ridge. The forest here is even higher, cooler, moister, and richer than the one on the south-facing slope before the junction. The understory is open and lush with herbaceous wildflowers; dark-barked black cherries are common in the well-spaced woods. The footpath passes through a shallow saddle on the ridgeline before slabbing back onto the north slope. With a little more than 200 yards remaining, the track passes Elderberry Spring, a small, rocked-in basin to the left. Licklog Ridge ends with an easy-to-moderate upgrade to its usually signed, three-way intersection with Big Frog and Wolf Ridge Trails near the high point of Big Frog Mountain (4,224 feet).

Because of its length and its upper-slope and ridgetop route, this trail affords numerous wintertime views through leafless trees. Looking to the left (east and southeast) you will see mostly low ridges and coves beyond the Big Frog Wilderness. To the right of the trail lie much higher ridges, most within the wilderness. A glance to the right (north) at roughly 0.6 mile offers a view of Chestnut Ridge. From the trailhead to Licklog Top, most of the prospects to the right (west and northwest) are of nearby Fork Ridge, across the East Fork Rough Creek valley. Beyond Licklog Top, most of the bare-branch views to the west take in Peavine Ridge as it rises to the south toward Big Frog Mountain. Chimneytop, a named knob on Peavine Ridge, is about a mile north of Big Frog.

Nature Notes

From mile 2.8, where it rounds a moist hollow, and for much of the next 0.6 mile, the trail passes through forest where Fraser magnolia (*Magnolia fraseri*) is more plenti-ful than along any other similar length of trail in the combined wilderness. Once the path regains the ridgetop, magnolia saplings often flank the treadway. One of three deciduous mag-nolias found in the wilderness, the Fraser is particularly easy to identify. It is a small- to medium-sized tree with smooth, light gray or light gray-brown bark. Its leaves—6 to 18 inches long and 3 to 8 inches wide, the second largest noncompound tree leaves in the Southern Appalachians—are crowded into whorls at branch ends. The richer the habitat, the larger the leaf. Saplings occasionally have jungle-sized leaves 7 to 9 inches wide and up to 20 inches long. The conspicuously eared (auric-

Fraser magnolia

ulate in botanese) base of the Fraser magnolia is diagnostic. The magnolia with a slightly larger, uneared leaf—the umbrella magno-lia (description on page 97)—is absent throughout much of the wilderness.

The Fraser magnolia's fragrant flowers, pale yellow and usually 6 to 9 inches in diameter, are larger than those of any other plant in the wilderness except the umbrella magnolia. Blooming usually begins at the lower elevations in early to mid-April, and moves up to the highest peaks by late April or early May. A Southern Appalachian endemic, Fraser magnolia is occasional to common throughout the combined wilderness.

The flame azalea, a tall heath in the same genus as rhododendron, is almost as inconspicuous without its flowers as it is conspicuous with them. At peak bloom this azalea is the most strikingly colored deciduous shrub in the Southern Appalachians, and is immediately identified by all who know its name. Particularly large and showy clumps are justifiably admired and photographed. But as soon as the fire has faded and fallen, the small leaves blend in with the rest of the understory and the shrubs go largely unnoticed until the next spring.

flame azalea

At mile 4.8 this trail curls up to and over Groundhog Ridge. For the next several tenths of a mile beyond the ridgetop, flame azalea uncharacteristically dominates the understory for short stretches. Known to many old-timers as wild honeysuckle, mature flame azaleas are usually only 3 to 10 feet tall. Occasionally, in rich habitats such as upper coves, treelike specimens grow 15 to 18 feet high.

The flowers appear before the leaves are fully grown. Clusters of five to seven blossoms near branch ends range in color from light orangish yellow to dark orangish red. Most of the azaleas at the upper elevations of Big Frog are either dark orange or very dark orangish red.

Flame azalea occurs as scattered individual plants or small clusters throughout the wilderness in the right habitat, usually oak-pine or predominantly oak forest. It grows at all elevations in the wilderness. Depending upon the progress of the season, blooming begins at the lowest elevations from mid-April to the end of the month and climbs to the broad crown of Big Frog by late May or early June.

Directions

The Licklog Ridge Trailhead can be most easily reached from Access Points 6 and 7.(See the detailed description of the Access Points at the beginning of this guide.)

Access Point 6: From the three-way FS 45–FS 221 intersection, turn left onto FS 221 and proceed approximately 3.3 miles to the trailhead on the right side of the road. Look for the beginning treadway, sign, and the bulletin board, which is 40 yards up into the woods. There is a small parking area on the opposite side of the road.

Access Point 7: From the paved, three-way intersection of FS 221, FS 65, and County Road 251, continue across the bridge over Tumbling Creek, then turn right onto FS 221. Proceed approximately 5.5 miles (the pavement ends after 0.1 mile) to the trailhead on the left side of the road.

Notes

We must recognize that all of our land is destined to be put to some human use. If any of it is to be preserved in its natural condition, it must be as the deliberate setting aside of it for our human use of it in a natural condition.

—Howard Zahniser

The Idea of Wilderness

WILDERNESS ADVOCATES SEE the Wilderness Act of 1964 as the most foresighted land-ethic legislation since the formation of the National Forest System. The concept of designated wilderness represents a progression of concern, a hard-won belief by the majority that some parcels of the earth should have their own heritage, should be allowed to become what they will, unmanipulated by humans. This act of preservation, a tithing of wildness for ourselves and for the future, is an important but as yet paltry beginning reparation for our abuse and misuse of the land and its life.

Those who oppose the concept of designated wilderness view it as a radical step that locks up resources. Let it be emphatically stated to them, however, that the idea is often a matter of preference—a matter of zoning really. Either we can choose to continue opening large areas of our Southern Appalachian forest to road building and logging in order to satisfy the incessant demands of a world crowded with people chanting more, more, more, like a mantra. Or we can choose to preserve, to lock up diversity and beauty—clear, unsilted streams, magnificent forests, views into wild and natural land—by designating significant tracts as wilderness. Even though the physical resources of these areas would no longer be available for extraction, we can still use them—recreationally, spiritually, scientifically—in their natural state.

Unlike Alaska and the western states, the central and eastern regions of our country have only three categories of federally owned wild land—national wildlife refuges, national parks, and national forests—where federal wilderness designation is possible. Within that immense expanse of our country east of the Rockies, from Texas to South Carolina, from Nebraska to Pennsylvania, federal owner-ship of those three types of wild land constitutes less than 5 percent of the total land mass. Some states within that region, especially those with flat topography and good soil, have little or no opportunity for wilderness.

Within that less than 5 percent, only certain areas—those that are roadless, predominantly publicly owned, and large (usually at least 5,000 acres)—are qualified to be considered for a roadless inventory, the first step toward designation. Once an area is inventoried as roadless, it still has to be sufficiently scenic and undisturbed—and often economically useless—for there to be enough support to continue the qualification process.

Although percentages vary from state to state, congressionally mandated wilderness within that region east of the Rockies is, at best, somewhere between 5 and 10 percent of the federal wildlands. Thus, designated wilderness over much of our country is a small fraction of a small fraction: two to three-tenths of 1 percent of the total land base. Even in our relatively wild South, with its mountains, swamps, and forests, the figure remains below 1 percent.

Unlike large sections of the Midwest, the South fortunately still has the opportunity for more wilderness. Our best opportunity lies within the national forests of the Southern Appalachians—the South's largest concentration of publicly owned land.

Especially in the highest and most remote mountains, road building and logging in the steep-sloped Southern Appalachians is destructive and costly. Bulldozing and stabilizing roads in this high-rainfall, mountainous terrain is so expensive that the federal government must subsidize it. The road building and logging damages watersheds, leaves the forest less diverse, harms certain wildlife species, and keeps the land in its ecological infancy. Spending money to subsidize destructive logging that yields little of the national lumber output makes neither ecological nor economic sense. This is especially true where we are further fragmenting the small amount of unprotected public land that remains wild and natural.

We are always faced with difficult land-use choices; designating wilderness is just one among many. But today at a time when the pace of life is increasingly frenetic—when ocean levels, global temperatures, and human populations are rising; when acid rain is falling and ozone layers are disappearing; when our collective actions lead to the daily extinction of species —it makes good sense to spare a few more teaspoons of wildness as havens for life and for human hope and renewal, protected both for and from us.

The Wilderness Act

The Wilderness Act of September 3, 1964, established the National Wilderness Preservation System, the first of its kind in the world. The idea of wilderness means different things to different people. Some describe any patch of woods bigger than their backyard as wilderness. Others won't call an area true wilderness unless it meets rare conditions: that it takes at least a week to walk across the longest part of it, that there is no sign of human habitation even from the vistas, and that all of the original predators are still on patrol. Knowing that the term is nebulous, as much spiritual as physical, the framers of the law attempted to define the qualities and purposes of wilderness. The following are salient ideas from the act.

A wilderness:

■ is an area of undeveloped federal land retaining its primeval character and influence, without permanent improvements or human habitation;

■ has at least 5,000 acres of land or is of sufficient size to make practicable its preservation and use in an unimpaired condition;

■ generally appears to have been affected primarily by forces of nature, with the imprint of man's work substantially unnoticeable;

■ is hereby recognized as an area where the earth and its community of life are untrammeled by man, where man himself is a visitor who does not remain, and which has outstanding opportunities for solitude or a primitive and unconfined type of recreation;

■ is devoted to the public purposes of recreational, scenic, scientific, educational, conservation, and historical use;

■ is preservation that will secure for the American people of present and future generations the benefits of an enduring resource of wilderness—unimpaired for future use and enjoyment.

What is permitted in wilderness?

■ Primitive recreation such as dayhiking, backpacking, and camping

■ Hunting and fishing in accordance with state and federal laws
■ Collecting berries, nuts, and cones for personal use
■ Scientific research compatible with wilderness values
■ Primitive facilities, if critical to the protection of the land
■ Nonmotorized wheelchairs

What is prohibited in wilderness?
■ New road construction
■ Timber harvesting
■ Structures of any kind, except those primitive facilities deemed necessary to protect the land
■ Mechanical transport (bicycles, wagons, carts)
■ Public use of any motorized vehicles or equipment
■ Removal of plants, stone, or moss for personal or commercial use
■ Removal of historical or archeological artifacts by the public

Wilderness Additions

Every ten to fifteen years the Forest Service is required to revise its overall management guideline—the forest plan. After weighing public input and recreational demands against its traditional role as timber producer, the Forest Service recommends additional wilderness acreage in each new plan. The designation process is straightforward; the decisions, however, are often controversial.

Before the Forest Service considers an area to be a candidate for wilderness designation, it conducts the often subjective roadless inventory. If a given tract is determined to be roadless, or nearly so, the Forest Service takes the second step—a wilderness requirements review. Following inventory and review, the Forest Service formulates its recommendations for wilderness additions and new wildernesses, which are then included in the draft forest plan and the accompanying environmental impact statement. After the draft forest plan is published, there is a public comment period of up to 120 days. The final forest plan, further revised and fine tuned, is the last step in the sequence for the Forest Service.

The Forest Service can only recommend; the U. S. Congress designates. Congress can designate more or less acreage than the report recommends, and they can also designate, if there is sufficient interest and pressure, at any time they choose. Normally, however, Congress waits until after the final forest plan to act. Even then, though, unless a potential wilderness bill has immediate sponsorship and support, Congress may table the proposal for several years.

The draft plans for both the Cherokee and the Chattahoochee National Forests are scheduled for completion by late summer of 2000. Following public comment and further revision, the final versions will appear during the summer of 2001.

The two potential additions to the Cohutta Wilderness are Ken Mountain and Foster Branch, both contiguous with the existing wilderness. The preliminary recommendation for the Ken Mountain tract, west of Ken Mountain along the northwestern edge of the wilderness, is a significant 933 acres. This addition would protect the Horseshoe Bend Trail and bring the wilderness boundary out to FS 51.

Foster Branch is located along the eastern side of the existing wilderness near Three Forks Mountain. Thus far, the preliminary recommendation for this tract is an uninspiring 181 acres, amounting to a barely meaningful boundary adjustment. Nearby, however, the prospects are much better. The Chattahoochee National Forest has made a preliminary recommendation for an entirely new, 10,000-acre wilderness—Mountaintown—immediately to the southeast of the Cohutta. While not technically contiguous with the Cohutta Wilderness, Mountaintown, if designated, would abut that wilderness from Potatopatch Mountain to Three Forks Mountain. Stretching away to the southeast, this potential new wilderness would be separated from the Cohutta by only one narrow, dirt-gravel road—FS 64.

On the Tennessee side, the news is not encouraging. Two logical additions would greatly enhance the integrity of the Big Frog Wilderness and its trail system. The larger and by far the more important of the two areas, north and west of the existing wilderness out to Forest Service roads 62 and 221, did not even pass the roadless inventory inspection. It failed despite the fact that there are no roads open to vehicular traffic in the entire tract.

Long north-south and skinny east-west, the second potential addition flanks the eastern side of the Big Frog out to FS 221. The Cherokee National Forest has made a preliminary recommendation for a token, 363-acre addition from this parcel.

The Cohutta–Big Frog is the westernmost anchor in the Southern Appalachian system of designated wildernesses. This system of high, wild gems sporadically dots the narrow corridor of mountains from western Virginia to northern Georgia. Though the Cohutta–Big Frog is the largest gem along that corridor, it is simply the largest among the conspicuously puny. You can walk most from one end to the other and still make it home for an early supper. The majority of Southern Appalachian wildernesses range from a mere 5,000 to 12,000 acres. At present, there is not one national forest wilderness, single or combined, over 50,000 acres in the eastern United States.

But this oversight can be remedied, and the Cohutta–Big Frog Wilderness should be the place to start. If the Big Frog were extended to its surrounding roads, a modest and reasonable addition of approximately 4,800 acres, the Cohutta–Big Frog would become the first decent-sized national forest wilderness in the East.

With this addition, plus those recommended for the Cohutta, the South would score a hat trick for the three categories of federal wilderness in the East. The Everglades has the largest national park wilderness (1.3 million acres) in the East; the Okefenokee has the most expansive national wildlife refuge wilderness (354,000 acres) in the East, and with sensible and prudent additions, the Cohutta–Big Frog would complete the sweep.

There are several practical reasons for moving the Big Frog's boundaries out to the surrounding Forest Service roads. First, it would protect the existing trail system. The beginning mileages of the six trails that start on FS 221 are vulnerable to roading and logging until they enter the wilderness. Secondly, it would help meet the inexorably growing demand for quality outdoor recreation. With the help of volunteers and hiking clubs, the trail system could be extended into the newly protected tracts for the use of hikers, hunters, and trout fishers.

The third reason for expanding the Big Frog to the Forest Service roads is the fact that a wilderness bounded by roads is easier to manage and easier to protect. For instance, once an ORV rider leaves the main road and heads down a logging road toward a wilderness, you have no way of knowing what he is up to and where he and his machine will stop. And once an ORV enters an area, it is extremely difficult to force the rider to stop exactly where you want. But where a wilderness borders the main road, as the Cohutta often does, any ORV rider that turns off the main road into the wilderness is in clear, unambiguous violation and is much more easily seen and reported.

Finally, a larger wilderness would protect wildlife. All of the Cherokee National Forest from the Georgia line northward to US 64, including the Big Frog Wilderness, encompasses the approximately 52,800-acre Ocoee Bear Reserve. Hunting bear is illegal throughout the year within the reserve. A sizable addition to the Big Frog Wilderness would give the reserve concept more teeth, would immediately

Southern Appalachian black bear

afford added protection for the wildlife in the area and, in time, would support a mature forest where den trees and hard mast would be more abundant.

But perhaps the most compelling reason to expand wilderness is the desire to experience the documented and imagined past again in the future. Since 1975 we have had the opportunity to set aside meaningful tracts of publicly owned Southern Appalachian forest. Our past failure to do so makes the present opportunity more important. If we have the vision to set aside large roadless areas now, if scientists and foresters restore a blight-free form of the chestnut, if natural fires are allowed to burn on the dry slopes and ridges, if.... I know, I know—if ifs and buts were candy and nuts, everybody would have a great Christmas. But these ifs are well within our grasp. With vision, research, and effort, a few large national forest wildernesses may once again approximate the primeval in appearance, function, and health. And some lucky backpacker may one day spot a pig-eating puma, an eastern cougar, as it lopes out of sight on Rough Ridge.

Environmental Guidelines

Before the Hike

■ **Limit group size** to no more than eight for backpacking and no more than twelve for dayhiking.

■ **Split large organized groups** into two or three smaller parties, allowing the groups to go to different destinations, travel opposite directions on the same loop, stagger their starts, or do whatever it takes to avoid overwhelming everyone and everything in their path.

■ **Educate large groups**, especially children, about the evils of littering and cutting across switchbacks before they leave the trailhead.

■ **Plan ahead**—remember that rivers with waterfalls and swimming holes, the Jacks and Conasauga, and major trail junctions with level ground and nearby water will be heavily used during warm-weather holidays and weekends.

■ **Take a lightweight backpacking stove** so you won't have to build fires for cooking.

■ **Repackage food supplies** in sealable bags or plastic bottles so there will be fewer boxes and tinfoil pouches to burn or carry.

On the Trail

■ **Travel quietly.** And, if you can, take breaks away from the trail to preserve solitude and to keep other hikers from having to hop-scotch around and over your gear.

■ **Don't litter**—not even the smallest of candy wrappers or cigarette butts. If you pack it in, pack it out—all of it.

■ **Don't be a hider**—a person whose consciousness is caught midway between right and wrong. The undersides of rocks should be salamander sanctuaries and tree hollows should be wildlife dens—not beer can repositories. And no one wants to see your misfired banana peel draped over the flame azalea.

■ **Remember that organic scraps are definitely litter.** Orange peels, peanut hulls, apple cores, and campsite compost piles crowned with eggshells and spaghetti noodles are not welcome sights in the wilderness. Either burn it or carry it out.

■ **Carry a plastic bag with you.** Help pick up what those uncaring louts have left behind. Take only pictures and litter; leave only footprints.

■ **Take your dump du jour at least 100 feet from the trail** and at least 150 feet from a campsite or water source. Dig a cat hole with boot heel or plastic trowel, then cover everything up well—please.

■ **Stay on the main trail** (preceding precept is a notable exception), and do not cut across switchbacks. Cutting across switchbacks tramples vegetation, starts erosion, and encourages more shortcut taking. Walk through, not around, muddy spots. If everyone goes around, the mucky areas, such as those on Rice Camp and Penitentiary Branch Trails, grow larger and larger.

■ **Step to the high side of the trail** so you don't cave in the lower side when stepping aside to let other hikers or backpackers pass.

■ **Don't pick, pluck, dig up, or cut up any flowers, plants, or trees,** not even the tiny ones you think no one will miss. Let offenders know of your disapproval gently and tactfully, at least at first.

No-Trace Camping

■ **Don't use worn out, naked-ground campsites** where the entire area is bare earth with eroding soil, damaged trees, and exposed roots. Let these areas heal. Use existing, well-established campsites in acceptable condition. Better yet, move well away from the trail and make a no-trace camp that will rarely, if ever, be used again.

■ **Do your best to camp 100 feet away from trail or stream.** It is often difficult, if not impossible, to camp 100 feet away from both the path and stream when walking a trail that closely parallels a watercourse. One side of the trail is too close to the river; the other quickly tilts into a steep-sided slope of rhododendron. But bending one rule is better than breaking two. Try fording the Jacks or Conasauga to the bank opposite the trail, then tuck in as far as you can. That way you will be well over 100 feet from the trail and maybe even 100 feet away from the river.

■ **Don't cut standing trees** or pull up or beat down vegetation to make room for your tent or tents. Fit in, tuck in—don't hack in.

■ **Don't enlarge an existing campsite.** There is no need for large groups to circle the wagons against the night. Again, fit in and tuck in.

■ **Absolutely no campsite construction**—leave the blueprints and hard hats at home: no boot bulldozing, trenching, digging latrines, hammering nails in trees, etc.

■ **Use biodegradable soap** and dispose of waste water at least 100 feet from camp and 150 feet from any water source.

■ **Don't wash dirty dishes directly in a spring or stream.** Don't use soap on yourself or your clothes directly in a spring or stream.

■ **Don't bury trash or food scraps.** Animals will dig them up.

■ **Don't spit your toothpaste on the campsite vegetation.** After a month of drought, heavily used sites look like bird roosts.

■ **Make your campsite look at least as natural as when you found it.** Replace branches, twigs, and leaves cleared for the sleeping area.

■ **Keep length of stay to one or two nights, if possible.**

■ **Wear soft-soled shoes in camp.**

■ **Avoid building campfires.** Take a lightweight, backpacking stove for cooking. If you do start a fire, keep it small and use only dead and down wood. Leave the saws and axes at home.

■ **Erase all evidence of a campfire** built with no fire ring. Scatter the ashes, replace the duff, and camouflage the burned area.

■ **Don't build fire rings**—tear them down.

■ **Never build a fire on a dry, windy day.**

Backcountry Courtesy

■ **Leave radios and tape players at home or bring headsets.**

■ **Don't take a dog into the wilderness unless it is well trained.** Even then, carry a leash so you can control your animal when necessary. Leave behind dogs that may growl or bark at other hikers. Do not take aggressive dogs—canine weapons—into the wilderness for protection. Creating stress for other hikers is unconscionable. If you fear being accosted on the trail, stay at home or buy a can of pepper spray. But leave that snarling, lunging dog at home.

■ **Take consideration**—do nothing that will interfere with someone else's enjoyment. It is considered insensitive to enter the wilderness with a very large group that will completely overrun and overwhelm other hikers.

■ **Keep as quiet as possible.** Drunken parties, war whoops, and loud radios are frowned upon, and downright rude. Especially on heavily used trails, such as the Jacks River during summer weekends, talking in normal tones helps preserve the illusion of isolation.

■ **Remember that campsites are first come, first served.** Don't whine, argue, or try to crowd in if someone already has the camp you really wanted.

■ **Help preserve the illusion of solitude, for yourself and others.** Make yourself as unobtrusive, as invisible, as possible. Use earth-tone tents and tarps and, if possible, camp far enough off the trail so that other hikers can't see you and vice versa. Please do not camp smack on the trail so that other hikers have to wind through your sprawling encampment just to follow the trail. Also, if possible, take lunch and rest breaks off the trail.

Tips for Beginning Hikers

THE COHUTTA–BIG FROG WILDERNESS is a forest of forty freedoms, where you use your own judgment, act on your own decisions, and fill out your own report card. No river patrol ranger whistles "ford" or "do not ford." All the potential lawsuits in the world will not keep you warm and dry. And that is exactly how it should be.

The wilderness, however, is a place where mistakes and mishaps are magnified. The good news is that most of the predictable problems—from blisters to becoming much wetter than you wanted—can be prevented with preparation and good judgment. The bad news is that inexperience—not knowing what to expect, what to do, or when to do it—often can preclude good judgment. In hiking, as in almost every other endeavor, ignorance and inexperience are liabilities. That is why it is so important for beginning hikers, especially backpackers, to start out slow and easy, build fitness and skill, then progress from there.

■ **Think of the "what ifs" before you leave home.** What if it rains or snows? What if you can't find a particular junction? What if your hiking partner can't handle the climb? What if someone takes the wrong turn? What then? The more of these questions you can answer or solve to your satisfaction before you set out, the better your trip will be.

■ **Prepare a reasonable hiking plan.** Match your route and intended pace with your level of experience and fitness. If you are a rookie, and unsure of your physical capabilities, try car camping and dayhiking first. That way you can increase your camping skills and gauge your mountain fitness level before planning your first backpacking trip. Factoring in pit stops, snack stops, rest stops, lowering-heart rate stops, and wildflower watching, etc., backpackers in the middle of the fitness bell curve average only between 1 and 2 miles per hour in mountainous terrain.

■ **Take as many of the ten essentials as your trip warrants.** Most how-to books list map, compass, whistle (three rapid blasts is the distress signal), flashlight with extra batteries, knife, matches, candle, first aid kit, extra food, and at least an extra heavy shirt as the ten essentials. My list of important items would include rain gear and hiking stick.

■ **Protect your possibles**—your food, extra clothes, matches, sleeping bag—from becoming wet. Devise a way to keep the contents of your daypack or backpack dry at all times. Backpackers who wear rain-suits rather than ponchos should have waterproof backpack covers. You may want to further protect your food, clothes, and sleeping bag with waterproof plastic bags. Trash compactor bags are cheap, sturdy, and waterproof. Overprepare to the point just short of obsessiveness.

■ **Take good care of your feet.** Too many times over the years I have seen backpackers sprawled out beside a trail, shoes and socks off, nursing blisters ranging from dime to half-dollar size. Blister pain does not have to be a mandatory part of your backpacking rite of passage. Moleskin, cushioning shoe pads, arch supports, and Second Skin should prevent or alleviate most foot problems. As soon as you feel a hot spot, stop and stick some moleskin on your feet. It will protect you from blisters for days and days. If you already have a blister, try Second Skin to ease the pain and cushion the area. Wearing two pairs of socks, the inner pair thin, moisture wicking ones, helps prevent blisters and increases comfort.

■ **Dress appropriately.** Shorts are fine for promenade trails where there are few deadfalls and wide treadways. But on wilderness trails, where deadfalls can be common and paths are often narrow, shorts do not always afford adequate protection. They might on some trails, but definitely won't on others. Tight-fitting blue jeans, no matter how good they look on you, are the worst kind of pants to wear hiking, especially when wet. Pick a pair that are lightweight, loose fitting, and fast drying.

■ **Take a hiking stick.** The most common hiking injuries are the result of sprains and falls due to bad footing or stumble-footedness. Wilderness and bad footing are practically synonymous. The best way to keep from falling is to carry that third contact point of balance, a stout hiking stick. It is especially important if you are day-hiking alone or backpacking. If you haven't fallen in the woods yet, you haven't hiked much. When you fall while wearing a backpack, you fall fast and hard.

I started using a hiking stick right after witnessing a backpacker take a rolling, elbow-smashing, downhill fall off the AT. Ever since, I have used a stick to help ford rivers, to brace on steep descents, to reduce leg strain on ascents, and generally to keep my balance so that I can look at wildflowers, trees, and mountains while walking. I have also used my stick to fend off aggressive dogs (once), to shove a reluctant rattlesnake out of harm's way (once), and to help hikers make long jumps between river rocks. Hiking sticks also come in handy as instant tarp poles during thunderstorms, and as throw-rope javelins to help hang the bear bag from a high branch.

■ **Take two tarps for your tent**, one for underneath and one to line the inside floor. Cut the tarps for a custom fit. Make sure you roll the outside edge of the bottom tarp inward well past the drip line of your rain fly. That way water that pours off your tent pools underneath the tarp, not between the tarp and tent floor. Tarp number two protects your tent floor and adds another moisture barrier. Cut this tarp a little larger than your tent floor so that the tarp's edges curl up against the tent's walls. Again, this is so that any water entering your tent stays beneath the tarp and away from your sleeping bag. Cheap tents and old tents are not waterproof. In fact, when it comes to tents, think "allegedly" waterproof.

■ **Carry an extra tarp.** Although it adds a pound or two to your pack, carrying a high-quality, 8' by 10' or 10' by 12' nylon tarp adds greatly to the comfort of a rainy camp. If there is only one tent, you can protect all or part of your tent and still have a dry area for cooking, pack storage, and loafing in front of the tent. If the group is larger, you can rig a tarp for a common dry area for cooking and trail talk.

■ **Make sure your water supply is safe.** For years, when my water bottles ran dry, I took pleasure from drinking cold, clear, presumably pure water straight from springs and high rivulets. But no more. The odds finally caught up with me, in part because harmful microorganisms are more prevalent than they were twenty-five years ago. While walking the trails in North Carolina's Joyce Kilmer–Slickrock

Wilderness, I suffered an attack of the Mini Watu—what Sioux Indians call water imps. My particular imp was Giardia; and attack is an apt word. Now I'm a born-again water purifier.

There are three general ways to purify water: boiling, filtering, or treating chemically. Boiling, because of the time and fuel required, is usually considered impractical. Water filters have become lighter and more effective over the years. Before buying one, make sure it will at least remove all particles larger than 0.4 microns. If you have had trouble with your water filter clogging up and slowing down, try tie-twisting a coffee filter around the pre-filter uptake acorn.

You can also use water purification tablets, available at most back-packing shops. How-to books and magazines recommend tablets that use iodine as their purifying agent. The iodine-based tablets are safer and more effective (and retain their potency longer after the bottle has been opened) than others. Recent publications have expressed health concerns associated with prolonged use of chemical tablets.

■ **Watch out for yellow jackets.** These fierce, ground-nesting, stinging insects reach numerical peak during late summer and early fall. Just as they reach this peak, bears begin to grub up their nests and eat their larvae. Thus when the dog days are over and it's time to start hiking again, these aggressive insects are numerous, edgy, and on full-pheromone alert. Although you will never be entirely safe from these little warriors, you can take a few, practical precautions to lessen the odds of being stung.

Wear long pants and, if you can stand it, wear a long-sleeve shirt too. During mid-October my wife, a friend, and I met a large group of backpackers finishing up a long loop hike at the East Cowpen–Rough Ridge junction. Most of these backpackers—members of a hiking club from Kansas City called the D.O.A., the Degenerate Outdoor Adventurers—were wearing shorts. Their encounters with yellow jackets were immediately obvious from their conversation and from their red, swollen legs. One backpacker, in obvious pain, had bandaged both legs from calf to boot top.

Leave the dogs at home—they are yellow jacket magnets. In a bug's brain, anything big and hairy is a bear. And once the chemical alarm goes off, these stinging insects don't do much deep thinking about the difference between a black lab and a black bear.

Take a minute to look for insects flying out of the ground before you throw off your pack and plop down. At the Panther Creek–East Cowpen junction, I came across a man who had taken off his pack and leaned up against a tree for lunch break. Unbeknownst to him, he had thrown his pack next to the entrance hole of a yellow jacket nest. It didn't take him long to find out. By the time I arrived, he had already been stung somewhere between five and ten times on the face and neck. We watched as over a hundred of the angry buggers funneled above his pack and sandwiches.

Develop a low-level, internal alarm that automatically goes off when your eyes see flying insects milling close to the ground.

Adopt-a-Trail

THE U.S. FOREST SERVICE has an "Adopt-a-Trail" program, which provides individuals, friends, families, and organizations the opportunity to do something worthwhile: to become Forest Service volunteers. The Forest Service provides a pat on the back, perhaps a patch, and all the equipment—saws, shovels, axes, shin-guards, plastic bags—you could possibly use or carry. Volunteers provide the time, energy, and enthusiasm needed to clean up and trim out their adopted trails.

The Forest Service, and indeed all those who use and respect the wilderness, will greatly appreciate your help.

If you are interested in becoming the foster parent of a wilderness trail, or a section of a trail, call or write the Ocoee Ranger District in the Cherokee National Forest or the Cohutta Ranger District in the Chattahoochee National Forest. (See the following page for addresses and phone numbers.)

Addresses and Maps

MOST OF THE COHUTTA WILDERNESS and the southernmost 89 acres of the Big Frog Wilderness are located within the Cohutta Ranger District of Georgia's Chattahoochee National Forest. Almost all of the Big Frog Wilderness and the northernmost 1,795 acres of the Cohutta Wilderness lie within the Ocoee Ranger District of Tennessee's Cherokee National Forest. For more information contact:

Chattahoochee National Forest

USDA Forest Service
Cohutta Ranger District
401 G.I. Maddox Parkway
Chatsworth, GA 30705
(706) 695-6736

USDA Forest Service
Supervisor's Office
1755 Cleveland Highway
Gainesville, GA 30501
(770) 536-0541
www.fs.fed.us/conf

Cherokee National Forest

USDA Forest Service
Ocoee Ranger District
RT 1 Box 348D
Benton, TN 37307
(423) 338-5201

USDA Forest Service
Supervisor's Office
P.O. Box 2010
Cleveland, TN 37320
(423) 476-9700
www.r8web.com/cherokee

Maps of the Chattahoochee National Forest, the Cherokee National Forest, and the combined wilderness are available from the Forest Service offices for a small fee. The combined wilderness map is entitled *Cohutta and Big Frog Wilderness Georgia-Tennessee.*

Topographic Quadrangles (1:24,000) are available from the United States Geological Survey: USGS, Branch of Information Services, Box 25286, Denver Federal Center, Denver, CO 80225, (303) 202-4700.

Index of Trails

Index of Nature Descriptions

Italics indicate illustration.

Other Books By Tim Homan

Hiking Trails of Joyce Kilmer–Slickrock and Citico Creek Wildernesses

The Hiking Trails of North Georgia

A Yearning Toward Wildness: Environmental Quotations from the Writings of Henry David Thoreau